TAKING FICTION FILM SERIOUSLY

TAKING FICTION FILM SERIOUSLY

A Philosophical Approach to Cinema Studies

MARIO SLUGAN

BLOOMSBURY ACADEMIC
LONDON • NEW YORK • OXFORD • NEW DELHI • SYDNEY

BLOOMSBURY ACADEMIC
Bloomsbury Publishing Plc, 50 Bedford Square, London, WC1B 3DP, UK
Bloomsbury Publishing Inc, 1359 Broadway, New York, NY 10018, USA
Bloomsbury Publishing Ireland, 29 Earlsfort Terrace, Dublin 2, D02 AY28, Ireland

BLOOMSBURY, BLOOMSBURY ACADEMIC and the Diana logo are
trademarks of Bloomsbury Publishing Plc

First published in Great Britain 2025

Cover design: Ben Anslow
Cover image: *The War Game* (1965). Directed by Peter Watkins.
(© Pathé Contemporary Films / Photofest)

A catalogue record for this book is available from the British Library.

A catalog record for this book is available from the Library of Congress.

ISBN: HB: 978-1-3505-0567-4
PB: 978-1-3505-0571-1
ePDF: 978-1-3505-0569-8
eBook: 978-1-3505-0568-1

Typeset by Integra Software Services Pvt. Ltd.
Printed and bound in Great Britain

For product safety related questions contact productsafety@bloomsbury.com.

To find out more about our authors and books visit www.bloomsbury.com
and sign up for our newsletters.

For Nomi

CONTENTS

FIGURES

ACKNOWLEDGEMENTS

This monograph has been brewing since Enrico Terrone and I started organizing a conference titled 'Documentaries and the Fiction/Nonfiction Divide' (Queen Mary University of London, 15–16 November 2019). Through conversations with him and other conference delegates it became obvious that there is much more to say about what fiction film is than I had in my book that was just coming out at the time (*Fiction and Imagination in Early Cinema*, 2019).

In the intervening years I have had the good fortune of discussing various aspects of the monograph at a number of conferences, workshops and annual meetings of learned societies, including Association for Studies in Fiction and Fictionality (2024, 2022, 2019), Society for the Cognitive Studies of the Moving Image (2022, 2021), Seminar on the Origins and History of Cinema (2021), European Society of Aesthetics (2021), Reel Borders Workshop (2021), Dubrovnik Philosophy of Art Conference (2021) and Domitor (2020). I would like to thank all those who found the presentations stimulative enough to comment. I have learned much from these remarks.

I have also profited immensely from acting as a co-investigator on the project 'Aesthetic Education through Narrative Art and Its Relevance for the Humanities' (2021–6) led by Iris Vidmar Jovanović at the University of Rijeka. The workshops and conferences organized as a part of the project – Exploring Artistic Engagements (2024), Aesthetic Education and Screen Stories (2023), and The People We End Up Being: Art, Ethics and Agency (2022) – and the conversations I had with the participants and especially with Iris made an indelible mark on my thinking.

Taking part in the online reading group on fiction run by Merel Semejin was no different. Next to Merel, for adding me to the group and for organizing a session on my own work I would particularly like to thank

Filippo Contesi for putting my piece on the list of potential readings in the first place. It was genuinely fulfilling to have analytic philosophers take a critical look at my ideas.

Maarten Coëgnarts, together with the three anonymous peer-reviewers, deserves praise for reading the whole manuscript – I can only hope I have addressed his and the reviewers' comments sufficiently.

I would also like to thank my spouse, Uuriintuya Batsaikhan, for comparing her intuitions with mine on a range of examples. It is always a pleasure to find a kindred spirit when it comes to having no imaginative resistance to all kinds of jokes and yarns.

Many thanks to Veidehi Hans as well, for pitching the project to Bloomsbury, organizing a very stimulative peer-review process, and bearing with me in figuring out the book cover.

This work has been supported in part by the Croatian Science Foundation under the project (UIP-2020-02-1309). Much of the book writing took place during the sabbatical at Queen Mary University of London from January to June 2024.

Chapter One is derived in part from an Article published in the *New Review of Film and Television*, 20 October 2022, 'Fiction as Challenge to Text-Oriented Film Studies', available online: https://www.tandfonline.com/doi/full/10.1080/17400309.2022.2132072. Another part of Chapter One has appeared as an Article published in *Studies in Documentary Film*, 7 May 2021, 'Textualism, Extratextualism, and the Fiction/Nonfiction Distinction in Documentary Studies', available online: https://www.tandfonline.com/doi/full/10.1080/17503280.2021.1923142. An earlier version of Chapter Five appeared as 'The Moral Problem of Fiction: Rethinking the Emotional Effects of Fictional Characters', in A. James, A. Kubo and F. Lavocat (eds), *Can Fiction Change the World?* 69–81, Oxford: Legenda. Finally, an earlier version of Chapter Seven appeared as 'What Counts as (Evidence of) Narrow Aesthetic Cognitivism', *European Journal of Analytic Philosophy*, 20 (2): 363–88, available online: https://doi.org/10.31820/ejap.20.2.6.

Introduction

Film theory is in no short supply. The same holds for philosophy of fiction. Yet, little has been devoted specifically to fiction film. Undoubtedly, classical and post-classical film theories alike have traditionally been about fiction film, but they have not been interested in defining what *fiction* in fiction film stands for. Conversely, philosophers of fiction have regularly claimed that their account is applicable to all media including film, yet they have rarely pursued such an application. In fact, to my knowledge there are only four monographs which are genuinely devoted to exploring what fiction film is – Gregory Currie's 1995 *Film and Mind*, Roger Odin's 2000 *De la fiction*, George Wilson's 2011 *Seeing Fictions in Film*, and my own 2019 *Fiction and Imagination in Early Cinema*. But even these have been geared towards their respective disciplinary readerships. Currie and Wilson are philosophers mostly read by philosophers while Odin and I as film scholars are typically read by other film scholars.

This monograph sets out to establish a firmer rapport between film studies and philosophy of fiction. In my own monograph (Slugan, 2019a), I have tried to do the same while focusing on early cinema. I still believe that early cinema is an excellent case study for understanding not only the historicity of the categories of fiction and nonfiction film but fiction and nonfiction in general. But I cannot blame philosophers for not reading a monograph with an admittedly niche focus and the film side of things weighing more on the balance of the book. With philosopher of art Enrico Terrone, I have tried to improve on this in a co-edited special issue of *Studies in Documentary Film*

(2021). This seems to have been a more effective attempt with the contributions at least recognized by philosophers (cf. Davies, 2022). At the same time, the issue tackled primarily the fiction/nonfiction distinction and did so, as the title of the journal suggests, from the documentary studies perspective.

Here my focus will be primarily on fiction with more weight given to theoretical than historical work. This will, of course, first involve the discussion of the fiction/nonfiction distinction. But the bulk of the attention will be on what fictional works are, how the works claim their membership in the category of fiction, what they demand of their audiences, and how audiences engage them in response.

I will be asking four main types of questions: disciplinary, historical, ontological, and phenomenological. The disciplinary ones include: What have been the assumptions of film studies and philosophy of fiction? What has been the focus of their attention in studying fiction? What have been their blind spots? Where does the dominant model for studying fiction come from? How can the two disciplines harness each other's strengths and offset their weaknesses? How can experimental studies contribute to the understanding of fiction? What is the future of the study of fiction?

Ontological questions concern the nature of fiction and related phenomena. What is fiction? What is a fictional work as opposed to the content of fiction? How do fictional works differ from nonfictional ones? Are there hybrid works? What is a mandate to imagine? What is imagination? What distinguishes imagination from other mental states like belief? How does film fiction differ from literary fiction? What are the typologies of different forms of imagining involved in film fiction? What are the different types of imaginative resistance? Is imaginative resistance a common phenomenon or an artefact of highly specific philosophical examples? Do emotions elicited by fiction films have fictional entities as their objects?

Historical questions find their way in the monograph as well. Has the definition of fiction changed over time? What is the relationship between genre changes and fiction? Can a work change its non/fictional status over time? How are mandates to imagine established? How do they dissipate? What are some of the historical examples of films that have crossed the boundary from nonfiction to fiction? Have there been crossings in the other direction as well? How does hybridity relate to such historical change? How are works which do not circulate publicly categorized?

The last set of questions pertains to audience responses. What do audiences actually imagine in response to mandates? Is imagination necessarily involved in the understanding of narratives and/or visual representations? What is the relationship between mandated imaginings, actual imaginative engagement, and imaginative resistance? Why is there considerable individual variability in imaginative resistance? Why do audiences have emotional responses to films about fictional entities? Is there anything paradoxical about the intensity of these emotions compared to the intensity of the same for real people? Are fictional narratives effective tools of narrative persuasion? Is there a difference in short- and long-term effects? Do audiences acquire knowledge and/or beliefs from fictional works? Are different age groups more susceptible?

The main answers to these sets of questions that I will be providing can be divided into criticisms and proposals. It is only natural to lead with the former. Film studies have undertheorized fiction and have missed the opportunity to draw on the developments in philosophy of fiction to grasp the importance of theorizing the category. Philosophy of fiction has focused on fictional utterances instead of works of fiction and has neglected film historical approaches to categorizing fiction and nonfiction. Film studies have dominantly approached fiction from a textualist perspective, whereas philosophy of fiction has done so from an intentionalist position, with neither of the approaches being able to account for the changes in non/fictional status of works. The understanding of fiction has been modelled on literary fiction in both disciplines. While film studies have shown a lack of interest in the phenomenon of imaginative resistance, philosophy of fiction has focused on examples from literary fiction neglecting film. Discussions of the emotional engagement with fiction film entities have neglected the moral problems of such consumption. Philosophers of fiction and even more so film scholars have not sufficiently engaged with empirical studies of belief acquisition in fiction film.

As a response to these criticisms, I offer the following key proposals. Fictional work is a work whose content the audiences are primarily mandated to imagine. The primacy of mandate is determined institutionally through a negotiation of production, promotion, distribution, exhibition, and reception factors. Works can change their non/fictional status in both directions over time. Literary fictions typically mandate propositional imaginings while film fictions standardly also mandate perceptual imaginings making their mandated imaginings richer. Imaginative resistance is a consequence of how richly audiences imagine, be it as a response to mandates or as a preferred engagement strategy. It is the free imaginings together with other real-life structures rather than mandated imaginings that cause emotions like fear in engagement with fictional works. Fictions are inefficient at changing real-life beliefs about the non-aesthetic world in adult audiences. Studies of fiction should become more interdisciplinary.

The monograph has a tripartite structure. In short, Part One defines fiction as primarily mandated imagining, Part Two explores the primacy of this mandate, and part three investigates the actual imaginative responses to fiction. The first two chapters constitute Part One and address the difference between fiction and nonfiction from the perspective of film studies and philosophy of art, respectively. This distinction will be understood in terms of primacy of mandate to imagine as opposed to the lack of such a mandate. The third chapter investigates the changing nature of the primacy of the mandate on historical case studies. Chapter Four addresses the core mandate that differentiates film from literary fiction – the mandate to imagine perceptually. The last part of the monograph and its final three chapters consider the audiences' actual imaginative engagement and its relation to three key responses to fiction: imaginative resistance, emotions, and beliefs. The summary for each chapter is as follows.

Chapter One proposes an institutional theory of fiction as a response to the lack of interest in theorizing film *fiction* in film studies. On this account, works serve as props which mandate social games of make-believe. The chapter also addresses significant disciplinary issues which issue from this undertheorizing. First, categorization of numerous films diverges significantly from the ordinary understanding of the fiction/nonfiction divide. Second, such categorization may lead to both misunderstanding of audience experience and ethical problems. Third, theoretical commitments revolving around indexicality although partially applicable to documentary cannot shed light on fiction contrary to numerous attempts to do so. Fourth, one of the discipline's key assumptions – fiction films change real-life beliefs – demands a theory of the relationship between fiction and belief that is currently absent in film studies. Closer scrutiny of the notion of fiction, I argue, is necessary to dispel these issues. The remainder of the monograph provides such an analysis.

An institutional theory is further developed in Chapter Two in conversation with philosophy of fiction. The chapter first moves away from the disciplinary focus on the non/fictional status of utterances to that of works. Building on the consensus view, fictional work is defined as one whose content the audiences are *primarily* mandated to imagine. The proposal is defended against three main obstructions. Concerning the inflation of the category, it is argued that imagination is relevant for the definition only if it is mandated and not if it is a part of the basic understanding of the work. The idea that fiction is best understood as genre does not mean that it cannot be defined in terms of sufficient and necessary conditions. Lastly, the argument that there is no special place for imagination in engagement with fictional works is belied by the general imaginative stance that must be taken to focus on film as a fictional representation as opposed to a recording of the profilmic.

The historical nature of the primacy of the mandate is explored in Chapter Three. It is argued that determining this primacy, i.e. assigning works membership in categories of fiction and nonfiction, respectively, is accomplished through indexing. Indexing is a process of providing labels for films through production decisions, promotional strategies, exhibition patterns, public classification, and critical and audience reception. Much like genre labelling, for the membership of a work to stabilize within a given category indexing needs to be accepted by audiences. And membership can always be relitigated through re-indexing. The chapter offers two case studies of such renewed litigation. *The Blair Witch Project* (Daniel Myrick and Eduardo Sánchez, 1999) originally constituted a documentary but was quickly transformed into a fiction film. *Neighbours* (Norman McLaren, 1952) initially belonged to the category of fiction, then moved to nonfiction following its Short Documentary Oscar win, and eventually returned to fiction where it remains. The chapter concludes with an analysis of hybridity as an effect of either competing public classifications or lack thereof.

Chapter Four turns to the question of what the mandate to imagine requires of audiences. The chapter starts with two taxonomies of imagination – according to the quality of the object of imagination (propositional, perceptual, experiential, objectual) and depending on whether the imagining involves imagining oneself experientially or not (from within or without). Differentiation of imagination from other mental phenomena like belief and memory follows. The distinction between propositional and perceptual imaginings allows us to argue that while literary fiction typically mandates only the former film fiction standardly authorizes both. When it comes to the core mandate about imagining audiovisual information, special attention is paid to Vsevolod Pudovkin's ideal observer and George Wilson's mediated imagining seeing proposal. Both versions of this imagining perceiving from within are refuted in favour of the view that audiences are supposed to imagine perceptually from without.

The focus of attention in Chapter Five is imaginative resistance or the phenomenon wherein audiences report difficulties in imagining what is mandated. While traditionally the phenomenon has been discussed on propositional examples from literary fiction in a speculative manner, this chapter shifts the focus to perceptual imaginings in film fiction supported by experimental findings. The key interventions are threefold. First, recent empirical evidence suggests that both the range of examples of imaginative resistance and the level of resistance among individuals are far more varied than philosophers allow for. Second, the more domains in which audiences imagine – vertical richness – the more likely it is they will be mandated to imagine clashing experiences of the object-prop incongruence type. Third, the more domain-specific details – horizontal richness – the audiences flesh out the more they risk imagining cognitively taxing contradictions. In other words, because film fictions typically mandate richer imaginings than literary fictions, the former are more fertile ground for imaginative resistance.

Chapter Six devotes itself to the relationship between mandated imaginings, actual imaginative engagement, and emotional effects in fiction films. While the debate has hitherto revolved around how emotional responses to entities that do not exist are possible and whether they are rational or not, this chapter treats the relative intensity of such emotions compared to those for real-life people as a moral paradox. Taking horror films as its key case study, it is suggested that the object of audiences' fear is not the mandated imagining about the fictional monster but the real-life structures instead. These include the audiovisual quality of the profilmic representations and strategies such as jump-scares which elicit fear reactions without involvement of mandated imaginings. Real-life structures also involve suggested but not mandated imaginings about the implausible yet not impossible existence and potential dangers of similar monsters. Framing the fear responses in terms of real-life structures instead of fictional entities disarms the moral dimension of the paradox.

The final chapter returns to the key assumption in film studies, shared in good part by philosophers of fiction, that fiction film influences real-life beliefs. The assumption is contextualized within the broader debate about the value of art and its potential for both epistemic harm and benefit. While film scholars have traditionally held a pessimistic outlook on the matter and aesthetic cognitivists an optimistic one, both agree that fiction impacts real-life beliefs. But while over the years both have suggested mechanisms of belief acquisition, neither has devoted sufficient attention to the question of whether beliefs are actually acquired through engagement with fiction. By turning to experimental studies of belief acquisition this chapter argues that fictional narratives as opposed to nonfictional ones are ineffective in imparting beliefs. This means that both narrow versions of aesthetic cognitivism and great swaths of ideology critique-driven film studies need to revisit their assumptions.

The future of this assumption is one of the proposed directions of research on fiction addressed in the Conclusion. While it is unlikely that fictional works influence real-life beliefs in adults, children and teenagers might be more susceptible. This, however, cannot be resolved through speculative work; instead, experimental research is needed. Ideally, this work should be interdisciplinary involving at the very least film scholars, philosophers of fiction, and experimental psychologists. This is a general lesson when it comes to phenomena on the intersection of mandated imaginings, imaginative engagement, and audience effects. The study of imaginative resistance would profit from establishing how rich the audiences imagine when engaging fictional works. The discussion of emotional engagement with fiction would do the same by investigating the object of emotions.

Simultaneously, this does not mean that all questions of fiction can be resolved through experimental work. Most of the disciplinary, ontological, and historical questions do not offer themselves as easily to such methods. But they would all profit from a greater interaction between scholars from different disciplines working on the category that people devote so much of their time to. What follows is an attempt in that direction.

PART ONE

THEORIES OF FICTION

1

Fiction as challenge to cinema studies

There is undeniably much more to cinema studies than studying film texts. For some time, film scholars have been interested in other objects of study including film technologies, industries, studios, promotional strategies, distribution networks, exhibition venues, censorship, and audiences among others. But despite these approaches, studies focusing on specific films, film structures, film genres, authorial oeuvres, national or local productions, stylistic epochs, film schools and movements, and the likes remain the bulk of scholarly production. Furthermore, such text-oriented scholarship primarily looks at fiction film. And this is true of all three traditional branches of film studies – criticism, history, and theory.

Next to privileging fiction film, the concept of fiction also organizes text-focused scholarship. The fiction/nonfiction binary presents a key taxonomical division in the field where it is fiction that is the default term against which the other is defined. For instance, documentary and experimental cinema are, at least in the first instance, regularly articulated in opposition to fiction. In the case of documentary, Bill Nichols writes that '[documentaries] tell stories that, although similar to feature fiction, remain distinct from it' (2017: 4). In calling for the study of experimental cinema, P. Adams Sitney also contrasts it to fiction film, i.e. '[to] this other cinema [heralded by] Griffith, Chaplin, Méliès', Eisenstein, von Stroheim, Dreyer, Bresson' (1978: 1).

Yet for all the organizing power that the concept of fiction has within the discipline, *fiction* in the notions of 'fiction film' and 'nonfiction film' rarely receives sustained treatment by film scholars with the discussion most often relegated to relatively brief opening remarks in documentary theories. Works of film theory more broadly, which, interestingly, regularly focus on fiction film, by comparison, may define what film is but are virtually never interested in defining *fiction* film.[1] That an entry for 'fiction' cannot be found in any of the widely used conceptual encyclopaedias/dictionaries of film studies – Edward Branigan and Warren Buckland's 2014 *The Routledge Encyclopaedia of Film Theory*, Anette Kuhn and Guy Westwell's 2020 *A Dictionary of Film Studies*, and Susan Hayward's 2023 *Cinema Studies* – is also symptomatic.[2] It is as though fiction is a given, hence something film scholars need not worry about.

In this chapter I argue that this leads to significant issues. In the first section I address the rare instances of film scholarship which devote sustained attention to the notion of fiction. According to the dominant approach – the textualist one – it is the form and content that determine the fictional or nonfictional status of a film. This is most visible among scholars of documentary film who regularly argue that discursive strategies such as misrepresentation and staging introduce fictive elements. But such accounts misconstrue the difference between fiction and nonfiction as a degree of truthfulness.

I argue in section two that the difference should instead be understood along the lines of the presence or absence of mandate to imagine as developed by Kendall Walton. In other words, fictional works are those whose content the audiences are primarily supposed to imagine. Nonfictional works, conversely, are those whose content the audiences are not primarily supposed to imagine. (A subset of nonfiction may further be defined in terms of mandate to believe.) Because under my institutional view of fiction the mandates to imagine arise through a negotiation between production, distribution, promotion, exhibition, and reception factors, this proposal has advantages over other extratextualist approaches. Unlike intentionalist accounts, an institutional theory of fiction can accommodate works like early train and trick films which have changed their non/fictional status over time. Contrary to reception-driven approaches, my proposal preserves the public nature of fiction and nonfiction categories.

In the third section I address the most detailed theory of fiction developed by a film scholar – Roger Odin's. Much like institutionalism it avoids the pitfalls of textualism and intentionalism, and to a good extent those of reception-driven theories. But ultimately, I argue that institutionalism should be preferred to Odin's approach for two main reasons. He assumes that only narrative forms can be fictional which is belied by non-narrative fictional work in different arts, including painting, literature, and film. Moreover, he models his theory of film fiction on linguistic forms of communication mistakenly assuming that fiction is originally a linguistic phenomenon.

I tackle the consequences of undertheorizing fiction in film studies in the fourth section. First, academic categorization of numerous films diverges significantly from the ordinary understanding of the fiction/nonfiction divide. Second, such scholarly categorization may lead to misunderstanding of audience experience and ethical problems alike. Third, theoretical commitments revolving around indexicality although partially applicable to documentary cannot shed light on fiction contrary to numerous attempts to do so.

Given its importance, I focus on the last consequence in the final section. Perhaps the key assumption of film studies is that fiction films change real-life beliefs. Yet, despite this assumption a theory of the relationship between fiction and belief is currently conspicuously absent from the discipline. Even more disconcertingly, film studies have been generally uninterested in investigating whether the assumption holds in the first place. Closer scrutiny of the notion of fiction, I argue, is necessary to dispel these issues. The remainder of the monograph provides such an analysis.

As a preliminary consideration it is important to say that in exploring the notion of fiction, I do not aim at any form of semantic policing. In ordinary language it is perfectly proper to call lies, fabrications, and made-up things, fictions. When Donald Trump insists that his first inauguration drew record crowds, we may legitimately refer to this as fiction. But we can easily distinguish this broad sense of fiction from the narrow one in which we say that, for instance, horror films are fictional, whereas TV reportages are not. In this narrow sense, Trump's claims are lies and not fiction. When I speak of fiction in this book, crucially, it is in this narrow sense. Moreover, I assume that it is this ordinary narrow meaning of fiction that the definitions proposed in film studies need to explain. Therefore, definitions will be faulty if they stray too much from this meaning without providing good reasons for doing so. Similarly, I propose that film theory, history, and criticism should also primarily focus on the ordinary narrow meaning of fiction for otherwise they risk equivocation between the narrow and broad meanings which are clearly distinct concepts.

Textualist approaches

The result of the relative lack of interest in fiction in film studies is that fiction is most often construed implicitly in terms of textual features. Many understand the fiction/nonfiction distinction in terms of presentational strategies and/or content alone: professional actors vs real-life amateurs, staging vs naturalness, fantastic stories vs everyday events, spectacular sets vs on-location shooting, animation vs live action. Traditionally, this dichotomy was exemplified by George Méliès' trick-films and the Lumière brothers' actualities. Whereas actualities depict everyday events, acrobatic feats, views of various locales, etc., fiction films include trick films, gag comedies, chase films, etc.

Although a useful heuristic, there are numerous counterexamples if the approach is treated as a strict categorization strategy. Despite animation's traditional association with fiction film there are numerous animated documentaries, including the almost completely animated *Waltz with Bashir* (Ari Folman, 2008) and *Tower* (Keith Maitland, 2016), which are nonfictions as Annabelle Honess Roe (2013) has argued and public classification has established. Conversely, TV shows like *The Office* (BBC, 2011–13) and films like *The Blair Witch Project* (Daniel Myrick and Eduardo Sánchez, 1999) make extensive use of documentary aesthetics. Yet they constitute fictions, nonetheless. It is even possible to imagine a fiction film identical to *The Arrival of a Train* (Lumière brothers, 1895–7) and a nonfiction one indistinguishable from *A Trip to the Moon* (Méliès, 1902). All that is necessary is a change in context. In the first case, a gallery projects a film indistinguishable from the Lumière brothers' film under the title *The Arrival of a Train in Freedonia, c.1900* inviting the visitors to make-believe viewing a black and white recording from the imaginary country from more than a century ago. On another occasion, the same gallery presents *A Recording of a Trip to the Moon*, now a film identical to Méliès', instructing the patrons to treat the film as a single-take documentary recording of one particular screening of Méliès' film.

More explicit treatment of fiction can be found on the opening pages of works of documentary theory. However, documentary theory also remains largely indebted to the textualist approach. In its earlier more radical instances, Michael Renov, for example, argued that 'all discursive forms–documentary included–are, if not fictional, at least *fictive*, this by virtue of their tropic character (their recourse to tropes or rhetorical figures)' (1993: 7, italics in the original). But fictive elements defined in terms of discursive strategies like exaggerated camera angles, editing, or narrative organization are far from the ordinary understanding of fiction. A World Health Organization video conference on Covid-19 outbreak shot with standard lighting does not become fiction if expressionistic lighting is used instead. It is true that, as Renov himself points out, 'documentary has availed itself of nearly every constructive device known to fiction (of course, the reverse is equally true)' (1993: 7). But, as Noël Carroll has argued (2003), this only points to problems with textualist accounts of the fiction/nonfiction distinction rather than demonstrates that the difference between the two collapses.

In a more moderate version of documentary theory, it is not discursivity in general but specific textual features such as the degree of fabrication that constitute fiction. As Bill Nichols puts it, 'The division of documentary from fiction, like the division of historiography from fiction, rests on the degree to which the story fundamentally corresponds to actual situations, events, and people versus the degree to which it is primarily a product of the filmmaker's invention' (2017: 8–9). For Nichols, the classification of *Nanook of the North* (Robert Flaherty, 1922) as documentary or fiction hinges on whether it is 'a plausible representation of Inuit life [or] Flaherty's distinct vision of it' (Nichols, 2017: 9). But the fact that Flaherty took liberties with Nanook's life, does not necessarily entail introduction of fictional elements. Rather, it means that what we are dealing with is a (deliberate) misrepresentation of Inuit life. Compare this to *Bowling for Columbine* (Michael Moore, 2002) where through creative editing Moore misrepresents that buying a gun takes shorter than it does. This does not introduce any fictional elements into the film. Rather, what we have is a documentary which despite presenting itself as a plausible representation fails to be truthful under closer scrutiny. This is no different from how Flaherty has Nanook hunt in traditional Inuit way no longer in use at the time of filming. In other words, Flaherty's distinct version of Inuit life is not something apart from its plausible representation but is precisely what is presented as the plausible representation (although this plausible representation is in fact a misrepresentation). In another variant of Nichols' vocabulary, Flaherty is not presenting us with *a* world, but still with *the* world – he is just misrepresenting it. In short, misrepresentation (deliberate or otherwise) does not constitute fiction, nor does it introduce fictional elements.

Another specific textual element often deemed to be fictive in documentary context is staging. Take, for instance, Springer and Rhodes' introduction to a volume on docufictions:

> For the authors in this collection, these intersections [between fiction and documentary] begin literally at the beginning of the cinema, blurring the lines between fact and fiction. *Blacksmith Scene* (1893), Edison and Dickson's first publicly exhibited film, purports to show exactly that: three blacksmiths working and enjoying a beer. But of course the men captured on film were not professional blacksmiths but Edison employees, and the film was staged and shot at the Edison laboratory.
>
> (2005: 6)

Here staging is meant both as manipulation of mise-en-scène and deception. Undeniably, the *Blacksmith Scene* was not recorded at the blacksmith's but in Edison's Black Maria studio with a specific set design, props, lighting, character placement, work choreography, etc., in place. However, since the manipulation of the mise-en-scène is a discursive trope in Renov's sense, it does not necessarily entail any fictive elements. Much like a presidential debate does not turn fictional simply because it includes a complex mise-en-scène of lighting, candidate placement, speaking rules, set design, etc., in front of a camera so is a recorded wielding and hitting of hammers and passing the bottle not fictional simply because it was staged in this sense. Matters do not change even when it turns out that the protagonists using these tools and enjoying a drink are not blacksmiths but actors. Precisely like with the Nanook example, then we are merely dealing with a (deliberate) misrepresentation. In other words, *Blacksmith Scene* remains nonfictional even in its deceptive aspects.

The last commonly invoked textualist feature I wish to address is indexicality. Unlike the preceding ones, indexicality is taken to be a standard marker of nonfiction. The most recent iterations of this view allow for non-indexical documentaries like animated ones (Nichols, 2017: 12).[3] But they do purport that if there is an indexical link between the image and its relevant content, then we are dealing with a documentary (Nichols, 2017: 24–8). Phrased in analytic philosophy parlance, indexicality is a sufficient but not necessary condition for documentary. The problem, I propose, is that indexicality standardly understood does not even extend to most non-animated documentaries and nonfictions, analogue and digital alike.

Since Peter Wollen (1969), indexicality has generally denoted an automatic causal link *and* some form of contact between the photograph and its object. Much like a pawprint is an index of a dog imprinted through its weight so is a photograph of Sun an index of Sun imprinted through its light. But what holds for photographs of light-emitting objects like Sun does not hold for a much broader class of objects including dogs (and typical subjects of documentaries) which only reflect light. In other words, while in the case of the pawprint dog is in direct contact with the sand, in the case of the photograph the dog is not the source of light but an object against which the light bounces off. This means there is merely indirect contact between the photograph and the dog via light. Things get even further removed once it is recognized that audiences virtually never watch the original negative print of a given documentary film. In the case of analogue films, the screened print would have gone through at least one photographic printing where a *new* source of light is shone through the original. In this step even the indirect contact where the relevant light touched both the object and the photograph is lost. (In digital cinema, copying does not even involve the image but its representation in the form of binary voltage states). Put succinctly, even if original negatives are indices of objects further prints are not (Slugan, 2017b).[4]

The problem with textualist approaches, then, is that textual features alone cannot determine whether something is fiction or not (or in between). To generalize Renov's claim, nonfiction genres can use representational strategies typical of fiction ones as much as fiction genres can deploy techniques standardly attributed to nonfiction ones. But this means extratextual features must play a key role in determining fictionality.

Despite some interest in the notion of fiction in the studies of documentaries and hybrid forms, only a handful of film scholars writing in English, French, and German have produced book-length investigations of the subject in the last twenty years, while in Italian, Spanish, Russian, and Japanese no such work has been written within the discipline in the same period if not longer.[5] The only study in German is an edited collection by Gertrude Koch and Christiane Voss (2009). The volume, however, is not interested in exploring fictionality's extratextual markers. Instead, its two best-known contributors – Gertrude Koch and Vinzenz Hediger – propose that films are fictionally indeterminate precisely because their medium properties understood as textual features are fictionally indeterminate.

When speaking of live-action recordings (documentaries and fiction films with live subjects and actors), Koch (2009), for instance, argues that they are both fictions and documentaries at the same time. They are documentaries because they document whatever was in front of the camera. And they are fictions because all such recordings are of people and things passed, i.e. of worlds which are now unalterable.[6] The insistence on fictionality of all such films is misplaced because it conflates the fact that the world of fiction like the one depicted in *Casablanca* (Michael Curtiz, 1942) is different from the world of documentary such as the one in *Roger & Me* (Michael Moore, 1989). Whereas it was never possible to speak to Rick from *Casablanca* for Rick never existed in the real world, in the case of Moore's film it was at least in principle possible to interact with the General Motors CEO Roger Smith in the late 1980s. The claim that all live-action films are also documentaries is undermined by Koch's assertion that animations are inherently fictional and that they, unlike live-action recordings, possess no documentary quality. But it is undeniable that if a film is made from hand-drawn pictures, then at the very least it is a documentary recording of those hand-drawn pictures and may even be a documentary of whatever those drawings depict as is the case with *The*

Sinking of the 'Lusitania' (Winsor McCay, 1918). As we can see, Koch is unable to reconcile the competing demands for determinacy and indeterminacy – both of which stem from the textualist approach to fiction.

Hediger (2009) goes even further in seeking to revive and combine the claims by Christian Metz (1982) and André Bazin (2004) that due to medium-specific properties all films are concurrently both fictions and documentaries. In the first case, he follows Metz's argument that '[e]very film is a fiction film' (1982: 44) because the cinematic signifier is present as an image of the object but absent as the object itself. But according to this logic all representations that single out an object are fictional. Portrait paintings denote a specific absent person with an image that is present. There are even automatic reproductions which do the same. Sound recordings, contrary to Hediger, are only the effects of the air vibrations that constitute the original sound, and not the same ontological object as the sounds that caused them. We do not capture air vibrations themselves but rather their effects which allow us to generate *new* waves (with the same relevant properties as the original ones). Regarding the film's nonfictional status, Hediger claims that all films are documentaries not because they record whatever was in front of the camera, but because as signifiers instantiated in a physical medium, they partake in the being of what they represent. Yet by this logic all representations are also documentaries because all representations instantiate what they represent through signifiers in a physical medium – colour pigments making up graphemes on book pages or forms in paintings, air vibrations constituting phonemes in spoken words, etc. This both undermines any claims to cinema's specificity and falls short of capturing the ordinary understanding of fiction/nonfiction.

Koch's and Hediger's emphasis on indeterminacy in its film-specific version can be understood as a part of a broader philosophical approach which argues that the fiction/nonfiction distinction is moot based on the idea that signification has no access to the real world, merely its representations (Derrida, 1976, Žižek, 1992, and Baudrillard, 1994). According to this view, our statements about the world never refer to the world itself but only to other statements. There is nothing but a chain of floating signifiers none of which is grounded in the actual world. And if that is the case, then what we take to be nonfictional statements are no different from fictional ones because the latter do not represent anything in the actual world either. Therefore, the argument goes, the fiction/nonfiction distinction is a mirage.

Extratextualist approaches

But even if no statements refer to the real world, we can still distinguish fiction from nonfiction (Konrad, 2016). According to the approach dominant in philosophical aesthetics (Stock, 2016), we can do so by following Kendall Walton's (1990) argument developed in *Mimesis as Make-believe* which construes fiction as mandated imagining. The key point to understand is that fiction should not be understood in terms of (linguistic) reference. Rather, it should be modelled on games of make-believe or imagining that children play with different props (toys, everyday objects, people, etc.). A typical game of make-believe, for instance, involves using Barbie and Ken dolls as props for imagining a couple lying on a beach and enjoying the sunset. In another, a child puts a wooden parrot on her shoulder and imagines herself a pirate with a taste for rum and adventure. Much like a child uses her doll as a prop for imagining various objects, people, and events, so do viewers use recorded sounds and images of say, Humphrey Bogart in *Casablanca*, as props to imagine Rick and the events of the film. The main difference is that whereas in children's games the mandate is most often explicit, in cinema and the arts in general it is implicit.

To return to the crucial point, the difference between fiction and nonfiction is not whether something refers to the real world or not, or whether something is true or false, but whether we are mandated to imagine it or not.

This understanding of fiction also explains why fiction (film) can regularly convey factual truths. Historical dramas often pride themselves on historical accuracy with *Zodiac* (David Fincher, 2007), for instance, conveying numerous facts about the eponymous murders and journalism business in San Francisco of the 1970s, among other things. This is not even a matter of degree, because a work could be factually completely true and remain fiction so long as on top of mandating the audiences to believe what is represented, they were also supposed to imagine it. That is why there are texts like Natalia Ginzburg's *Family Sayings* (1965) and Javier Marías' *Dark Back of Time* (1998) which are treated as fictions despite being factually (almost) completely accurate. And that is why we can also conceive of a completely accurate historical drama, say, a hundred per cent true version of Steven Spielberg's *Lincoln* (2012) which is still fiction.

In film scholarship, it is among those writing in English that Walton's influence can be found. This is because the debates about fiction in film have been relegated to the outskirts of the discipline to be picked up mostly by those interested in applying philosophical aesthetics to film studies. It is no surprise then that in the last thirty years it is mostly analytic philosophers who have produced monographs on the subject. Gregory Currie (1995) was the first to develop an extensive theory of film fiction in terms of imagination as a part of a broader theory of pictorial representation in film. Currie's key questions – whether we are supposed to imagine ourselves present at the fictional event represented and whether fiction films have fictional narrators – are also picked up in a book-length contribution by George Wilson (2011). Most importantly for this discussion, in their version of Walton's theory, the key extratextual features for determining fictionality are authorial intentions – audiences are mandated to imagine so and so if and only if the author intends them to do so.

Elsewhere (Slugan, 2019a) I have offered a different version of Walton's theory to argue that a film's fictional status is temporally unstable. I have proposed that whether something is fiction or not – i.e. whether there is a mandate to imagine so and so – is not defined solely through authorial intention and/or textual features but arises from a negotiation between production, promotion, distribution, exhibition, and reception strategies the results of which may change over time. For instance, whereas audiences today treat films like *The Arrival of a Train* as a nonfictional recording of a train pulling into station, at the end of the nineteenth century such films were both promoted and received as invoking the fiction of imagining a train launching out of the screen and into the auditorium. Conversely, whereas present-day audiences imagine the fiction of an astronomer enduring a string of fantastical misadventures in a film like *The Astronomer's Dream or the Man in the Moon* (Méliès, 1899), its contemporaries billed and understood it as 'a life motion picture reproduction of a celebrated French spectacular piece' (*Philadelphia Inquirer*, 4 September 1899, 10), i.e. as a nonfictional reproduction of a magic theatre performance.[7] Such negotiations are also the reason why animated films like the aforementioned *Waltz with Bashir* came to be accepted as documentaries.

A scholar who was initially relatively close to this institutional approach but went on to espouse intentionalism on par with Currie and Wilson is Carroll. In his earlier work, Carroll pointed out that audiences generally have information about whether film is fiction or nonfiction beforehand, because films come labelled or indexed as such by '[p]roducers, writers, directors, distributors, and exhibitors' (1983: 237). However, despite maintaining the value of indexing, Carroll's latest position is that the necessary criterion for fiction is the authorial fictive intention after all: '*x* is a fiction only if the sender intends the audience to imagine the propositional content of *x* for the reason that the audience recognizes that this is what the sender intends' (2003: 204).[8] Where Carroll parts ways with Walton is in arguing that a subclass of nonfiction relevant for film studies – viz. films of presumptive assertion – is defined by the mandate to *believe*: 'the maker of a film of presumptive assertion not only intends that the audience adopt the assertoric stance to his film, but he also intends that the audience understand his film' (2003: 207). But we have already seen that fictions can mandate beliefs at the same time as they mandate imaginings. In other words, *pace* Carroll mandating beliefs is not logically contrary to mandating imaginings. Both can be operational at the same time. It is possible to imagine things that (we believe) are true (UK prime minister is Keir Starmer), false (UK prime minister is Jeremy Corbyn), and do not exist (a silver unicorn) alike. The virtually fully factual re-enactment of Queen's Live Aid performance in *Bohemian Rhapsody* (Bryan Singer, 2018), for example, does not render that part of the film nonfiction because there is both a mandate to believe *and* a mandate to imagine the performance. And, as argued earlier, there is a mandate to imagine not because of some textual feature like the presence of professional actors. Rather, this is because *Bohemian Rhapsody* has been indexed as a fiction film and because audiences – the factor that is missing in Carroll's list of indexing agencies but plays an important role in institutional negotiations I advocate for – have accepted this indexing.[9]

The decision between the intentionalist and the non-intentionalist approaches hinges on what we take to better describe the ontological status of cultural texts such as religious mythologies. From a non-intentionalist perspective, ancient texts like the *Epic of Gilgamesh*, Hesiod's *Theogony*, or narrative parts of *Pyramid Texts* invite present-day readers to imagine various deities and as such constitute fictions. But for ancient Mesopotamians, Greeks, and Egyptians it is fair to say that these works articulated sets of real-life beliefs about the actual world. From an intentionalist standpoint, however, the present-day treatment of these mythologies is irrelevant. It only matters how the authors/compilers of these texts intended them to be understood. And given that they were meant to be believed they are nonfictions. However, all other things being equal, any definition of fiction needs to start from the ordinary understanding of the term which is in line with the non-intentionalist account. In the case of film, intentionalists will have problems with works like *Tracked by Bloodhounds* (Selig Poliscope Company, 1904) – today firmly indexed and viewed as fiction – because they would need to categorize them as nonfictions given that they were originally intended and advertised as such: 'NEGATIVE ACTUALLY MADE [...] OF ACTUAL OCCURRENCE' (Selig Polyscope Company Catalogue, 'Tracked by Bloodhounds', Supplement 17, 1905, 1, 3, capitalization in the original).

Roger Odin's theory of fictivization

The non-intentionalist approach I have espoused (Slugan 2019a, 2021b, 2022a) is closer to perhaps the most widely read work on fiction by a film scholar in the last two and a half decades – Roger Odin's *De la fiction* (2000) whose English translation is yet to appear.[10] In it, Odin continues developing his semio-pragmatic approach from the 1980s and 1990s according to which the status of fiction also does not hinge on textual parameters. Instead, the film's status depends on whether it is *read* as fiction. More precisely, Odin speaks of modes – categories and classes of films – which include the documentary and the fictional mode among others. Importantly for him, no film is inherently a documentary or a fiction film. Rather, modes are effects of reading strategies – operations in Odin's terminology. Although Odin has changed the number of operations over the years – in his 2000 monograph there are five broad operations – the key feature of the fictional mode is that it deploys all operations. So, for instance, whereas the documentary mode makes use of the following four operations – diegetization, narration, mise en phase, and the construction of actual enunciator – the fictional mode also deploys the final operation – fictivization. This fictivization, crucially, is the conferring of fictional status onto both the enunciator and the addressee which results in not having to take the film's content as real. Though in principle spectators can employ any operation to any film they want, in practice their reading strategies are constrained by institutional considerations such as whether the film belongs to commercial cinema, arthouse cinema, non-theatrical cinema, etc.

Although neither defines fiction in textual terms, in contrast to Waltonian approaches, imagination for Odin is not at the core of fiction. Instead, it is fictivization. Moreover, in Odin there is no such a thing as a *mandate* to imagine something irrespective of whether the mandate comes from the author (Carroll, Currie, Wilson) or is negotiated (Slugan). Rather, there is primarily the willingness of the spectator to apply the operation of fictivization in line with or against institutional constraints. In other words, Odin's position could be described as spectator-centric for it is up to the viewer to deploy fictivization or not. However non-intentionalist my approach might be, in it, readers privately applying fictivization or not could not confer fictional status on a film. Under this framework, when film changes from nonfiction to fiction, it is due to broad audiences publicly classifying it as fiction with promotional strategies usually following suit.[11] In Odin it would suffice for spectators to privately read a film against the institutional grain to transform, say, a documentary into fiction. This could easily lead to the hegemony of the author simply being replaced with the hegemony of the reader.[12]

This, for instance, is the key problem with other extratextualist approaches heralded by some documentary scholars like Dirk Eitzen (1995) and Vivian Sobchack (1999) who propose that it is spectatorial experience that defines the status of a film:

> On first viewing (for people who do not know the film's secret), *No Lies* [Mitchell Block, 1973] is labeled as a documentary, perceived as a documentary, and interpreted as a documentary. For all intents and purposes, it *is* a documentary.
>
> (Eitzen, 1995: 94)

> One viewer's fiction may be another's *film-souvenir*; one viewer's documentary, another's fiction.
>
> (Sobchack, 1999: 253)

Put succinctly, if a viewer experiences a film as non/fiction, then it is non/fiction. The strength of this view is that it also allows for historical change of non/fiction. But the problem is that it falls afoul the ordinary understanding of these categories. It is true that spectators can, say, view *The Favourite* (2019) as a nonfictional recording of whatever was in front of the camera during the shooting of Yorgos Lanthimos' film. But although the spectators may experience it as nonfiction, *The Favourite* is still ordinarily understood as fiction. Reception-driven approaches simply replace ordinary public categorization with personal experience. But for categorization purposes the point is precisely to understand how public categories come to be understood as ordinary rather than change the definition by fiat.

Contrary to Sobchack and Eitzen, Odin is sufficiently aware of the importance of institutions in regulating reading strategies so that in his account there is far less space for negotiating about the film's fictional status in practice than in principle.

The main problems with Odin's account lie elsewhere. The first concerns the relationship between modes and fictivization. Although fictivization distinguishes fictional and documentary mode, fictivization is also part of the instructional mode whose main point is to convey a message. This means that Odin does not have a firm criterion for defining fiction – fictivization is a necessary but not a sufficient condition of fiction. Moreover, Odin's taxonomy also puts on the same hierarchical level what should be a subcategory in his framework. Films like *The Boy with Green Hair* (Joseph Losey, 1948) and *Neighbours* (Norman McLaren, 1952) certainly deliver an anti-war message but they do so through their fictional storylines. In other words, from Odin's perspective, instructional mode should be better understood as a subclass of the fictional mode.[13]

Another issue is the discrepancy between Odin's modes and accepted categorization. Odin insists that musicals do not belong to the fictional mode because they alternate between fictivization of the story and spectacularization of the musical numbers. In the latter, Odin argues, performers are seen as performers and not as characters. But although there are differences between these aspects of the musical, it is regularly the case that numbers still perform a narrative function. *Summer Nights* from the opening of *Grease* (Randal Kleiser, 1978) undeniably demonstrates John Travolta's and Olivia Newton-John's skills as performers but it certainly also tells us how Danny and Sandy spent their summer vacation.

The third point concerns Odin's commitment to John Searle's (1975) account of fiction as non-deceptive pretence. According to Odin, in the fictional mode the spectator constructs the actual enunciator as Searle's non-deceptive pretender. But there are deceptive pretences which are fictions. For instance, the advertising campaign behind *The Blair Witch Project* following its Sundance premiere which I discuss in detail in Chapter Three demonstrates that the filmmakers intended the spectators to be deceived into thinking the depicted events actually took place, yet the film was already fiction by that time.

The next issue pertains to the fictional mode's relationship to narration. According to Odin, this mode necessarily entails narration. Insistence on narration is a reading strategy variant of the textual idea that only narratives can be fictions. But there are fictions which are not narrative. Paintings like *Prometheus Bound* (1611–12) by Peter Paul Rubens or sculptures like *The Rape of Proserpina* (1621–2) by Gian Lorenzo Bernini depict singular moments in mythical events which are fictional. They do not purport to represent some actual or historical states of affairs like nonfictions do. Similarly, there are non-narrative fiction films which depict singular moments as well. *Carousel* (Adam

Berg, 2009) is a short film which represents a moment in a fictional shootout between police and armed robbers by having a camera traverse the urban battlefield while all the characters are frozen.[14] In Odin's vocabulary, these paintings and films invite diegetization – the construction of an imaginary world – but not narration because such a world can be constructed based on description alone. So, if there are non-narrative fiction(film)s, it is also possible to fictivize without narrating.

Finally, Odin models all modes on linguistic communication between 'the actant director and actant reader' (1995: 227) which regularly involve assertions. The fact that the two need not share the codes of communication is precisely what allows the spectator the freedom to apply different reading strategies. But this does not negate that there is still an object of enunciation in Odin – irrespective of whether it is decoded or not. After all, fictivization in Odin is the operation which supplements the actual enunciator (actant director) and the actual spectator (actant reader) with their fictive versions with the consequence that the enounced flowing between the two which would otherwise be true/false is no longer treated as such. When watching *Metropolis* (Fritz Lang, 1927), for instance, it is irrelevant whether the enounced like Rotwang kidnapped Maria is actually true or not. In Odin's words, 'the spectator no longer feels interpellated as a real person having to take seriously what is narrated to him' (Odin 1988: 128).

The issue here is that fiction films need not involve any such true/false enunciations – assertions – to begin with. Again, non-narrative fiction films illustrate this best. *Carousel*, specifically, invites the spectators to imagine a shootout. But to do so the film does not *assert* something like '(t)here is a shootout' which is then fictivized. Rather, as the camera moves around the combat zone, the film presents images of the gun battle from various vantage points. Asked to describe the film, both the director and the spectators may well use the assertion '(t)here is a shootout' and they would be perfectly correct in doing so (as I have been). But, again, this does not mean that as an audiovisual text this film asserts anything. After all, based on the absence of predicate structures in images and the processing of visual data alike, it has been argued at length that images of x do not simply translate into statements like '(t)here is x' (Bordwell, 1985, Carroll, 2008). In short, visual depiction is not the same as linguistic assertion. (Not even all utterances amount to assertions – merely vocalizing 'shootout' does not assert that there is a shootout.)

The main advantage of Walton's approach over both Odin's semio-pragmatics and intentionalist accounts, then, is that it does not use linguistic communication as a model for understanding fiction. Instead, it resorts to children's games of make-believe. This view, unlike Odin's, allows for fictions which need not be narrative, need not involve any assertions, and even need not constitute communication. By simply make-believing a one-eyed parrot on her shoulder, for instance, the child is not only not making any assertions, but she is also not even communicating anything to anybody. What she is doing is using a plastic parrot as a prop in a game of make-believe. And it is props rather than assertions or objects of enunciation more broadly that are readily applicable to all forms of fiction. Rubens' painting and Bernini's sculpture discussed above are props for imagining Prometheus' and Proserpina's plight, respectively. The images and sounds in *Carousel* are props for make-believing a shootout as much as the images and sounds of Bogart in *Casablanca* are props for imagining Rick. And in fictions which are replete with assertions such as literary fictions, it is simply that assertions are props for imagining characters and events. Particular strength of Walton's theory is, therefore, that by replacing assertions and objects of enunciation with props, it privileges no medium of fiction over another.

Consequences

At this point, we need to remind ourselves that the view that extratextual features are crucial for a film's fictional status, irrespective of whether it is

Walton's or even Odin's version of it, has had little traction in film studies. The general lack of interest in these debates and the prevalent ideas that textual features alone define the film's fictional status leads at the very least to problems of categorization. Fiction films are identified as nonfictions and vice versa. Numerous nonfiction films are regularly said to be partially fictional because they share textual features with fiction films. And, if Walton's theory is correct, that fictional status may even change over time is left unrecognized.

But miscategorization is not the sole consequence of this lack of interest in the notion of fiction. Other outcomes are of greater importance for they relate to theoretical claims, audience responses, and even to a key assumption in film studies. Concerning theory, there is little recognition of how the notion of fiction makes the emphasis on the special relationship between the image and its profilmic object a moot point. When it comes to audience responses, miscategorization leads to faulty affective responses and may even lead to ethical problems. Finally, the assumption, taken for granted in film studies, that fiction films generate real-life beliefs demands both an empirical verification and a theoretical explanation from a position which is invested in articulating the concept of fiction.

The immediate consequences of the lack of interest in the notion of fiction relate to logical coherence and the scope of some widely influential film theories discussing ontological properties of the medium. Numerous theorists including most notably André Bazin (2004), Siegfried Kracauer (1960), Peter Wollen (1969), and Stanley Cavell (1979) have argued for the existence of a special ontological link between the photograph and its profilmic object. Kracauer, for instance, puts it like this: 'film is essentially an extension of photography and therefore shares with that medium a marked affinity for the visible world around us. Films come into their own when they record and reveal physical reality' (1960: ix). But the emphasis on this special ontological relationship, as Carroll puts it, 'implies strange results by ontologically misplacing, so to speak, the focus of our attention' (1988b: 148). Given their ontological commitments, the proponents of this theory should be forced to say that in fiction films like *Casablanca* it is the actor Dooley Wilson and not the fictional piano-player Sam that is primarily represented. Yet, this ignores the fact that when watching photographic fiction films, it is usually the fiction that interests us more than the actors or profilmic objects.[15] In other words, there is an incongruence between the focus of theoretical commitment (the profilmic) and the focus of actual viewing (fictional world).

Moreover, the special link between the photograph and its object cannot tell us anything about the ontology of *fiction* film. This is, first, because fictions cannot be recorded directly. Photographic film can only record the profilmic which can then be used for building fictions. Second, the special ontological link cannot serve as a border between fiction and nonfiction either because there are, as we have seen, animated documentaries.

Concerning audience responses, given that correct categorization is the basis for proper responses, miscategorization leads to reactions which may be aesthetically, scholarly, and even ethically dubious. Between the two potential miscategorizations, confusing fiction for nonfiction has less at stake. The most that the spectator is risking is the fate of an anecdotal rube who stops the performance of *Othello* believing that the actress playing Desdemona is really in danger. The comparative danger for film scholars is to misunderstand the institutional experience of films in question. For instance, even if Walton's theory of fiction is incorrect and early train films were always nonfictional, the analysis of early cinema (Slugan, 2019a) demonstrates the importance of imagination for the initial promotion and reception of these films. Take the example of Hale's Tours – simulations of train travel through projection of phantom rides (films taken with a camera placed on the locomotive) in an auditorium made to look like a train car and popular between 1905 and 1910. Exemplifying the standard understanding of Hale's Tours as a hyper-realistic nonfictional phenomenon, prominent film historian Lauren Rabinovitz argues that these rides instilled the false belief of actually taking a ride in contemporary audiences:

> Early accounts of these movie rides are reminiscent of the inventive reports regarding the reception of the earliest Lumiere films… [The installation manufacturers] organized a theatrical experience for the cognitive convergence of sensory information as the basis of illusion that "you are really there."
>
> (Rabinovitz, 2012: 84, 86)

But the analysis of contemporary promotion and reception materials demonstrates that it was the imaginative engagement rather than false belief that informed the institutional experience of these films. Here is a typical review following the premiere of American Mutoscope and Biograph Company's 1897 *The Haverstraw Tunnel* phantom ride which the company was only too happy to include in its Bulletins and further promote imaginative engagement as a response strategy: 'by the exercise of the very slightest imagination, [the spectator] can fancy himself [*sic*] perched upon the cow-catcher of an American locomotive tearing along at the rate of sixty miles per hour' (Niver, 1971: 36). In other words, much like the earliest audiences were never naïve enough to mistakenly believe that they are in any danger while watching films like *The Arrival of a Train*, so the spectators of Hale's Tours were hardly gullible enough to be fooled into believing that they are taking a train ride.[16] Instead, they imagined taking one. And this institutional experience risks being lost when nonfictional traits of a phenomenon, i.e. its relationship to beliefs (instead of make-beliefs), are unduly emphasized.

Whereas the miscategorization of fiction films as nonfictions may lead to misplaced affects and behaviours as well as to scholarly misunderstanding of the institutional experience, confusing or even willingly reading nonfiction films as fictions may lead to ethical problems. Let us consider the effects of confusion, on the one hand, and free application of reading strategies, on the other, starting with the latter. Consider *Fire at Sea* (Gianfranco Rosi, 2016) – Golden Bear winner and documentary about the plight of migrants trying to reach European shores. In a strong version of Odin's framework espoused by Eitzen and Sobchack, the spectator is perfectly free to apply fictivization in her reading of the film. This means that she is completely free not to take the film seriously. From this perspective, what is narrated is no longer a real-life tragedy but something to be easily dismissed. It is not only that this type of wilful reading will not lead to any action relating to the plight, but it is not even that it will generate the bare minimum when it comes to an ethical response to such events – acknowledgement of their truth.

Ethical issues also arise in the other case where fiction and nonfiction are not merely effects of reading strategies and the miscategorization stems from the insistence on textual features as markers of fictional status. *The Act of Killing* (Joshua Oppenheimer, 2012) – a documentary in which perpetrators of Indonesian Killings of 1955–6 re-enact their crimes – presents an excellent illustration of the problem. Because of the extensive use of re-enactments, the film is regularly seen as a mixture of nonfiction and fiction. As Bill Nichols puts it:

> Usually, documentaries embed reenactments as acknowledged reconstructions (fictional representations) of historical but originally unfilmed events within a larger context of nonfiction representation. But this need not be the case, as The Act of Killing amply demonstrates in a befuddling, disturbing, and illuminating manner. [...] Befuddlement arises when a clear distinction between fictional and documentary representation fails to materialize.
>
> (Nichols, 2013: 25)

According to Nichols, re-enactments are fictional representations. But this cannot be the case for a couple of reasons. The first is that this is a textual feature and as such is neither necessarily fictional nor necessarily nonfictional. Re-enactment is meant as a recorded staged representation of an event that took place. Yet these can easily be nonfictional. Consider a situation in which

I wish to convey to my friends how my speech at my relative's wedding looked like. I stand in front of them, take a glass, and make the speech anew. To the best of my recollection this is a reasonable reconstruction of the event and as such a nonfictional representation of the same. And in the light of the discussion of Koch's view above, nothing changes if instead of doing this directly in front of my friends, I record the re-enactment and post it on our WhatsApp group. In fact, as the discussion of *Nanook of the North* reveals, I could also be completely misrepresenting how my speech looked like in order to, say, present myself as wittier than I was, but this would not make the re-enactment fictional – it would just make it a deliberate misrepresentation.

Moreover, most of the re-enactments in *The Act of Killing* cannot be fictions precisely because they are presented as veridical accounts of the killings, i.e. plausible representations in Nichols' vocabulary, without inviting imaginings. For instance, Anwar, one of the main perpetrators, restages in detail how he used metal wire to 'optimize' the extrajudicial killings. And this is also what makes re-enactments nonfictions from both Odin's and Walton's perspective. From Walton's position, the re-enactments are not fictions because the audiences are not supposed to make-believe that these killings took place in such a way. Rather, the audiences are supposed to either confirm the plausibility of these representations by believing in them (as per the official Indonesian history) or deny it (from a critical humanist perspective) and make moral judgements based on that. Certainly, it is true that other re-enactments in the film are often stylized using visual tropes from gangster films, among others. But again, as the discussion of discursivity has demonstrated, these are textual features which cannot determine on their own whether something is fiction or not.[17] For Odin, the point of fictivization is not to take what is represented seriously. Yet the killings the perpetrators are re-enacting surely took place. Undeniably, the re-enactments are regularly misrepresented as heroic deeds and as such certainly involve gross falsehoods, but they nevertheless make a claim to how things happened. Not believing and denying the perpetrators' version is, crucially, distinct from not taking them seriously. The former is necessary for a minimum of an ethical response whereas the latter gives such a response no chance.

Furthermore, to equivocate between fictional and fantasmatic representations and say that these 'gangsters live inside fantasmatic representations of their past and present state of mind [...] that seems so far removed from the frame within which most viewers conceive of reality' (Nichols, 2013: 25) opens the dangerous door of equating these pathological outlooks with fictions. For both Walton and Odin fictions are neither to be believed or disbelieved. Instead, they are to be imagined (Walton) or not to be taken seriously (Odin). But the perpetrators' delusional representations in *The Act of Killing* constitute a country's official line to be believed in. Conflating delusions and fictions risks making the question of belief and therefore potential ethical responses superfluous.

An unexplored assumption

But perhaps the most important reason why the notion of fiction should be given more importance in film studies is the fact that the concept informs one of the key assumptions behind the discipline. Text-oriented film scholars are regularly interested in questions of representation. There is an abundance of studies focusing on the representation of gender, sexuality, race, class, ethnicity, minorities, disability, etc., in fiction film. And the underlying reason for the interest in these matters is the assumption that 'how social groups are treated in cultural representation is part and parcel of how they are treated in life' (Dyer, 2013: 1), i.e. that 'images of people on film actively contribute to the ways in which people are understood and experienced in the "real world"' (Benshoff and Griffin, 2011: 3). In other words, one of the core assumptions is that representations (fictional and nonfictional alike) influence audiences' attitudes, intentions, beliefs, and even behaviours relating to those representations.

When it comes to fiction, however, these assumptions need to be squared with the ordinary understanding of fiction (also captured in Walton's and Odin's technical accounts) according to which fiction is precisely something that, contrary to nonfiction, in principle does not generate beliefs and does not lead to action. For instance, it is common-sense to say that after watching *Super Size Me* (Morgan Spurlock, 2004) the audiences are supposed to believe the events of the film (that the director went on a thirty-day McDonald's diet) and the film's message (that fast food is unhealthy) and that they should at least consider acting accordingly. At the same time, having seen *Godfather* (Francis Ford Coppola, 1972) it is also commonplace to say that the audiences are *not* to think that any of the events represented took place *nor* that all Italian Americans are mobsters, let alone act on these beliefs and stereotypes.[18]

Yet film scholars have generally lacked interest both in testing these competing assumptions or in the results of these tests. Interestingly, the most recent meta-analysis of persuasive effects of narratives in general demonstrates that although narratives are effective means of changing attitudes, intentions, beliefs, and behaviours the results for *fictional* narratives are more ambiguous (Braddock and Dillard, 2016). In other words, the authors conclude that more empirical work is necessary to determine the actual effects of fictional narratives, especially when it comes to generating beliefs. Moreover, Braddock and Dillard's meta-analysis of fictional narratives does not distinguish between video, audio, theatre, and verbal text narratives and therefore cannot say what role, if any, the medium plays in potential belief generation. Furthermore, the study also focuses only on the immediate effects but does not consider whether the effects persist over a longer period – another point assumed by film scholars. This is clearly not to say that film scholars should be responsible for undertaking empirical or meta-analytic work of this type, but it is to claim that it should be at least recognized that the disciplinary assumption is precisely that – an assumption in need of empirical demonstration.

A related concern pertains to the current lack of interest into what, if the assumption of persuasive effects in fiction film is true, the psychological mechanism of this persuasion is. It is clear how, for instance, stereotypical representations of people and groups in nonfiction, given that nonfiction presents itself as plausible representation, may instil beliefs in these stereotypes. It is, however, far from obvious how such representations in fiction could do the same.[19] For this a theory of the relationship of fiction to belief is necessary.

There is undoubtedly more or less explicit understanding among film scholars that 'we are all constantly bombarded by images, ideas, and ideologies' and that 'these constructs are consciously and unconsciously internalized by everyone' (Benshoff and Griffin, 2011: 11). In the tradition drawing on Louis Althusser's (2001) work on ideological state apparatuses and Stuart Hall's (1973) accounts of encoding/decoding, the idea is that the audiences are more prone to accept those representations which reinforce the dominant ideology. Moreover, stereotypical representations accumulate and in the absence of alternative representations the sheer plethora of such representations become treated as the default account of the world. One film with negative stereotypes might not make a difference, but a steady diet of such films will. For instance, given that Italian Americans are often depicted as members of organized crime and that the dominant ideology is replete with such stereotypes, it is no wonder that film viewers will come to see the Italian American community as threatening and violent. But as I argued earlier, although this makes sense for nonfictional representations, the theoretical problem is precisely to explain why we would count *fictional* representations of this type (whether there is one or a plethora of them) towards our default worldview if fictional representations are what we merely entertain or imagine but do not take seriously.

One influential strand of psychoanalytic film theory running from Brecht did speak of cinematic illusion or 'impression of reality' where, due to the conflux of the properties of the apparatus, the medium, and the realist narrative form, spectators were at least momentarily said to have been fooled into believing the content of fictional representations. Metz (1982: 69–74, 101–9) offered the theory's latest notable explicit account of the problem with an appeal to the concept of disavowal which allows spectators to simultaneously believe something and not believe it.[20] Although the spectators know perfectly well that what they are seeing is fiction, on some level they still believe in it. Moreover, there are also moments when the spectator is briefly overwhelmed and enters a dreamlike state in which the credulous spectator takes over from the uncredulous one.

But these ideas have been criticized extensively by cognitivists and psychoanalytic theorists alike and have lost currency. Cognitivists have pointed out that there is no need for recourse to incompatible or wavering beliefs to describe the impression of reality. Other concepts such as the focus on the represented content rather than representational strategies (Carroll, 1988a), imagination (Currie, 1995), and narrative absorption (Hakemulder et al., 2017) do the job. It should be added that whatever wavering is said to take place during screening dissipates after it, i.e. the impression of reality is not a long-term effect. Moreover, even the later defenders of psychoanalytic theory have argued that we should distinguish pathological disavowal in which the same thing is believed and not believed from normal disavowal in which the same thing is merely entertained while not believed in (Allen, 1997: 135–43). Crucially, it is the normal rather than pathological disavowal that is characteristic of fiction film. These critiques clearly call for an alternative explanation as to how fiction film could potentially elicit beliefs, yet since then film scholars have generally not met this demand.

Theoretical models offering answers to this call can be found in other disciplines. Some psychologists have proposed the availability heuristic – a process of generating beliefs based on access to vivid examples (Kahneman and Tversky, 1973). Following a fiction film depicting nuclear war, people evaluate such an event as likelier.[21] Others have argued that people mentally represent both false and true information as true by default and that additional mental effort is necessary to 'unbelieve' it (Gilbert, 1991). Building on the idea that understanding entails default acceptance of what is understood and on the experiments with literary fictions, it has been argued that people engage fictions in precisely the opposite way than Samuel Taylor Coleridge (1817) suggested. Instead of 'willing suspension of disbelief' there is a 'willing construction of disbelief' (Gerrig and Rapp, 2004).[22]

Philosophers have criticized these accounts and presented their own. Availability heuristic is unlikely to generate long-term beliefs because, by definition, vivid examples fade with the passage of time (Currie, 2020). Automatic belief in all information is also doubtful because pragmatic considerations must take place before any such automatic acceptance takes place (Sperber et al., 2010). Understanding hyperbole such as 'I died of embarrassment' is precisely to see them as not literally true. Similar pragmatic consideration must therefore precede rather than follow the understanding of fictional representations.

Instead, we may come to believe fictional representations for other reasons (cf. Sullivan-Bissett, Bradley, and Noordhof, 2017). Currie (2020), for instance, proposes two mechanisms – significant overlap of truths and fictional truths and the confidence in the author's beliefs. In the first case, because even the most fantastical stories abound with real-life truths fictional representations which are not explicitly marked as fantastic are also tacitly assumed to be true. *Independence Day* (Roland Emmerich, 1996), for example, can be easily assumed to provide true information about the visual appearance of numerous US landmarks (before they are spectacularly blown up). In the second, it is assumed that fictional representations diverge from real-life truths only as a part of the author's narrative design so if they have no obvious story-function they are accepted as true in real life as well. A background stereotype such as the Black maid Lottie in *Mildred Pierce* (Curtiz, 1945) may be easily accepted because of its lack of effect on the main storyline.

But there are problems with this account as well because it still makes it difficult to explain which fictional representations will be believed and which not. Concerning the truth overlap, the convention that characters speaking English in films about Ancient Rome is not marked as a fantastic element, yet it is hardly claimed that spectators enjoying a steady diet of historical films believe that Ancient Romans spoke English. When it comes to authorial design, that characters are good-looking rarely has a story-function, yet audiences do not come to believe that an average person in real life is as good-looking as an average actor. So, what is the answer?

The point of this chapter was not to decide which of the theories sketched out here is correct. Rather it is to draw attention to their existence and relevance for film studies. More generally then, this chapter will have hopefully shown the importance of theorizing the notion of fiction not only for the taxonomical organization of the field and the problems stemming from categorization but also for one of the discipline's key assumptions – that fiction films influence real-life beliefs. The remainder of the book will explore in detail these and other questions which become apparent once the notion of *fiction* in fiction film is taken seriously. To do so, the next chapter fine-tunes the definition of fiction through an engagement with theories of fiction in contemporary philosophy of art.

2

Philosophy of fiction

In Chapter One I have tackled the rare instances of sustained theorizing of the category of fiction in film studies focusing on Roger Odin's work, argued why they fall short, and proposed an alternative that I have referred to as institutional theory of fiction. I have also briefly explained that the theory builds on Kendall Walton's understanding of works of fiction as props prescribing imaginings or mandating games of make-believe. But I have said little about the advantages Walton's theory of fiction has over its competitors motivating its application to film in the first place. Nor have I discussed the challenges to his view of fiction stemming from both Walton's own idiosyncrasies and the current debates in the philosophy of art.

I will start, therefore, with a general outline of competing theories of fiction to explain the reason behind choosing Walton's framework. While, inspired by Walton, most theorists of fiction in the tradition of analytic philosophy consider imaginative engagement on the part of the audience to be the key feature of fiction, unlike Walton, they treat linguistic fictions as the model on which to build general theories of fiction. Walton, instead, sees children's games of make-believe as basic forms of fiction allowing us to develop a theory of film fiction which is not merely an application of theory of literary fiction to film but one indebted to a phenomenon that precedes language. Moreover, Walton's approach – unlike the dominant intentionalist accounts – allows for an institutional view of fiction necessary for explaining how works can change their non/fictional status over time. But even Walton is primarily interested in fictional utterances or what is true in the fiction than whether a work is fiction or nonfiction.

Concerning Walton's peculiarities, he has been clear that his project is not about capturing the ordinary understanding of the distinction between fiction and nonfiction. Instead, he is primarily interested in games of make-believe which for him are typical of representational arts in general rather than a smaller subset of those representations that are ordinarily referred to as fiction. When it comes to visual representations such as paintings and photographs, Walton is unequivocal that these should also be treated as fictions because they necessarily prescribe imaginings. In the case of film, this clearly inflates the category of fiction film out of proportion. Therefore, in the second section I offer a form of Waltonian theory which is a far better fit with the ordinary language categories of fiction and nonfiction and which does not treat visual representations as fiction by default.

In the third and longest part of the chapter, I take up current challenges to Walton's view that something is fiction if and only if the audiences are supposed to imagine its content. Recently, Walton himself has renounced his earlier position to argue that mandated imagining is only a necessary but not sufficient condition for a proposition to be fictional. Others have claimed that we should give up on trying to identify necessary and sufficient conditions for fiction in terms of prescribed imaginings, because nonfiction regularly mandates imaginings while fiction commonly authorizes beliefs. In response, I argue that while the above is true, the necessary and sufficient condition for a work of fiction is whether it *primarily* mandates imagining its content regardless of whether it also mandates beliefs in part or even in whole. Primacy, furthermore, is not a matter of completeness but of what one is supposed to do first and foremost.

Crucially, as I explain in the last section, the source of this primacy is the placement of the work in what, in a competing institutional account, Catharine Abell's calls fiction institutions. Unlike for Abell, however, in my account the placement is not secured by authorial intentions but through indexing, i.e. the negotiation between factors of production, promotion, distribution, exhibition, reception, and public classification.

Consensus theories

As Derek Matravers explains, since Walton's seminal work (1990) the consensus among scholars working on the nature of fiction in the analytic tradition of philosophy of art has formed around two points: 'that what it is for a proposition to be fictional is for there to be a mandate to imagine it and that the mental state of imagining a proposition can be given a functional definition that distinguishes it from believing that proposition' (Matravers, 2014: 2–3). Although the remarks were written more than a decade ago, with notable dissent by Stacie Friend and Derek Matravers, the consensus for the most part still holds. In this section I address the consensus view and reserve the third section for dissenters.

In his 1990 monograph, Walton explains fiction in terms of games of make-believe or imagining. In what is now a classic example, children are playing an imaginary game in a forest in which coming across a stump means encountering a bear. In this game, it is fictional – fictionally true in the world of the game – that a stump is a bear. In other words, when a child stumbles upon a stump, she is mandated to imagine that she has come across a bear. For Walton, fictional works are much like collections of such stumps. They are objects – Walton refers to them as props – which prompt our imaginative engagement. The main difference between children's games of make-believe and engagement with fictional works is in how the imagining is authorized – the mandate. Whereas in the former the authorization is explicit – children have expressed among themselves the rule that they should imagine a bear for every stump – in the latter the mandate is implicit.

A particular strength of this account, as I already foreshadow in Chapter One in relation to Roger Odin's work, is that it moves away from the dominant approaches in philosophical aesthetic, film studies, and literary theory alike which model fiction on literary fiction. These approaches usually start from declarative sentences or assertions understood as propositions and ask what makes these propositions fictional. If they are interested in fiction in other media, the scholars then treat these other media as though they are offering propositions.[1]

Once fiction is understood not primarily as a language phenomenon, but as a prop-led game of make-believe linguistic utterances just become one prop among others. Sentences making up Cervantes' *Don Quixote* (1605, 1615) are props as much as the image that is Sandro Botticelli's *The Birth of Venus* (1480), the sculpted marble of Gian Lorenzo Bernini's *Apollo and Daphne* (1622), a performance of Shakespeare's *Hamlet*, sounds forming *The Flight of the Bumblebee* (Nikolai Rimsky-Korsakov, 1899–1900) and *The War of the Worlds* (Orson Welles, 1938), or sounds and images constituting *M* (Fritz Lang, 1931) are.[2] Put differently, much like 'he made up his mind to call himself "Don Quixote"' mandates us to imagine the content of the phrase, so does the shadow of Peter Lorre and his words 'What is your name?' in the opening of *M* authorize us to make-believe that a stranger has approached a child in the street. But unlike with the example from Cervantes, Lorre's shadow and voice also mandate imaginings about how the stranger's shadow looks and voice sounds. I will discuss these non-propositional or perceptual imaginings in detail in Chapter Four but for now suffice it to say that they cannot be exhausted in propositional descriptions of the story conveyed.[3]

Walton's other great strength is that he recognizes that fiction is a social category and that as such it may change over time and may even differ from place to place (1990: 91). In other words, he allows that the mandate for how to engage a work has a history of its own. This is contrary to most philosophers for whom the mandate issues from authorial intentions which are fixed (Currie 1990, 1995, 2020, Davies 2015, Stock 2017). This is usually spelled out in terms of Gricean theory of communication where the author not only intends that the audiences make-believe the content of the proposition but that the audiences recognize that they are supposed to make-believe this from the proposition that is being communicated. Even in a recent modified account which prefers Austin's speech theory to Grice, what changes is the condition under which the authorial intentions are secured, not that they are the starting point (García-Carpintero, 2013).

In the previous chapter, I have argued that intentionalist theories are vulnerable to examples like trick films which were originally intended to be regarded as recordings of stage tricks but are currently treated as fictions of magical events and train films which were initially intended to evoke imaginings about the trains' looming presence yet are nowadays seen as actuality recordings of locomotives pulling into station. This deserves further clarification because it risks conflating two things – the discussion of what is fictionally true and whether a work is fictional or not.

As can be gleaned from Matravers' quote, most theorists are primarily interested in the definition of fictional utterances or what is true in fiction as opposed to whether a work is fictional or not. Because the two are seen as related they risk conflation, and I have undeniably been guilty of this (cf. Slugan, 2019a). While this does not invalidate the key points theorists have made – it certainly does not negate my claims that works can cross the fiction/nonfiction divide in either direction over time – it is worthwhile to keep the distinction between fictionality of utterances and works alive. In the Introduction, my criticism of intentionalism was from the latter perspective. While it is immediately applicable to those who like García-Carpintero (2013, 2021) define a fictional work in terms of authorial intentions, it deserves further clarification for those who are more interested in fictional utterances (Currie 1990, 2020, Stock 2017).[4] In fact, even Walton (1990, 2015a) is, in his own admission, primarily interested in what makes propositions fictional. For him, originally, 'a proposition is fictional [...] if it is to be imagined' (1990: 40).

For fictional utterance theorists propositional fictionality easily translates into fictionality of work when all the propositions are fictional (cf. Stock, 2017: 150). The inclusion of interrogatives and other non-declarative forms in fictional works does not pose a problem either because it is the story content what counts expressed through a string of utterances (Davies, 2015). From this perspective, a film like *The Four Troublesome Heads* (Georges Méliès, 1898) is a fictional work for Currie, Davies, and Stock because it is a string of utterances about a conjurer manufacturing, juggling, and disappearing multiple heads intended exclusively for make-believe. This, however, belies the original filmmaker's intentions – engage the film as a recording of a famous stage trick.[5]

The reason for being pedantic here is that from the perspective of fictional utterance theorists most fictional works are *patchworks* of nonfictional and fictional statements rather than sets of fictional utterances alone. In Victor Hugo's *The Hunchback of Notre-Dame* (1831) there are many sections about the medieval culture and rules of sanctuary which the readers are supposed to believe as opposed to imagine. James Cameron's depiction of how the titular ship broke in half in *Titanic* (1997), similarly, was intended to be believed by audiences as an accurate representation of the event. What is the precise relationship between the fictionality of statements and the fictionality of works, then? Is there a ratio of such propositions that the works need to satisfy to count as fiction?

Walton seems to suggest that so long as works contain some mandate for imaginative engagement they should be treated as fictions (1990: 72). Some like Currie (1990, 2020) explicitly refuse to spell out the connection between the two in terms of necessary and sufficient conditions, insisting that their focus is on utterances. Stock (2017: 150) also refrains from clarifying the connection merely stating that sets of fictional utterances generally do not respond to fictional works. David Davies (2015) stakes an intermediary position wherein the unit of analysis is narrative – generally larger than single propositions but smaller than fictional works – and moves from there to fictional works.

The first problem here is that Davies suggests that the presence of a narrative is 'plausibly a necessary condition for something to be a *work* of fiction' (2015: 42, italics in the original). Not only does he reserve his proposal for narrative fiction, but he denies that there is non-narrative fiction. As I already argued in Chapter One, however, this is belied by paintings like *Birth of Venus* and sculptures like *Apollo and Daphne*. They both capture moments in the lives of mythical beings, and we are supposed to imagine how these – the birth and the foiled embrace – look. Davies might resort that there is no mandated imagining here – much like encyclopaedic entries provide nonfictional verbal descriptions of mythological beings so do Botticelli and Bernini offer nonfictional visual descriptions. Even if we granted this, however, Chapter One also reminds us that there are fictional non-narrative films like *Carousel* (Adam Berg, 2009) for which no equivalent argument can be made. This is hardly a nonfictional description of a non-existent shootout – it is a shootout that we are supposed to imagine.

Further trouble for Davies stems from his inclusion of an additional criterion for fictionality. Roughly, fidelity constraint holds if the narratee correctly assumes that the narrator organized the narrated events in the order the narrator believes they actually took place. A narrative is fictional if it consists of authorially intended fictive utterances, and its organizing principle is *not* the fidelity constraint. A work is fictional if it contains at least one fictional narrative and if the work is organized according to the principle which is *unlike* the fidelity constraint. This allows Davies to correctly eliminate philosophical and scientific works which use thought experiments – fictional narratives – from fiction because their organizing principles are like fidelity – the goal is to get the reader to assume that this is how the author believes the reality to be. Davies (2015: 50–4) spends much time discussing borderline cases such as didactic works and parables where it is unclear whether the dominant organizing principle is like fidelity – conveying general truths about the world – or unlike fidelity – entertaining through prescription to imagine. However, there are already less complicated fictional works which comprise only one fictional narrative and respect the fidelity constraint on the level of narrative – the organization of events – but are nevertheless fictional. *The Assassination of the Duke of Guise* (Charles le Bargy and André Calmettes, 1908) is a one-reel film which presents actual events in the sequence the authors believe they happened – from Duke's mistress luring him to Henry III to his assassination by king's henchmen.

More importantly, as Friend (2012) reminds us, audiences are more interested in classifying works than in categorizing specific utterances or narrative chunks that make up a work. After all, fiction and nonfiction are, much like genres, appreciative categories which are approached as a whole with different attitudes and for different purposes. Histories are usually read to learn about their subject matter (although it is unlikely that the reader thinks the whole book will be of relevance) while horror movies are watched for a good scare (though we don't expect them to be scary from start to finish). These are important points to keep in mind in the third section but before that we need to address Walton's tendency to inflate the category of fiction.

Walton's idiosyncracies

One peculiarity of Walton's view is that for him 'pictures are fictional by definition' (Walton, 1990: 351). On this view, pictures are a subclass of depictions or perceptual representations, including visual, aural, tactile, etc., representations. In other words, these are 'representation[s] whose function is to serve as a prop in reasonably rich and vivid perceptual games of make-believe' (Walton, 1990: 296). This clearly is a very broad understanding of fiction and needs to be addressed by anybody who wants to uphold the difference between fiction and nonfiction film in a Waltonian framework. Elsewhere (Slugan, 2019a: 18), I have argued that there is a string of visual representations including anatomical atlases, zoological and botanical guides, cross-sectional views, etc., whose function is primarily to illustrate. This means that they serve not as props for perceptual make-believe but as tools enabling visual recognition of the subject depicted. Therefore, I claimed, Walton's blanket statement about pictures cannot hold.

But that did not address the key reason behind Walton's idiosyncratic claim. As I mentioned earlier, Walton is more interested in building a theory of fiction than having results of it coincide with the categories as they are used and understood in ordinary language. So, the dismissal of Walton's view about pictures based on standard delimitations of nonfictional and fictional visual representations does not go to the heart of the matter as Walton understands it. The reason why pictures, and by extension, all films are fictional for Walton, is because to engage a visual representation is to see the lines, pigments, colours, etc., that make it up as the subject depicted. This is an example of what Richard Wollheim (1980) refers to as seeing-in or the phenomenological experience of recognizing an object of representation in the configurational properties of the image.

When looking at *Girl with a Pearl Earring* (Johannes Vermeer, 1665), for example, visual imagination is necessarily deployed to turn the brushstrokes of colour pigment into the eponymous girl. As Walton puts it, the 'imagining of a viewer [...] is not deliberate, but a spontaneous response to the marks on the canvas; she just finds herself imagining in a certain manner as she looks at the picture' (2008: 137). When looking at photographic representations visual imagination is similarly needed for seeing gradations of light and shadow as depicted objects. In other words, typical cognitive processing of visual representations for Walton necessarily involves visual imagining which plays a key role in transforming the visual array into the object of representation. And this processing is also what explains the phenomenology of engagement with visual representations (cf. Walton, 2008).

There are a couple of ways of responding. We could follow Matravers (2014) and Enrico Terrone (2020b) in marshalling evidence from psychology of vision which suggests that imagination does not play a role in the comprehension of visual representations. We could also echo Carroll (1995) in proposing that the processing of visual representation need only involve the faculty of visual recognition which does not necessarily entail any input from visual imagination. Put differently, if Walton accepts that the comprehension of linguistic text – transformation from the linguistic sign into what it represents – does not necessarily involve any imagining, then why assume that visual comprehension – transformation from a visual sign into its representation – cannot function in the same way?

Walton's response is that perceptual representations (depictions) and linguistic ones are fundamentally different. This can be explained by pointing out that while through a particularly evocative writing style a textual description can prompt the reader to imagine seeing (e.g. the first time Tolstoy introduces Karenina), it cannot prompt the reader to imagine the act of reading the words as one's seeing of the relevant content. Only a picture can prompt a viewer to imagine the viewer's actual seeing of the canvas' configurational properties as the viewing of the object depicted (Walton, 1990: 293–4). And not only is the picture able to do so but in standard cognitive processing of images it necessarily does so.

My strategy therefore is to deny that the necessity of imagination as a part of comprehension of representations turns those representations into fictions. Novel findings in psychology of vision may yet furnish evidence that imagination is a typical part of processing of visual representations after all. But even if that were to be the case that would not transform those representations into fiction. The reason is because the *mandate* to imagine is not a description of the presence (as opposed to absence) of imagination in the causal mechanism of comprehension. Mandate to imagine is not about the psychological reality of what mental processes are needed to secure comprehension of a work.

Rather, mandate to imagine is a normative category about what to do with the representation once comprehension has been secured.[6] Even if comprehending each frame in a film required visual imagination, this would not make the film fictional because the mandate is about what to do with the images once comprehended.[7] Returning to the example of trick films from Chapter One, the mandate is about whether the images are to be used as props for imagining various fantastic events or, in the case of the mandate's absence, taken simply to be recordings of a magic theatre play.

Photographs add a further wrinkle to the discussion. For Walton (1984), although photographs and pictures are both depictions, the two are essentially different insofar as the former are, in his vocabulary, transparent and the latter are not. Briefly, photographs are transparent because they allow us to see their objects in the same sense visual prosthetics like mirrors, binoculars, telescopes, microscopes, etc., do – actually but *indirectly*. Walton argues that in the way we actually see a person *through* the mirror in front of us although the person is in fact around the corner or behind us, this is also how we see people and objects in photographs. We really do see them albeit indirectly. Whether this holds or not need not concern us here. The important thing is that for Walton in photographs there is another layer of fictionality not present in pictures. Pictures are necessarily fictional because the very experience of seeing-in entails spontaneous imagining. Photographs are doubly so because, next to seeing-in, the experience of watching photographs for Walton also entails fictionally seeing their objects *directly*, i.e. as though they were in front of us. So, when looking at a photograph of our deceased grandma we actually see her indirectly and fictionally see her directly, i.e. as though she was in our presence.

In my previous work (Slugan, 2019a: 17–9), I reasoned that there is no need for recourse to imagination to explain this phenomenology of presence. Because all visual prosthetics afford this phenomenology, it is not specific to photography and photographically derived cinema but to visual prosthetics in general. I was, however, wrong in thinking that this could iron out the wrinkle because what Walton is after is precisely the reason behind this phenomenology of presence and not whether it is specific to photography or not. For him, the presence is explained because photographs (and visual prosthetics) prescribe imagining that we see the object directly.

But this again returns us to the distinction between what is required for securing the basic understanding and experience of a representation and what attitude to take towards that representation once this has been secured. As I argued earlier whether imagination is necessarily involved in this basic engagement is irrelevant for whether something is fiction or not, because the mandate is a social category and not a psychological mechanism. Certainly, engaging works of fiction oftentimes involve spontaneous imaginings where we are not consciously aware of the mandate to imagine. But as we will see in more detail in the next section this is not because fiction is necessarily processed like this – basic comprehension of texts and narratives requires no imagination either. That there is frequent spontaneous imagining in engagement with fiction, rather, is because most of the time the implicit mandate is clear (i.e. there is no doubt as to whether something is fiction or nonfiction) and the audiences have learned to follow such mandates automatically.[8]

Before proceeding it should be noted that Walton himself has recently argued that his view of fiction is only half right. Whereas in his key monograph (1990) he held that the necessary and sufficient condition for a proposition to be fictional is for the audiences to be supposed to imagine it, in his revised account he argues that authorized make-believe is only a necessary condition (2015a). This is so, because there are instances of works where audiences are supposed to imagine something, but this is not a part of the fictional world. His main examples are what he refers to as iconic meta-representations such as paintings within paintings and dream sequences or illusions in films. For Walton the issue is that because the dream sequence in, say, director's cut of *Blade Runner* (Ridley Scott, 1992) mandates the audiences to imagine seeing a unicorn it also mandates us to imagine that there is a unicorn (imagining seeing x implies imagining x exists). But there is clearly no unicorn in the world of *Blade Runner* (only in Deckard's dream). This, however, is only a problem if we subscribe to Walton's theory of depictions as necessarily fictional which we have seen there is no need to.[9]

But Walton claims meta-representations are also problematic in their literary and narrative forms, i.e. in stories within stories. In *One Thousand and One Nights* Scheherazade tells many stories. Given that we are mandated to imagine the content of those stories this makes them, according to his original definition, fictional or true in the world of *One Thousand and One Nights*. But many stories that Scheherazade narrates are fictional in *her* world, not true. Again, in his view, there are prescribed imaginings which are not true in the relevant fictional world, i.e. the framing story. This, however, obtains only if in engaging such narratives there is a collapse of the levels we are supposed to imagine. Surely, what we are supposed to imagine is not just the content of Scheherazade's stories but *that* the content is told by Scheherazade. It is one thing to imagine in Scheherazade's first story – The Story of the Merchant and the Jinnee – 'that there was a certain merchant who had great wealth' and another 'that Scheherazade is recounting that there was a certain merchant who had great wealth'. It is the latter we are supposed to do, not the former.[10]

His point that there are many works which misdirect us has more substance to it. For most of the film, in *Fight Club* (David Fincher, 1999) we are supposed to imagine that Jack and Tyler Durden are two different people. By the end, of course, it turns out that they are one and the same biological individual. But this should not cause much concern. We can simply revise our account of what is true in fiction by saying that the relevant mandated imaginings are those which are operational upon consuming the whole work. What we need to remember, moreover, is that Walton's concern is about what is fictional *in* the work. The next two critics are rightfully more interested in the question of criteria for determining whether a *work* is fiction or nonfiction.

Current challenges

Stacie Friend's objections

In a series of pieces over more than a decade, Stacie Friend has launched an influential critique of the idea that the difference between fictional and nonfictional works can be cashed out in terms of the distinction between mandate to imagine and mandate to believe. First, prescribed imagining cannot be a sufficient condition for fiction because there are many nonfictions that mandate imagining. As Friend notes, many histories include prescriptions to imagine their content either implicitly through evocative writing style or explicitly like Simon Schama's *History of Britain*: 'imagine its [Disraeli' country house's] terraces full of peacocks, and the sense of Disraeli the sorcerer – or magician, as his friends and enemies liked to say – becomes more plausible' (2003: 259). Similarly, animated natural history documentaries like *Walking with Dinosaurs* (BBC, 1999) authorize audiences to imagine that they have travelled back in time or at the very least to imagine seeing the dinosaurs in their prehistoric habitat. The opening voice-over (by Kenneth Branagh) certainly invites the following: 'Imagine you could travel back in time, to a time long before man. Back across 65 million years.' If prescribed imagining was sufficient for fiction, this would make numerous histories and documentaries fictions, yet this is obviously not the case.

Second, if the prescription to believe as a sufficient condition for nonfiction is appealed to distinguish fiction from nonfiction that will not do either. The reason, as Friend points out, is that many fictions regularly mandate beliefs. Realist novels and social dramas standardly authorize believing that the subject covered and the setting in which it takes place are accurately depicted. *The Wire* (HBO, 2002–8), among other things, prescribes believing that Baltimore is ridden with drug trade. Similarly, period dramas like *JFK* (Oliver Stone, 1991) do not merely authorize audiences to imagine the story around the assassination of the eponymous president but also to believe that JFK was the president of the United States, that he was assassinated in Dallas, Texas in 1963, and that, along with other things, the times have been reasonably accurately portrayed.[11] *JFK*, in fact, goes much further than that insofar Stone has clearly stated that his intention was to convince the audiences that Lee Harvey Oswald was merely the fall-guy in a deep state conspiracy to assassinate the president. For Friend, despite their firm categorization, there is even more to believe in *JFK* – a fiction – than it is in *Walking with Dinosaurs* – a nonfiction.

This is why, to Friend's mind, we should abandon the search for necessary and sufficient conditions for works of fiction and nonfiction. Instead, she proposes that we treat fiction and nonfiction as genres, categories which are not merely classificatory but play a role in appreciation as well. Importantly, the classification is not based on necessary and sufficient conditions but on a combination of standard, variable, contra-standard, and categorical features. Standard traits are the ones that typically place the works that exhibit them in a genre. In film fiction, for instance, they include professional actors, made-up stories, fantastical beings and settings, 'all persons fictitious' disclaimers, etc. Variable features are ones that have no effect on classification. Whether a film is in colour or in black-and-white or whether it is German or French production is irrelevant for classifying it as fiction or nonfiction. Contra-standard properties are those that typically exclude a work from a genre. In film fiction, again, we do not usually expect to find no narrative or exclusively non-visual representation of characters. But exceptions occur. *Carousel* is a non-narrative traversal of a moment in a gun battle frozen in time but is still a fiction film despite the contra-standard property. The protagonists (and perhaps even the whole story) of the fictional *First and Last Men* (Jóhann Jóhannsson, 2020) are never presented visually but are conveyed exclusively through voice-over narration.[12] The trouble with current theories of fiction is, from Friend's perspective, that what they hold to be the sufficient and necessary condition of fiction – prescription to imagine – is merely a standard trait. They also do not take into consideration categorical features which include authorial intentions about how the work is to be classified and how it is currently classified or indexed.

Friend is right to treat fiction (and nonfiction) as a genre for many reasons. Categorical features undoubtedly play a role in categorization. Differentiation between standard and contra-standard traits allows for historical change in the category by tracking how contra-standard features can become standard or variable ones over time. At one point in time, what continues to be standard features of documentaries – direct look at the camera, non-actors portraying main protagonists, and handheld camera – were all contra-standard features of film fiction. Conversely, rich cinematic re-enactment and animation which were once contra-standard traits of documentary, are still standard features of fiction.[13] But while it would indeed be foolish to look for necessary and sufficient conditions for many genres, Friend's examples do not show there are no such conditions for fiction in general. She only shows that they do not hold in their current form.

It is true that some theorists explicitly deny that mandated imagination and authorized belief can be operational at the same time for the same part of the fictional work (cf. Currie, 1990). But this is not a constraint for the institutional theory proposed here. In Friend's vocabulary, under my proposal, mandated imagination is a standard feature of fiction, while prescribed belief is merely a variable trait. Moreover, sufficient and necessary conditions can be spelled out as follows: a work is fiction if and only if its content is *primarily* mandated to be imagined. One way to understand what 'primarily' means is to cash it out in terms of completeness. But as we will shortly see, while completeness is an example of primacy, not all forms of primacy boil down to completeness. Rather primarily will be best understood as *first and foremost*.

Construed in terms of completeness, primacy allows us to properly categorize fictions which regularly mandate beliefs. So, irrespective of whatever we are supposed to believe in realist novels, social dramas, period works, etc., audiences are oftentimes mandated to imagine the whole of the content of the work including the things that they are also supposed to believe. Contrary to the idea that fictional works are a patchwork of distinct fictional and nonfictional parts, some sections are *both* to be believed and imagined.[14] Even if we are supposed to believe the opening sentence of Leo Tolstoy's *Anna Karenina* (1878) about familial un/happiness, we are certainly supposed to imagine it as well as a framework for the story that follows. Similarly, while we are likely supposed to believe the archival footage of Charles de Gaulle is a recording of his actual visit to Cambodia in 1966 near the end of *In the Mood for Love* (Wong Kar-Wai, 2000), we are also mandated to imagine that the French president visited the country around the time the film's protagonist was making his pilgrimage to Angkor Wat.

Completeness also allows for accurate categorization of evocative histories and documentaries like *Walking with Dinosaurs*. In the case of Schama's *History of Britian* it is not the whole content that is to be imagined, only parts of it. In *Walking with Dinosaurs* there are also sections which are, clearly, not to be engaged imaginatively. Quickly after the opening lines, the narrator says: 'But this series will also take you much further [than 65 million years ago]. Back to the Jurassic period.' There is no explicit prescription to imagine that the series will do so, rather the point is to believe Branagh that the show will also represent an earlier period in pre-history. In fact, even in the opening invitation to imaginatively travel back in time it is only part of the content of the BBC's show that we are mandated to imagine. We are not supposed to imagine a *narrator* inviting us to time-travel, but rather *believe that Branagh* is inviting us to do so. In other words, there is a content that envelops the imaginary content of *Walking with Dinosaurs* and this envelope – roughly, Branagh's act of narration through voice-over – prescribes beliefs rather than imaginings.[15]

Here opens the first crack in treating primacy as completeness. If Branagh's act of narration is part of the relevant content to be engaged under a mandate, then we should also treat voice-over narrators in fiction films as part of the content to be imagined. So far so good. But if we have included extradiegetic elements into relevant content, then how can we not include other elements external to the diegesis such as nondiegetic music? Yet the point of elements such as nondiegetic music is precisely that the audiences are not supposed to imagine it playing somewhere in the story world. And even if we resolved this somehow, Enrico Terrone (2020a) reminds us of what he calls Brechtian films – films in which a whole section of the audiovisual track may be nondiegetic. In *Big Short* (Adam McKay, 2015), for instance, Margot Robbie in a bubble bath interrupts the storyline to explain to the audiences what subprime mortgages are.[16]

Furthermore, there are cases when the content of a work is to be simultaneously completely believed and imagined. While he can think of no film examples Manuel García-Carpintero (2021) informs us of literary works like Natalia Ginzburg's 1963 novel *Family Sayings* whose content is completely to be both believed and imagined. What makes the novel fiction is that it is *primarily* to be imagined – the mandate signalled both by the author's preface and the categorization of the work as a fictional novel rather than a memoir or an autobiography. As I have mentioned in Chapter One, it is also possible to conceive of an equivalent fiction film, say a star-studded period drama not unlike *Lincoln* (Steven Spielberg, 2012) which boasts itself on having reconstructed a certain historical event as accurately as possible and without introduction of any additional material. So long as the film is indexed as fiction through promotion, movie database classification, inclusion in relevant festival circuits, etc., the audiences would be mandated to primarily imagine its content.[17]

In fact, there is at least one film which completely mandates its content to be believed and imagined – *The War Game* (Peter Watkins, 1966). The audiences are both mandated to imagine the events following a nuclear strike on the UK in the then-near future and to believe that the events depicted are how things would unfold were there to be a strike. The mandated contents are, importantly, simultaneous and complete.[18]

I am certainly not the first to consider primacy as the necessary and sufficient criterion for fictionality of works. Walton (1990: 94), Currie (2020: 23–4) and Terrone (2020a) alike have floated the idea of primacy. Terrone shares my view but does not develop it as he focuses on defining documentary instead. Currie does not pursue it either, but this is so because he is clear that he does not want to define the fictionality of a work. Walton argues against primacy as the main criterion preferring simply the presence of mandated imagining. One line of his argument hinges on the idea that we cannot define *nonfiction* in terms of primacy of mandated beliefs (or more broadly construed understanding). But this does not prohibit us from defining *fiction* in terms of primacy of mandated imaginings.

The other line is to claim that 'promoting understanding is arguably the primary objective of many paradigmatic works of fiction' (Walton, 1990: 94). But he provides no examples. I am not denying that this is often an important function of many fictional works but in the absence of examples it is difficult to launch a specific response. Perhaps he has in mind didactic fiction like fables.[19] If so, while the messages they convey are vital, they are, as I argued in Chapter One, still not primary. Walton could retort that I am not appreciating the work properly if I deny the primacy of the message in La Fontaine's *The Ant and the Grasshopper* (1668). But this gets us to the question of how primacy is determined. One way is to ask which of the two could we lose in engaging the work and still call the engagement minimally appropriate. I suggest that if we overlooked the message about the importance of one's own labour, we could still appreciate the work as an imaginary tale of the ant and the grasshopper. If, by contrast, we got the message about industriousness but not that we are supposed to imagine the tale of the two animals we could hardly say that we engaged the work appropriately even minimally. The mandated engagement is more fundamental to the understanding of the fable than is getting the point. And we still have the other and more important way to determine primacy as I will show on example of a didactic film *Neighbours* (Norman McLaren, 1952) in Chapter Three – indexing.[20]

While this is a monograph about fiction rather than nonfiction, it should be quickly pointed out here that there is no equivalent definition of either nonfiction or documentary in terms of mandated primacy of belief. At first inspection, it works for *Walking with Dinosaurs* where the point is to primarily convey the belief that the dinosaurs looked and sounded as they are depicted on screen. However, as Carl Plantinga (2005) points out, not all documentaries can be cashed out in terms of his asserted veridical representations which are meant to cover prescribed beliefs in both claims about the subject matter depicted and the perceptual appearance of the profilmic. Mandate to primarily believe in the appearance of what is represented is not the best way to describe poetic documentaries like *Bridge* (Joris Ivens, 1929) which are geared more towards aesthetic appreciation. Enrico Terrone's (2020a) recent proposal that documentaries should be understood in terms of primarily mandated perceptual beliefs – beliefs that in the relevant sensory domain objects appear *like this* – also does not address that poetic documentaries *primarily* authorize a different type of engagement. Furthermore, prescription to primarily believe is also too broad a criterion for defining documentaries, for there is a range of moving images which are not documentaries – TV news, live broadcasts, etc. – but are primarily to be believed. Even if we insist with Terrone (2020a) that the relevant category within which documentaries are delineated is moving image artworks rather than simply moving images, there are still subcategories of moving image artworks that are not documentaries including comedy specials and at least some pornography and sex tapes (e.g. *Pam & Tommy Lee: Stolen Honeymoon* [Tommy Lee, 1995]).[21] In other words, as scholars of documentary film have long recognized, documentaries are a better bet than fiction for Friend to treat as genre without sufficient and necessary conditions of membership.

One last point about nonfiction before returning to the discussion of fiction. Given that nonfiction involves far more experimental forms than poetic documentaries, nonfiction cannot be defined in terms of prescribed beliefs about content of any kind. Films like Peter Kubelka's *Arnulf Reiner* (1960) do not provide any forms of asserted veridical representations and as such cannot mandate any beliefs about them in the first place. But this does not mean there are no necessary and sufficient conditions for nonfiction. I suggest that nonfiction films are those whose content the audiences are *not* primarily mandated to imagine. Friend (2012) argues that nonfictions are not negations of fictions in the sense of terms which are logically contradictory, i.e. not A as opposed to A. That is true, for, as she points out, chairs and cars are not fiction, but that does not make them nonfiction. However, within the category of *films* nonfiction is logically contradictory to fiction. In other words, every film that is not fiction is nonfiction.[22]

Does that mean that there are no hybrid films? As already highlighted in Chapter One, it certainly means that documentaries which include what is usually referred to as fictive elements are not fictional works in any way or degree. Even documentaries that involve mandates to imagine should not be thought of as hybrid but merely as including variable elements.[23] Similarly, docudramas are not hybrids because they include prescriptions to believe. But this does not necessarily exclude the possibility of hybrid's existence. This is because it might presently be indeterminate whether there is a mandate to *primarily* imagine.

Consider Johanna Vaude's visual essay *Extreme Is My Name* (2020) which consists of meticulously edited clips from films by Kathryn Bigelow.[24] On the one hand, the montage could be treated simply as an exercise in establishing eyeline matches, matches on action, etc., where the audiences are merely prescribed to believe that this is a collection of clips from Bigelow's films. On the other, it could be argued that skilful edits establish connections across films that build a new narrative that one is prescribed to imagine – starting with protagonists from different films noticing each other across shots and culminating in a violent shootout across locales. At this point the question arises whether the audiences are primarily mandated to imagine the new storyline or are they primarily to engage the work as a virtuoso demonstration of editing. In fact, *The War Game* is another example of a hybrid film because it is currently unresolved what its primary mandate is. This is the reason why in the discussion above I never specified in which category it falls. The answer in both cases is unclear because, as I already pointed out in Chapter One, textual features alone cannot determine whether something is a fictional work or not.

Surely this contradicts what I have been saying above about Schama's narration and Branagh's voice-over. Given that I have written that their narration establishes a mandate to make-believe by using the words 'imagine', does that not mean that textual markers can establish work's fictionality after all? No. It only means that there are textual features which can establish whether a part or the whole of the content is to be imagined, the whole content still being distinct from the work.[25] It is true that by having the 'imagine' instruction precede the whole text and/or reappear through the text as a reminder, Schama could have prescribed imagining the whole of the content of his *History of Britain*. But this would still not guarantee that the work is fictional because it would not ascertain whether the content is *primarily* to be believed or not. For that indexing is necessary.

Previously (Slugan, 2019a: 27–8), I have argued that there are some instances where textual markers determine that a work is fictional. I have based this on a claim that if the *direct* content of a representation is a non-existent object, then it necessarily mandates imagining. Direct representational content meant that the representation is not embedded in another representation. For instance, the word 'unicorn' directly represents a non-existent object – a unicorn. But an analogue photograph of a unicorn directly represents only a horse with a horn attached to it, i.e. it is a representation of something that represents a unicorn. On this logic, a linguistic representation of a unicorn necessarily mandates imagining because the very act of considering a non-existent signified entails imagining it. The analogue photograph, by contrast, does not entail any such imagining because the signified could always be construed as a horse with a tacked-on horn, rather than a unicorn. Now, because, unlike analogue photographs, digital images which are not photographically derived are direct representations, I reasoned that this means that any film that includes such images is necessarily fiction. But this is wrong for three reasons. Direct representation – linguistic or otherwise – of a non-existent object does not necessarily mandate imaginings – comprehension need not involve imagination. Even if it did, and even if every frame of a CGI film – let us call it *Unicorn* – included images of the unicorn, as the discussion of Walton's idiosyncratic view of visual representations evinces, it would not determine on its own whether the film as a work is to be imagined because it is the social mandate and not cognitive processing that counts. The last reason is that the content is not the same as the work. With the right labelling and context, say 'Recording of *Unicorn*' in a gallery space to modify an example from the previous chapter, the film could still be treated as a nonfictional recording of one screening of that film.

Friend has astutely noticed that categorical features are important for determining whether a work is fiction or nonfiction. Had Ginzburg published her work as a memoir instead of novel, it would constitute nonfiction. It is indexing that generates the context for deciding whether a content is to be primarily imagined or not. In fact, indexing can serve to undermine the weight given to contra-standard features. The key reason why Truman Capote's *In Cold Blood* (1966) – an evocative description of actual murders case deploying novelistic techniques – is nonfiction is because the *New Yorker* agreed to publish the work as nonfiction. At the time, novelistic techniques were contra-standard to literary nonfiction. Had the publisher refused Capote, it is likely that the work would have been labelled as fiction and that the audiences would nowadays be primarily mandated to imagine its content. It would have certainly not been as influential as it has been in the sense of transforming contra-standard traits into variable ones. The same holds for *Waltz with Bashir* (Ari Folman, 2008) which significantly contributed to making animation no longer a contra-standard but variable feature of documentary by being labelled a documentary.

This is not to say that indexing will determine the non/fictional status of a work forever or that the existing label cannot be challenged. In my previous monograph (Slugan, 2019a), I have argued that prior to the existence of labels of 'fiction film' and 'nonfiction film' numerous train rides – nowadays treated as actualities – have been effectively indexed as fictions through promotion and reception. Conversely, many trick films – indexed today as fiction – have been advertised and received as recordings of magical stage tricks. In these cases, originally intended effects wore off and reception strategies changed leading to re-indexing. Train films were no longer advertised (as inviting imagining about the relationship to the train) and as the novelty of such films wore off the audiences no longer recognized the originally intended mandates to imagine. Terms like 'actualities' and 'nonfiction' were applied to them to clinch the deal. Similarly, trick films were no longer promoted as recordings of magic theatre, the audiences started treating the images as props in the game of make-believe, and the category was labelled as 'fiction'.

But changes in indexing can work in different ways as well. Indexing can be challenged and even overturned because the work contains contra-standard properties. Capote was criticized for fabricating many elements of the story, but the 'nonfiction' label stuck. This was not the case with *A Million Little Pieces* (James Frey, 2003) which was initially published and received as a hard-hitting memoir of drug addiction.[26] However, once it came to light that Frey made up many parts of the story, readers who felt cheated by this were refunded, and the publisher reclassified the work as fiction. The example of *The Blair Witch Project* that I treat at length in the next chapter demonstrates how marketing strategies can navigate audience responses without blowback. This shows that fiction is not simply whatever we label as 'fiction' because the label still must be accepted. And the matter can always be relitigated.

To summarize, I agree with Friend that fiction and nonfiction are best understood as (super)genres which exhibit standard, contra-standard, variable, and categorical properties. But unlike Friend I claim that it is still possible to define fiction and nonfiction in terms of sufficient and necessary conditions. Moreover, whereas both of our models allow for change as to what counts as a fictional work, for Friend this primarily means that the criteria for what counts as fiction changes over time. It is only after *In Cold Blood* that evocative novelistic descriptions of actual events can be easily classed as nonfiction. Earlier they would have almost certainly been categorized as fiction. Under my proposal, it is not that criteria change because necessary and sufficient conditions for what fiction is, remain the same. Rather, what changes is whether a given work satisfies these conditions, a phenomenon which is best tracked by investigating the history of labelling and, in the absence of those, promotional strategies and reception practices.[27]

Derek Matravers' intervention

While despite her criticism Friend still sees the fiction/nonfiction distinction as fundamental, Matravers' (2014) critique is more radical. He not only denies that fiction can be defined in terms of mandated imagining, but also that there is a functional difference in engaging fiction and nonfiction which can be cashed out in terms of the difference between imagination and belief. According to him, if the key difference between imagination and belief is that, in principle, belief in the content of representation leads to action whereas imagining the same content does not, there is no functional difference in engaging history or fiction. In both cases we cannot do anything about the content of representation.[28] If we read a history in which captives are beheaded for not converting, we cannot help them any more than we can help Anna Karenina from jumping under the train. So, while in general Matravers does not deny the difference between imagination and belief in terms of action potential, because there is not even a theoretical chance for action when engaging both fictions and histories there is no point for him even in introducing imagination to our descriptions of engagement with fiction. In other words, both histories and fictions involve the same types of comprehension processes which enable the reconstruction of narrative meaning. Any invocation of imagination beyond narrative comprehension is superfluous.

A further consequence of this is that a far more important distinction than fiction and nonfiction is the difference between representations which afford what Matravers dubs, on the one hand, confrontation relations and, on the other, representation relations. First, Matravers has a narrower understanding of representation than usual: 'information about what is happening or has happened in other places' (2014: 53). He essentially equates representation with narrative, while allowing there could be some less interesting forms of non-narrative representations. Second, if a representation makes it even remotely possible to act on, then it puts us in confrontation relations. A warning that a wolf is coming is such a representation as much as a report about a drought in a distant land because even in the latter case we could in principle go there and help with the relief efforts. In other words, if the representation forms relevant beliefs which could be acted upon then audiences are put in confrontation relations. Last, if, by contrast, it is impossible for us to act when faced with a representation, then we are put in representation relations. This, for Matravers, puts all fictional work and reports about the past in the same category.

As a first response, it does not seem that even under Matravers' framework fiction is a subordinate category to works affording representation relations. There are ways of helping fictional characters unlike historical ones. Sherlock Holmes was originally killed off by Conan Doyle in *The Final Problem*

(1893) because the author wanted to focus on more artistic work. But under the pressure of fans and commercial considerations Holmes was eventually resuscitated in *The Adventure of the Empty House* (1903). And this is no one-off. Endings are regularly changed, and film characters' lives are often saved following the airing of pilot episodes and focus group screenings. In this way, Head Nurse Carol Hathaway survived her originally successful suicide attempt and Julianna Margulies went on to star as one of the protagonists of *ER* (NBC, 1994–2009) for six seasons.

Different indexing of the same representation, furthermore, can change whether audiences are put in confrontation or representation relations. Were the exact same warning about an approaching wolf issued fictionally, it would not lead to any defensive actions. In fact, framing representations of 'what is happening' as fictional would regularly put the audiences in representation relations rather than confrontation relations. Note that what is actually happening does not matter, the important thing for Matravers is the representation of it and whether the representation produces relevant beliefs about it. After all, it might turn out that the news report about the drought was mistaken and that there was no emergency but as far as it caused relevant beliefs it put audiences into a confrontation relation.

When it comes to comprehension, I agree with Matravers that at the basic level fiction and nonfiction are processed the same. In engaging literary texts, the audiences first comprehend the meaning of the words, sentences, and narrative (characters, locations, time, events, and their causation) or what Matravers calls basic meaning and mental models. Only after this has been secured, they may have an attitude such as belief to what has been understood. First we understand that the captives have been decapitated for refusing to convert and only then we come to believe it or not. But while this coincidence of narrative comprehension for fiction and nonfiction works for literary narratives because of the nature of the linguistic sign, it is different with photographic film.

Certainly, the same mechanisms apply to fiction and nonfiction alike when an image is comprehended. An image capturing Lupita Nyong'o in *Twelve Years a Slave* (Steve McQueen, 2013) and her receipt of the Academy Award is first and foremost processed as an image of the actress. But if we are properly engaging McQueen's film, we are not *narratively* understanding *Twelve Years a Slave* as a progression of documentary recordings of Nyong'o and other actors performing on the set of a Hollywood production, but as a story about antebellum slavery in the United States with Patsy as one if its tragic protagonists. In other words, if Matravers is claiming that the same narrative comprehension underlies engagement with all fiction and nonfiction, this clearly does not apply to photographic film. It will not help to say that 'understanding a narrative is a matter of working out the content of the narrative from its surface structure' (Matravers, 2013: 155) because depending on whether a film is fiction or not, the surface structure is, unlike in literature, different.

Matravers is, of course, aware of what film philosophers refer to as a two-tiered system of representation (Hopkins, 2008) and film scholars as the difference between the profilmic and what the profilmic stands for (Nyong'o as opposed to Patsy). But his argument that there is no need to involve imagination in comprehending such representations in his one chapter devoted to film, even if it were valid, would apply only to illusionistic or photographically verisimilar films.[29] This is so, because as he himself points out, while in illusionistic films audiences directly engage with the embedded representations because the embedding representation is self-effacing in non-illusionistic ones they do not. In other words, while the photographically verisimilar profilmic allows for direct access to Patsy making her story in the illusionistic *Twelve Years a Slave* the surface one, in non-illusionistic films like *Dogville* (Lars von Trier, 2000) the audiences would primarily see Nicole Kidman as Nicole Kidman in costume rather than as Grace. This leaves unanswered how precisely is Grace's story understood in Matravers' account. Put differently, fiction/nonfiction categorization is key because it guides the comprehension of what the relevant or, in Matravers' terms, surface narrative is.

This is, of course, the point I was making elsewhere (Slugan, 2019a). It is the application of the imaginary attitude through the establishment of mandates to imagine that transforms early trick films from actualities of magic theatre performances into fiction films. And it is the dissipation of the mandate to imagine that transforms early train films from fictions of presence into nonfictional recordings of trains pulling into stations. Put in yet another way, Matravers' focusing on the difference in potential for action between imagination and belief misses the point when it comes to describing the role of imagination in engaging works. It is not that imagination needs to be introduced into theoretical accounts of fiction to explain why audiences do not act on what is represented. Rather, imagination is there because it genuinely changes the nature of engagement including understanding of what the relevant or surface content is. This content may be narrative, as in the case of narrative fiction films as opposed to narrative nonfiction films, or non-narrative, as in the case of early cinema where the question was whether to engage something as a prop to begin with or not. And this is missed if we, as Matravers does, do not investigate historical change.

Matravers might respond that even if this were true, it only applies to film. It does not change anything about literary texts for which I have admitted that the underlying narrative comprehension is the same across fiction and nonfiction. But while the effects might not be as radical as in film, the point about the global attitude towards the text cashed out in terms of primacy which is key for different types of engagement with fiction and nonfiction still applies. Take Matravers' example of Tolstoy's *War and Peace* (1869), which he claims is, from the perspective of imagination and belief, engaged with in the same manner as with Faber du Faur's vivid memoir *With Napoleon in Russia*. But again, the point is not to focus on the potential for action. Matravers admits as much when he 'grant[s] that the relation between the former [*War and Peace*] and subsequent belief is less straightforward than the relation between the latter [*With Napoleon in Russia*] and subsequent belief' (Matravers 2014: 47) and devotes a chapter to the difference in acquiring beliefs from fiction and nonfiction, respectively. For Matravers the difference is because in fiction it is never quite clear which propositions are to be believed. But he does not think this is the reason to invoke imagination. Simply pointing out that we are dealing with fiction as a category suffices – we need not specify some special mental state that describes engagement with fiction.

Yet there must be not only some attitude but also a mandate for that attitude involved. In many forms of nonfiction audiences not only form beliefs but are also primarily mandated to believe. Cautious scepticism towards the content and reading for entertainment is what Matravers does mention when giving some of the reasons why belief acquisition is not as straightforward in fiction. But even if we treat these not only as attitudes but as mandates as well, they are certainly no better than the consensus view that imagination is what is mandated. Both cautious scepticism and entertainment are more widely applicable to nonfiction than imagination is. Academic writing, journalism, and documentaries alike profess their ideal consumer is critical. There is a whole genre of infotainment across media while true crime has proven immensely popular given its entertainment value. The two cannot even be necessary conditions for fiction. Because cautious scepticism is an attitude towards propositions, it cannot be a part of the mandate for fictions which involve no propositions or assertions as explained in Chapter One (literary forms without predicates, majority of painting, photography, etc.). Entertainment as a mandate does not work well as a description of what audiences are supposed to do when engaging non-propositional fictions like mythical paintings either. Similarly, there are narrative fictions like James Joyce's *Ulysses* (1919) or *Finnegans Wake* (1939) whose primary mode of engagement is hardly one of entertainment. The obvious advantage of imagination here is that, as Manuel García-Carpintero (2021) reminds us, even Friend never manages to deny that mandated imagination of at least some of its content is a necessary condition for a fictional work. She only produces an example of a fictional work that is completely true, but this does not mean that its propositions are not to be imagined.

Admittedly, Matravers' goal is not to define fiction but rather give some reasons why belief acquisition is not as straightforward as in nonfiction. His main reason for why imagination cannot do the job is because he finds faults with how imagination is explained under the consensus view. For this he mainly discusses Currie's (1990) definition of imagination as simulation and Kathleen Stock's (2011) account of imagining propositions in relation to existing beliefs. But theirs is not the only way to think about imagination and I outline one such alternative in more detail in Chapter Four. At present suffice it to say that because Matravers focuses on narratives he directs his critiques predominantly at discussions of propositional imagination (Currie and Stock), i.e. imaginative attitude towards parts of the work which are propositional, or which express propositions. But even in mostly propositional works propositions are not the only thing to be engaged with beyond mere comprehension. Schama's history and *Walking with Dinosaurs* mandate imagining things like terraces and peacocks and travelling in time, respectively. These are not propositions, but objects and experiences. And fiction typically mandates such imaginings as well. As I have argued, moreover, fiction can be completely non-propositional (e.g. most forms of sculpture, painting, some forms of music). There the mandated engagement will also be non-propositional. And most importantly, as Matravers himself admits, audiences can also have an attitude towards the work as a whole. And that is what my emphasis on the primacy of mandated imagining captures – the global attitude towards a fictional *work*. It is the general attitude towards what we are to engage which under the banner of imagination covers different forms of non-propositional and propositional engagement. In mainly propositional works which also involve local mandates to believe like *War and Peace* this global attitude casts doubt on what exactly to believe. But this overall attitude also prepares the audiences for non-propositional imaginary engagement.[30]

And this returns us to the point that Friend was making – fiction and nonfiction are categories of appreciation in the sense that they are approached in different ways. While at the basic level, comprehension is the same across these (super)genres – narrative for literature and image recognition for photographic film – it matters for engagement whether a work is fiction or not. Usually, fiction will be consumed for entertainment and nonfiction for edification. Fiction will typically entail greater attention paid to the style and nonfiction to veracity. These may be thought of as standard features of the genre from the perspective of how they are engaged. What I have been arguing is that primary mandated imagining is not only a standard feature but a necessary and sufficient one.

A competing institutional approach

I will conclude with how my proposal relates to another account which can be described as institutional. In an original and thought-provoking monograph, Catharine Abell (2020) argues convincingly for the importance of what she refers to as fiction institutions in engaging fictions. For Abell, institutions provide solutions to cooperation problems by providing rules. Driving presents one such problem wherein to avoid colliding with the car going in the opposite direction, the two drivers need to choose some strategy. The crash will be avoided if both drive either on the left or on the right side of the road. The trouble is that the strategy depends on what the other driver is doing and thinking, and the two cannot agree beforehand what strategy to adopt. Institutions solve such cooperation problems by providing external rules which single out one of the possible solution strategies. In the UK, for instance, the institutional traffic rule is to drive on the left while in the rest of Europe it is to drive on the right. In other words, if drivers follow the rule, they can be sure they will avoid a crash. Importantly, while the rule is relatively arbitrary in the sense that it could be either of the two options, it is not absolutely arbitrary in the sense that it must have been one of the two options because only these two solve the problem.

Fiction institutions are also here to solve cooperation problems. The main cooperation problem for Abell is how to communicate an imagining, i.e. how to ensure that the audiences will engage in imagining the content offered through fictional utterances. According to Abell, audiences cannot appeal to either (reconstructing) authorial intentions or decoding texts, for instance, to correctly imagine that in George Eliot's *Middlemarch* (1871) Dorothe regrets marrying Casaubon despite this never being explicitly stated in the text. Instead, the audiences must follow certain rules provided by fiction institutions to imagine this implied content.

While Abell's discussion is illuminating when it comes to what precisely counts as fictional content and how it is secured, the inclusion of at least one fictive utterance for her is only a necessary condition for something to be a fictional work. The demand for *primacy* of mandated imagining in my definition of a fictional work also implies that there needs to be at least one fictive utterance in it. On this we agree.[31] In her definition the fictive utterance condition is the second one:

A work is fiction if and only if:

1. there is a practice of fiction such that audiences' responses to the series of utterances by which that work was produced are intended to conform to it; and
2. at least one utterance in the series by which it was produced is governed by a content-determining rule that regulates that practice. (Abell, 2020: 37)

It is the first condition that on cursory inspection appears like my only one. This is so because it specifies that 'Works of fiction differ from works of non-fiction only in respect of the *source* of their prescriptions to imagine. Works of fiction alone prescribe imaginings as a consequence of the institutional contexts in which they are produced' (Abell, 2020: 40, italics in the original). In other words, her theory is institutional because the source of the mandate to imagine is the placement of the work in the institution of fiction and not authorial intentions for prescribing imaginings. As she clarifies, a disgruntled author might churn out a novel just to get out of a contract with the publisher, without intending any imaginative response by the eventual audiences. Such a novel would still count as fiction because it was placed in the institution of fiction. On this we also agree.

But there is an important point of disagreement. In her final analysis, the placement in this institution of fiction is secured by authorial intentions: 'a work is fiction only if its author has certain intentions regarding the whole series of utterances by which it is produced' (Abell, 2020: 24). For the disaffected author's work to be fiction she must 'intend[] that audiences' responses to [her novel] conform to a practice of fiction' (Abell, 2020: 40). Put differently, for Abell it is only the content of fictive utterances that is a problem to be solved by institutions and not the categorization of works. Different historical and cultural institution fictions can vary only in rules for how the content of fictive utterance is to be determined and not in assigning membership in the category of non/fictional works. This means that her theory also cannot handle examples like early train and trick films because for her intentions about placement fix a work's status in time once and for all.

In my account the work's placement in fiction institution hinges on the negotiation between factors of production, promotion, distribution, exhibition, reception, and public classification. And this original indexing can always be relitigated and the work placed in nonfiction institution instead. In Abell's vocabulary, this process of indexing and re-indexing can be understood as its own indexing institution which provides a solution to the cooperation problem of categorizing works by placing the work in fiction institution or nonfiction institution. The indexing institution's two main rules are:

> If the work is indexed as fiction, then you are mandated to primarily imagine its content.
>
> If the work is indexed as nonfiction, then you are not supposed to primarily imagine its content.

The second part of the book will open with illustrating in more detail the mechanics of indexing on the examples that have been renegotiated or are yet to be negotiated. In other words, it will concern itself with how primacy of mandated imagining is established and lost.

PART TWO

FICTION AS PRIMARILY MANDATED IMAGINATION

3

The temporally unstable primacy of mandate

While in the previous chapter I have regularly spoken about treating fiction and nonfiction as genre, I am starting the second part of the book by setting out to clarify how a film might change such a genre over time. Readers familiar with film theory might point out that all this looks very much like Rick Altman's (1999) pragmatic understanding of film genre which also dismisses any necessary and sufficient conditions for the category and instead gives considerable attention to institutional classification practices. If that is the case, why approach the matter in such a roundabout fashion starting with Stacie Friend's modification of Kendall Walton's ideas and not resort to Altman directly?

Although it is true that Altman makes a point that the changing categorization applies to all communicative practices, his focus is on literary and film genre. Friend, by contrast, explicitly tackles fiction as genre so I have addressed that discussion first. Additionally, while I have used Altman's model of genre formation elsewhere (Slugan, 2022b) it cannot be immediately applied to fiction and nonfiction, because it is based on substantivization of adjectives. According to Altman, genre names are established in such a way that the adjective that described a type of genre in the previous cycle becomes a standalone genre with the adjective now transformed into a noun. For instance, a type of drama is first described as a *comic* drama and then once the audiences start treating this type of film as a genre of its own the adjective 'comic' becomes a noun: comedy. In further genrification a subgroup of comedy known as romantic comedy crystallizes, and the adjective 'romantic' is again eventually substantivized into a noun and genre called romance. No such labelling informs 'fiction' and 'nonfiction film'. The two are, unlike Altman's genre, for the most part mutually exclusive categories.

Furthermore, for Altman, producers and critics are key agents in the process of genre formation. On the one hand, the critics identify a genre through industry or critical sources, describe the films which are regularly listed as members of such genre, and then start the analysis of the genre based on the films' common features. On the other, the producers identify the most financially successful films, single out their characteristics and replicate them, accompany this extraction in promotional terms, and if successful repeat the same process. While these are not irrelevant processes for indexing fiction and nonfiction, they operate on a finer level of granularity usually already within the categories of either fiction or nonfiction. Moreover, indexing involves a wider range of actors than genrification as presented by Altman – promotors, distributors, exhibitors, and public classification platforms like movie databases all play an important role as well. What is more, the labelling offered by one set of agents may be vehemently litigated by another as we have already seen in the previous chapter on the example of *A Million Little Pieces* (James Frey, 2003) and will expound on in detail here.

One final important difference is that the categorization need not necessarily explicitly involve labels. Elsewhere (Slugan, 2019a), I have shown how films shifted between categories of fiction and nonfiction not based on any 'fiction' or 'nonfiction' genre labels – for these were not in use for film at the time – but through the analysis of explicit and implied mandates articulated in the discourse surrounding those films. And even here, where I focus on the period after these labels have been established in discussions about film, the indexing process cannot be fully described just by looking at which genre labels were applied when. For details, I provide three examples, each with their own specific traversal of boundaries between fiction and nonfiction, starting with a work which has moved from nonfiction to fiction.

In the first section I briefly outline two distinct phases of *The Blair Witch Project* (David Myrick and Eduard Sánchez) promotion prior and after the January 1999 Sundance premiere and the purchase of the film's distribution rights by Artisan. I argue that during the original phase of promotion, *The Blair Witch Project* constituted a documentary film because the audiences were mandated to believe the events depicted in the film rather than make-believe them. Although die-hard fans who followed the original website, the newsletters, and fan websites would have been in the know that the content of the film and its historical context were invented, this information was hidden from baseline engagement with the producers' website, the two 'trailers' that appeared on *Split Screen* (John Pierson, 1997–2001), and initial radio and press coverage. As importantly, the Sundance catalogue description for the film did not include either 'dramatic' or 'documentary' label. While the second phase of the official promotion after the Sundance led by the distributor Artisan pushed the mandate to believe even more strongly (with even IMDb playing along by listing the actors as missing), the reviews following the premiere and the increased attention in trade press categorizing the film as fiction made indexing the film as documentary virtually impossible.

I discuss a film whose fictional status initially moved in the opposite direction in the second section. *Neighbours* (Norman McLaren, 1952) started off as a fiction film about a friendship descending into murderous violence, albeit with much more limited promotion and coverage than the chapter's previous example. With the nomination for the Academy Award for Best Short Documentary in February 1953 and the win in the category next month, the film was transformed into a work which should be primarily treated as a parable about the need to love one's neighbour to be believed in. Interestingly, by present-day the film has reverted to its original fictional status mandating the audiences to primarily imagine the story of warring neighbours.

I conclude with an outline of a hybrid not as a work which contains fictional and nonfictional elements – for the mandate to imagine and the mandate to believe, as we have learned, regularly appear together – but as a work whose indexing has not resulted in stable categorization. This can be because the work has not garnered sufficient attention from parties involved in indexing or because influential contributors to the process are continuing to offer competing classifications.

The Blair Witch Project

The Blair Witch Project opens with the words 'In October of 1994, three student filmmakers disappeared in the woods near Burkittsville, Maryland while shooting a documentary. A year later their footage was found.' What follows, the introduction suggests, is that very footage shot by now missing and presumed dead Heather Donahue, Michael Williams, and Joshua Leonard, and edited by Myrick and Sánchez upon its recovery. Textually, the film has a quality of raw footage made by an inexperienced, and as it progresses, an increasingly frightened crew. At the same time, the events that the film depicts have been invented and no such disappearance took place.

For scholars who have provided detailed discussions of the film's promotion (Johnson, 2001 and London, 2024) and reception (Schreier, 2004), the fact that it was invented means that the film was always fictional. On my institutional view of fiction, however, the invented content is but one textual parameter which cannot define the status of a work on its own. From this perspective, while the textual features limit the range of promotion and distribution strategies, and exhibition contexts and audience responses, it is the negotiation between all these parameters that needs to be analysed to ascertain the (changing) non/

fictional status of a work. In this light, *The Blair Witch Project* started off as a nonfictional film and turned into fiction after its premiere.

The Blair Witch Project officially premiered at the Sundance Film Festival in the Park City at Midnight section on 23 January 1999. By morning the film rights were picked up by an independent distributor Artisan Entertainment for $1.1 million (*Variety* 8 September 1999: a2). Following the theatrical release on 14 July the film would go on to earn almost $250 million making it one of the most lucrative films relative to the original budget of $100 thousand for the Sundance premiere and $750 thousand for the wide release.[1] As many commentators have recognized, an innovative marketing campaign including an online website which developed the film's background contributed to the success. Crucially for us, this background, much like the film as a text, was presented as a factual history to be believed.

As Johnson (2001) and London (2024) have shown, the promotion unfolded in two phases separated by Artisan's purchase of the film rights. Up to that point, it was the filmmakers and their production company Haxan Films who led the campaign through 'investment trailers', the film website, and the newsletter. The second phase was led by Artisan through the revamped website, TV and book tie-ins which further develop the Blair Witch lore, and more traditional newspaper, radio, and TV advertising. Johnson and London are interested in dispelling the myth both that Artisan came up with the online marketing strategy (they only built on Haxan's existing website) and that the online strategy was key for the film's commercial success (other factors like traditional outlets had a significant role as well).

For the establishment of the mandate, as I already noted, the promotion by producers and distributors can only go so far because other factors like exhibition context and reception reports are as important, for it is there that the proposed indexing is accepted or renegotiated. That is why to understand the categorization of *The Blair Witch Project* next to analysing promotion we also need to investigate how the trade press reported on the project, how the festivals where the film was presented categorized it in their catalogues, and once the film premiered how the film was labelled by the reviewers.

Much has been said about the website and the deliberate presentation of information therein as factual. While far from irrelevant, of more importance for the establishment of the mandate in the first phase of promotion and reception were the *Split Screen* trailers and the trade press reports on these which preceded the establishment of the original website in June 1998. The same is true of the radio show call-in by an early fan in October 1998. The reason is that the trailers, the press reports, and the call all had a wider reach than the website which started attracting larger amounts of visitors only after this phone-in. In the first two days after the call, the website saw 2,600 visits and only two weeks later did the website log its 7,000th visit since going live (Johnson, 2001: 73).

The project had its first national exposure in the form of an 'investment trailer' on 15 August 1997, in season 1, episode 10 of *Split Screen* – a half-an-hour TV show about American independent film run by John Pierson and airing on Independent Film Channel and sometimes Bravo.[2] The trailer consisted of three parts. The first described the more than 200-year-old legend of the Blair Witch and the mysterious deaths and disappearances that have been linked to her through the ages. The second focused on three students who have disappeared in the early 1990s while making a film about the witch, the police search for them, and the discovery of the students' footage. The final part was the interview with the Haxan filmmakers Myrick, Sánchez, and Gregg Hale in which they claim that they have been hired to conduct a private investigation using the found footage. Crucially, all three segments were presented as factual with the 'deadpan' interview arguably contributing the most to the establishment of the mandate to believe. The same day, *IndieWire* described the content of the first trailer as a factual matter further contributing to this mandate: 'Local filmmakers Ed Sanchez [*sic*], Dan Myrick, and Gregg

Hale of Haxan Films have secured permission to document the first public examination of the footage, hoping that it will solve the mystery of the missing crew' (15 August 1997).[3]

Based on this trailer Pierson's production company Grainy Pictures provided further financing for the project which allowed the team to shoot the content of the found footage whose edited form would essentially constitute the film shown at Sundance. This resulted in a second trailer that premiered on the first episode of season two of *Split Screen* on 6 April 1998.[4] While this trailer was again presented as factual, in his introduction to the segment Pierson expressed some scepticism about what follows and invited the viewers to visit the grainypix.com message board and address the question 'Is it real?'.[5]

The ensuing debate directly inspired Haxan team to develop a website for the film (London, 2024: 91–2).[6] Started in April/May 1998, the website was fully functional by June 1998 (Johnson, 2001). While the original website content (www.blairwitch.com) is no longer available, according to London (2024: 94–5) who conducted interviews with Sánchez and Monello who developed the website, between July and October 1998 it included 'Contact Us', 'Contents', 'Mailing list', 'Post', 'The Story of the Black Hill Disappearances', and 'Timeline' sections. Crucially, there was no information on production or release dates. Although 'Biographies' and 'Credits' sections which would have revealed the invented nature of the project existed, they were hidden. Instead, the focus was on the Timeline section which provided the backstory of the Blair Witch-related murders and disappearances over the years. Between July and October, the website was incrementally updated to further develop this backstory and provide fresh information on the missing students. The audiovisual material included their photographs from college, photographs of their recovered equipment, forensic photographs of Josh's car found in the woods, audios and videos from the found footage, and pages from Heather's journal.

As Johnson and London have reported, it is undeniable that those who extensively engaged with the website, spent some time on its message boards talking with the filmmakers, and subscribed to the newsletter would have found out and/or been told by the Haxan team that the work should be understood as fictional. But while this fan community was certainly committed it was not large – before the October 1998 radio call-in visits measured in hundreds.[7] More importantly, the general structure of the website meant that a typical web-surfer who spent a maximum of a few minutes on a site would have come away from the Blair Witch website thinking that the content of the found footage should be believed. In other words, committed fans here should be understood more as an extended group of people with whom detailed information about the project is shared (beyond filmmakers, producers, investors, family, and friends), rather than as broad audiences for whom the mandate is actually offered.[8]

This much is clear from another key event leading up to the Sundance premiere. Independently from the Haxan team, one of the film's earliest fans – Jeff Johnsen – single-handedly afforded the project its biggest exposure since the second trailer.[9] In October 1998, Johnsen phoned in on the Los Angeles-based radio show *The Mark & Brian Show* and went on to converse with the hosts about the film and the website for half an hour. Crucially, when asked whether it was real he responded: 'You know, I am pretty sure it is' (quoted in Johnson, 2001: 72). That even a fan who was in the know decided to present the film and the Blair Witch backstory as something to be believed when talking to the general audience, means that the public-facing campaign was one that sought to establish a mandate to believe.

More visits certainly also meant more engaged fans and newsletter subscribers in the know, but it also meant more casual web-surfers mandated to believe. And, more importantly, even with these increased visits which before the January Sundance premiere numbered in the thousands, it was the trailers, *Variety* report, and radio call-in that had wider exposure than the website at the time. And they all pushed the mandate to believe.

Another crucial reason to think that at the time of premiere *The Blair Witch Project* was indexed as nonfiction is the way that the film was presented during its original exhibition context – the 23 January 1999 premiere. It is worth listing the Sundance Film Festival catalogue entry in full:

> U.S.A., 1998, 87 min., color/black & white
> DIRECTORS/
> SCREENWRITERS/EDITORS:
> Eduardo Sanchez [*sic*] and Daniel Myrick
> PRODUCERS:
> Greg Hale, Robin Cowie
> COPRODUCER:
> Michael Monello
> EXECUTIVE PRODUCERS:
> Kevin J. Foxe, Bob Eick
> CINEMATOGRAPHY:
> Neal L. Fredericks
> PRODUCTION DESIGNER:
> Ben Rock
> MUSIC:
> Tony Cora
> PRINCIPAL CAST:
> Heather Donahue, Michael Williams, Joshua Leonard
>
> Picture yourself stranded in the woods, paralyzed by the night, and bombarded by the aural and physical evidence of your deepest, darkest phobias. If you've ever faced the demons of the night, you'll understand the rich psychology of fear that permeates "The Blair Witch Project," a film which catapults us into the seat of pure, unadulterated, primordial

horror. “Friday the 13th,” eat your heart out - this is bone-chilling, soul-stirring, cardiac-arrest-styled terror, made all the scarier by its exacting authenticity.

Shot in real time on video and 16 mm film, “The Blair Witch Project” is the firsthand account of three student documentary filmmakers who venture into Maryland’s remote Black Hills to discover the truth about the local scaremonger, the mythical Blair Witch. After the trio disappear without a trace, their footage is unearthed one year later, revealing a terrifying account of the events which marked their final days. It is an edited compendium of the purported filmmaker’s findings that forms the harrowing content of “The Blair Witch Project.”

Brilliantly blurring the lines between fact and fiction, “The Blair Witch Project” redefines the horror genre with sheer cinematic ingenuity, urgency, and invention. Deftly building suspense through sound, visuals, and performances of unparalleled realism, “The Blair Witch Project’s” violence is psychological, not physical; nary a drop of blood is spackled onscreen. But the result is none-the-less frightening, as the cameras bite into the heart of darkness, documenting the emergence of evil and the mounting hysteria of its unwitting victims.

– Rebecca Yeldham[10]

Although at the time Sundance differentiated between dramatic and documentary film, there is no unequivocal information about the film type here.[11] And because *The Blair Witch Project* was not included either in the Dramatic or Documentary competition, but in the Midnight section the relevant category cannot be inferred from this placement. At first, the description emphasizes the mandate to believe the film content: ‘shot in real time’, ‘the firsthand account of three student documentary filmmakers’, ‘their footage is unearthed one year later', 'it is an edited compendium'.[12] This is somewhat tempered by the opening of the last paragraph – 'Brilliantly blurring the lines between fact and fiction' – but from this alone it is impossible to infer what the fictional elements are or in what part of the film the lines are blurred. On its own, the description does not suggest that the content of the found footage itself is invented. At most, the film is presented as a hybrid and certainly not as fiction alone.

Given that the Sundance premiere was accompanied by the distribution of missing persons posters with the faces of Donahue, Williams, and Leonard, and that they heeded the producers' request not to participate in any interviews, it is safe to conclude that at the time and even in the original exhibition context the audiences were mandated to believe the film's content.[13] Again, I am not denying that die-hard fans would have known that the film content is invented but this does not change the overall promotional drive nor the original exhibitors' description of the film in mostly documentary terms. As I have argued in Chapter One, that something is invented does not necessarily make it fictional – in the context of mandate to believe it just makes it a misrepresentation.

Immediately following the screening, however, the mandate started to be renegotiated. Because *The Blair Witch Project* was the first film at the festival to be sold it generated a lot of coverage. The trade press and reviews regularly identified the film as fiction. *Variety* described the film as 'horror mockumentary' and 'psuedo-documentary' using '"discovered" footage' (25 January 1999: 10, 42). *Los Angeles Times*, similarly, labelled it a 'low-budget thriller' (25 January 1999: 174). *Filmmaker* published an interview with the filmmakers where they openly discuss how the film was shot (Winter 1999).[14] Reviews by audience members who saw the film either at Sundance or at various sneak previews throughout the country that followed also started appearing on IMDb. Among 102 reviews published between 1 February and 13 July 1999 not even one claims that the film is nonfiction while most are either explicit that it is fiction or implicit about its fictional status (inferable from comments about the acting or shooting style).[15]

Undeniably, in the second phase of the promotion the discussion board and other elements pointing to the invented nature of the film's content such as film credits were removed from the revamped website (Schreier, 2004 and London, 2024). Updated in April 1999, the webpage now opened with an introductory video of what would become the opening of the film: 'In October 1994 … ' The video then faded into the main webpage with 'Mythology', 'The Filmmakers', 'The Aftermath', and 'The Legacy' sections.[16] The mandate to believe was now pushed even more through the inclusion of further factual-looking details such as the photographs of the search for the missing students and new interviews with the relatives and police and private investigators. In fact, IMDb reportedly deferred to this strategy by listing the protagonists as missing and presumed dead on the film's main webpage.[17]

But as I argued in the previous chapter, promotional and distribution strategies are only a part of the negation process that is indexing. In the end, the category needs to be accepted through reception to stabilize. And starting from the premiere at Sundance, reviewers regularly labelled the film as fiction. This was not only professional commentators and critics in the trade press and newspapers but also nonprofessional audience members. It should not be forgotten that the film had its international premiere in May 1999 at the Cannes Film Festival before the wide theatrical release in July. This again offered both professional and nonprofessional reviewers the opportunity to categorize the film as fiction, which they seized. Writing in *Chicago Sun-Times* Roger Ebert did so by citing how Sánchez and Myrick organized the shoot and how some audiences 'think the film has to be real' because of its 'documentary look' (20 May 1999).[18] Both before and after Cannes, *New York Times* reported on the film as 'mock-documentary' and 'pseudo-documentary' (2 May 1999, 21 May 1999). Just to give another example, this time from European reception of the Cannes festival, Dragan Rubeša clearly stated that the film was made with professional actors and followed the principles of Dogma-95 (1999).

This is, again, not to deny that some audiences thought the film was nonfiction even after the July release.[19] But this is far less often than the commentary like Ebert's suggests. Margit Schreier (2004) analysed more than a thousand English and German newsgroup discussion posts from June 1999 to February 2001. Among ninety-five people who discussed the film's ontological status, fifty-eight classed the film either as fiction or hybrid, thirty-nine were temporarily uncertain about its status, and only two insisted that it was nonfiction. And more importantly, the key to indexing is not what the audience members thought the film was but how their public contributions to the negotiation impacted the categorization. Because even nonprofessional audiences generally identified the film as fiction on message boards and as reviewers and professionals regularly did the same, the reception side of the negotiation pushed for the mandate to imagine. While the website remained the same during this period, after the July premiere the actors also started giving both televised and press interviews, making it clear that they were not missing and further undermining the mandate to believe which started to be replaced with the mandate to imagine immediately following the Sundance premiere.

It is true that around the time of the theatrical release the website that Artisan updated in April 1999 saw another surge in visits with 213,000 unique visitors between 8 July and July 14 with the number peaking at 648,000 two weeks later (London, 2024: 103). But this does not mean that the film was a hybrid for some time in July 1999 – its mandate suspended between the promotional push for belief on the webpage, on the one side, and the authorization of imagination through cast and crew appearances, trade press reports, and reviews, on the other. While the number of more than a million unique visitors to the website insisting on the mandate to believe was undoubtedly high for the time, this is no greater than the number of people that would have seen the TV coverage of filmmakers Myrick and Sánchez, on the one hand, and lead actress Donahue, on the other, on 'Good Morning America', CBS' 'This Morning' and 'Saturday Morning', and NBC's 'The

Today Show' coming clean and supporting the mandate to imagine (*Variety*, 8 September 1999: a2). And we should not forget about the coverage in the printed and online national press that would have had a similar reach. More importantly, the distributor's website was only one parameter in the indexing process. At that point, the indexing process included not only the promotion through the cast and crew interviews, but also press and online reviews. We should also not forget that in the exhibition context, the film came with 'this is a work of fiction' disclaimer. Put schematically, according to the institutional model of fiction proposed here, up to its premiere at Sundance the film was documentary and following it fiction.

Neighbours

Around the time of its release, the short film *Neighbours* followed the opposite trajectory. The work depicts two men whose friendly relationship is strained by the appearance of a flower dancing on the border of their properties. The disagreement about whose property the flower lies on leads to a more and more violent exchange of blows and eventually to the demise of both. The film ends with its message spelled out in numerous world languages and bookended by its English version: 'Love Your Neighbour'. Stylistically, the film is made by pixilation, a stop-animation technique using live actors. The soundtrack produced by directly scratching the edge of the filmstrip also contributes to its experimental appearance.

Starting as a film whose fictional story was the focus of the mandate, following the nomination and the win of the 1953 Academy Award for the Best Documentary Short, *Neighbours* transformed into a work whose message took centre-stage in the rearticulation of the mandate. In other words, while both elements – the story to be imagined and the message to be believed in and adhered to – are present in the film, the renegotiation of the mandate had shifted the primary focus of audience engagement. To put it schematically once again, while prior to the Oscar Award the film was a fictional work about two feuding neighbours, afterwards it became a didactic illustration of the anti-war message about loving one's neighbour to be followed and believed in.[20]

While the film was originally conceived around the exploration of experimental techniques – pixilation and direct sound writing – when it comes to its content, McLaren clearly had both the story and a message in mind from the preparatory stages (Dobson, 1994: 225). The film was initially supposed to be about traffic safety, but once his employer – the National Board of Canada – informed him of funding available for films promoting democracy, the topic changed. Very quickly McLaren conceived the story about two people exchanging blows and the filming commenced shortly thereafter (Dobson, 1994: 225)

Produced by the National Board of Canada and shot in the summer of 1951 the film had very limited distribution in Canadian art cinemas and, unlike *The Blair Witch Project*, virtually no public promotion (Ohayon, 2011 and Dobson, 2017).[21] While the reactions at home were muted, the film garnered more attention abroad. In the UK, it premiered at the Edinburgh Film Festival in August 1952 with the following account appearing in the *Manchester Guardian*:

> The range of the Edinburgh Film Festival (devoted to works documentary, realist and experimental) is nicely illustrated by the contrast between a film that might be called "Love thy Neighbour" and another that should be entitled "Eat thy Neighbour". The first, by the Canadian Norman McLaren, is a parable called *Neighbours*. Here the director marries for the first time the naturalistic image of the living actor to a hand-made setting, and joins the result to the synthetic sound "drawn on the celluloid" which we know from his earlier cartoons. The parable is savage as is brief. In adjacent gardens innocent of fences, two neighbours smoke their pipes in amity; but a marigold springs up between them, fills them with desire, divides them.

> The mood is farcical, the audience is led laughing uproariously into a nasty little corner where Mr McLaren, without warning, kicks it in the teeth.
>
> There is no parable about Walt Disney's "Nature's Half Acre", the third in the series which has already produced "Beaver Valley" and "Seal Island." No loving here; the bee is caught by the spider, and the spider is caught by the mud-dauber, and so ad infinitum; all this in close-up and sumptuous colour. The human comedy takes its precarious place between these extremes, and has been represented by a moderately good version by Max Ophuls of three stories by Maupassant.
>
> (23 August 1952: 3)

At the very opening the film is explicitly contrasted to a nature documentary that also appeared at the festival – James Algar's *Nature's Half Acre* (1950). Placing Algar's film in the lineage of his earlier *Seal Island* (1948) – 1951 BAFTA Best Documentary nominee – and *Beaver Valey* (1950) – 1951 Berlin Film Festival and 1952 BAFTA Best Documentary winner – firmly secures its documentary status. Undeniably, the explicit contrasting genre at the beginning of the review is 'experimental' and not fiction film.[22] But this does not mean that the fictional status is somehow denied to *Neighbours*. After all, Ophüls' film – *Le Plaisir* (1952) – in this trichotomy of the festival's range belongs to the 'realist' category, but the film clearly was and remains fiction. What secures *Neighbours*' fictional status is that while the *Manchester Guardian*'s description clearly recognizes the allegorical nature of the film, when it comes to the distinction between fiction and nonfiction the emphasis remains on the fictional storyline – the neighbourly setup, the disturbance, and the hint of a violent finale.

The same emphasis on the story to be imagined can be seen in the French trade press announcing the film's upcoming appearance at the Venice Film Festival (20 August–12 September 1952): 'Two neighbours live in friendship. A flower comes to grow on the dividing line of their properties. For the possession of this flower, the two friends come to fight to the death' (*La Cinematographie Francaîse* 30 August 1952: 14).[23] Moreover, by pointing out that 'Jean-Paul Ladouceur and Grant Munro [are the] main actors in *Neihgbours*', the film is connected to the standard feature of fiction of the time – live action.

This classification, however, started to shift once the film was nominated for the Documentary Short Oscar in February 1953 thanks to its limited theatrical release in the United States (*The Exhibitor* 25 February 1953: 16). In fact, a piece that was 'read to a meeting of the British Kinematograph Society on 4 February 1953' can explain how the mandated shift in the focus from a story to be imagined to the message to be believed took place (Hoare 1953: 176). In it, Hoare points out that educational film can do more than just present facts from different domains of scientific knowledge: 'the greatest power of the film is in its emotional effect ; its power to change or develop what the Americans call "attitudes"' (Hoare, 1953: 176). Once Hoare listed *Neighbours* as an example of such a film, it is easier to see how the understanding of the film as educational in this wider sense must have been similar to the line of thinking that allowed the Academy to nominate *Neighbours* in the Documentary Short category (it was also nominated in the Short Category but won only the former).

With *Neighbours* winning the Oscar for Documentary Short on 19 March 1953, the mandate to believe gained further and decisive momentum. The award was widely reported in the trade press and general dailies alike. Among others, *LA Times*, *The Journal*, *Motion Picture Daily*, *Variety*, *Motion Picture Herald*, *The Exhibitor*, and *Canadian Film Yearbook* carried the news.[24] Moreover, as an Oscar winner, *Neighbours* became a sought-after commodity among exhibitors around Canada, the United States and elsewhere. In fact, it became the most popular National Film Board of Canada film with 108,000 theatrical bookings by 1987 (Dobson 1994: 223). As the description of the list of that week's screenings in *The Exhibitor* evinces, Oscar in the documentary category became the key exhibition context further regulating audience focus:

Color Documentary

NEIGHBOURS. Mayer-Kingsley. 8m. If only for its innovation in technique this should be a good Technicolor short subject. Add to that a startling type of humor and a moral of "love your neighbor", and this becomes a memorable, original film. By speeding up or reversing the film, some startling effects are achieved. When a dancing flower pops up in the backyard, two seemingly friendly neighbors are fascinated with it. There develops a quarrel as to whose property contains the flower, and a fight ensues. The fight, captured by trick photography, is fast and furious. In the course of the fisticuffs, the neighbors kill each other, and on their graves each has his own dancing flower. This subject was judged the best short subject documentary, and given an Academy Award in that classification. It was produced by Norman McLaren, and was made by the National Film Board of Canada. EXCELLENT

(8 April 1953: 3499)

To summarize, it is not that the story to be imagined somehow disappears but rather that the focus shifts from this imaginative engagement to a belief and an ought-to attitude that the audiences are supposed to espouse towards the film's moral.

Importantly, the changes in the film's status do not stop here. While I will not go into detail as I did with the shift from fiction to documentary, *Neighbours* has by now reverted to fiction. This much is clear from present-day public indexing. *Rotten Tomatoes* lists it as comedy. On IMDb it is tagged with 'stop motion animation', 'animation', 'comedy', and 'short' labels. *Letterboxd* has it as 'animation' and 'comedy' and its description as an 'Oscar-winning short film' conveniently drops the fact that the award was for the Documentary short. While *Neighbours* appears in the 'Animated Documentary' entry on Wikipedia, the page states that the 'award is somewhat considered a mistake'.[25]

Even the producers and the most famous awarder have backtracked on their classification. In a press release accompanying a retrospective of

Oscar-winning documentaries from 2005, the Academy writes: 'Documentary Short Subject winners "Benjy" (1951) and "Neighbours" (1952) are among a group of films that not only competed, but won Academy Awards in what were clearly inappropriate categories.'[26] Since 2011, the blog of the National Board of Canada, which previously jumped on the opportunity to bill the film as a documentary following its win, reads that the 'film won many awards over the years, but strangely they were in the documentary category, even though it had no documentary elements in it' (Ohayon, 2011).

The categories are inappropriate and the win strange, of course, only if we think about documentary from a textualist perspective which sees the representation of non-actors, real locations, lack of staging, etc., as constitutive of documentary. On this view, it would also be strange to treat *Walking with Dinosaurs* (BBC, 1999) as a documentary. But once we think about the category as a subset of works which operate under the mandate to primarily believe their content, there is nothing strange about the Academy's decision to not only treat *Neighbours* as a documentary but award it with an Oscar.

Hybridity

I will conclude the chapter with a note on hybridity. In the section on *The Blair Witch Project*, I briefly considered the possibility that the film was a hybrid during a few months of competing mandates to believe and imagine after the Sundance premiere and before the wide theatrical release. Under this model hybrid is better understood not as work which contains both fictional and nonfictional elements, but rather as one in which the placement of the work in the institution of cinema and the discourse surrounding the placement has not yet produced a stable indexing. While I have argued against the view that *The Blair Witch Project* was ever hybrid because the mandate to imagine became the dominant force in the process of indexing immediately after the January

Sundance premiere and considerably before the renewed online promotional campaign started in April, this does not mean that there are (or were) no hybrids. This may be because there are simultaneous strong competing views and/or presentation strategies, but it may also be because the work has not had substantial exposure and/or has not generated sufficient debate.

Extreme Is My Name (Johanna Vaude, 2020) discussed briefly in the previous chapter fits under the latter rubric. Made for channel ARTE, the film can be found on YouTube and has little more than 12,000 views.[27] The YouTube description does not specify any genre, and the comments below are generally positive evaluations of the film. A brief blurb reasoning its inclusion among the *Sight and Sound* best video essays of 2020 does not discuss fiction/nonfiction labels either.[28] In short, Vaude's film is a hybrid or, more precisely, neither yet fiction nor yet nonfiction because it has not gone through the indexing process despite being placed into the institution of cinema.

This does not mean that most film works are currently hybrids despite that most of them have generated even less discussion than *Extreme Is My Name*. The potential for hybridity only occurs when appealing to standard and contra-standard features for categorization as explained in the previous chapter does not get us far (most often it does). In their current use, for instance, my home videos are nonfiction despite never being uploaded anywhere and not seen and let alone discussed by anyone. (Of course, they could be fictions if I put them out as such and the labels were accepted.)

In fact, visual essay as a genre seems to me to be the best place to explore present-day hybridity. It is a genre for which not only its standard and contra-standard features have proven notoriously difficult to define (cf. Rascaroli, 2009, Alter and Corrigan, 2017), but whose very label is not that firm ('audiovisual criticism' and 'video essay' are just two contenders). At the same time, the genre has grown very popular in the last decade among filmmakers and critics alike spurring considerable attention by film scholars, inclusion in film studies curricula, establishment of festival circuits and, as we have seen, yearly best of roundups. While many now-classic visual essays are currently firmly indexed as nonfiction – *Night and Fogg* (Alain Resnais, 1956), *F for Fake* (Orson Welles, 1976), or *Sans soleil* (Chris Marker, 1983) – many more like *Extreme Is My Name* still await classification.[29]

By contrast, the status of other films is unclear because of strong competing categorizations. Peter Watkin's 1966 *The War Game* is a poignant example. The film depicts a likely and horrendous scenario of how a nuclear strike on Britain in the late 1960s would unfold and what its consequences would entail. Originally commissioned by BBC as a documentary, it was deemed too horrific and out of line with the official propaganda on the matter, that it was shelved. Instead, Watkins took it on the theatre circuit and ended up winning the Academy Award for Best Documentary Feature in 1967. The film also features on the 2014 (and updated in 2019) *Sight and Sound*'s Greatest Documentaries of All Time list.[30] At the same various movie databases and Wikipedia all list it either as fiction or hybrid: IMDb (drama, war, docudrama), Rotten Tomatoes (drama), Letterbox (war, TV movie, docudrama). In other words, because of competing categorizations by influential indexing actors the verdict on the film's status is still out.

The important thing to keep in mind is that the debate can sway things one way or another. Here, I will not put my hat in the ring because much like with *Extreme Is My Name*, I am genuinely uncertain how best to engage with *The War Game*. It is undeniable that the audiences are supposed to imagine the harrowing events of a nuclear attack on Britain. But it is no less deniable that they are also supposed to believe that what is represented is a very likely scenario of how things would have unfolded were an attack to have happened in the late 1960s. What is primary here I honestly cannot say. And even if I made the argument one way or the other, it is important to remember that it would only be one minor contribution in the indexing process which involves producers, distributors, exhibitors, audiences, and other public classifiers.

4

Mandated imagination in fiction film

While in Part One I have argued that a fictional work is one which primarily mandates imagining, in the opening chapter of Part Two I have shown how mandates are established within an institutional framework. Here I will focus on the imagining part of the 'primarily mandated imagining'. I will start with a general account of imagination and how it differs from other comparable mental phenomena. The opening section will provide a non-exhaustive taxonomy of imagination and briefly explain the differences between, on the one hand, imagination and, on the other, various mental states and processes.

The second part of the chapter will be devoted to how imagining relates to the (audio)visual nature of film as a medium. Specifically, I will outline the general difference between imagining *propositionally*, on the one hand, and imagining *perceptually* and imagining *perceiving*, on the other. While imagining propositionally involves imagining only the content of words and sentences and is typical of mandates in literary fiction, imagining perceptually and imagining perceiving encompass imagining in at least one perceptual domain such as vision, hearing, smelling, touch, taste, etc. In film, the imagination is clearly in visual and aural domains. Focusing on these two types of imagination in the case of imagining objects, whereas imagining perceptually involves only forming visual and aural mental images without the accompanying perceptual fields and forecloses any spatial relationship towards the objects imagined, imagining perceiving typically involves the perceptual fields thereby opening the door for imaginary spatial relationship towards the imagined objects. From another perspective, imagining perceptually is imagining from without in the sense that it involves no imaginings about oneself as experiencing something, while imagining perceiving is imagining from within, i.e. imagining oneself experiencing perceiving.

In the last section, I will specify the content of mandated imagination when engaging fiction films. In other words, I will propose that the answer to the question of what precisely audiences are supposed to imagine when viewing film images raised by everyday moviegoing reports such as 'we see Frodo' and 'we jump to a scene of murder' is – to imagine perceptually. In film studies, traditionally, it has been assumed that we are supposed to imagine ourselves to be like Vsevolod Pudovkin's ideal observer who has a privileged ghost-like access to the fictional world, moving together with the camera and seeing and hearing everything it sees and hears while occupying its vantage point. This is one version of imagining perceiving. Since the 1990s, however, this view has come under increasing pressure from philosophers working on film who have proposed instead that alternative forms of imagining perceiving and/or imagining perceptually constitute our mandates. I will argue that while Pudovkin's account is far more robust than philosophers would have us believe, it is imagining perceptually that best describes what we are authorized to imagine when watching film fiction. One reason is that when compared to adjacent cultural series (first-person shooters, VR, etc.) which mandate Pudovkin's ideal position, the mandate in standard fiction film is noticeably different. The main reason, however, is that no version of imagining perceiving can answer the question of what the audiences are mandated to imagine in situations involving different forms of split screens.

Crucially, when we turn to the discussion of what and how we are *mandated* to imagine in perceptual domains it will be important to keep phenomenological accounts of imagining distinct from normative demands about imagining. It is undeniable that different people will have their preferred phenomenological viewing strategies when it comes to imaginative engagement. But this is the domain of phenomenology or actual viewing experiences which will be addressed in more detail in the first chapter of Part Three in the discussion of the puzzle of imaginative resistance. Here, instead, I will be focusing on what audiences *should* imagine as a baseline for a common understanding of a societal game of make-believe that goes under the name of fiction film.

The ontology and psychology of imagination

Put as pithily as possible, imagining is a mental representation of phenomena without a commitment to those phenomena.[1] For instance, it is possible to imagine a silver apple without a commitment to whether such a fruit exists or not, or that Bernie Sanders is the president of the United States without a commitment to whether such a claim is true or not. In other words, imagining is merely supposing or representing hypothetically a certain state of affairs.[2] It is an *as if* attitude towards something.

The above examples also point to one important taxonomy according to the type of the phenomenon imagined.[3] Propositional imagining is imagining that *p*, i.e. that something is (or is not) the case. In the Sanders example we have already seen that it is possible to imagine propositions that are false, but it is also possible to imagine propositions that are true such as that Margaret Thatcher was the first female prime minister of the UK.

Another type of imagining is objectual imagining where certain entities are imagined. The example of the silver apple has already shown that it is possible to imagine non-existent entities, but it is no less possible to imagine existent ones such as a hippopotamus. The entities in objectual imagining may be of different kinds including things and beings, linguistic objects (imagining *a word, a question*), mathematical objects (*a number, a matrix*), events (*a funeral, a trip*), complex structures (*a nation state, an ideology*), etc.

One last broad type of imagining is experiential imagining where one imagines performing certain activities or experiencing certain phenomena. For instance, it is possible to imagine *going to the movies* or *seeing a xenomorph*. There is an important difference, then, between imagining that there is a person called Sherlock Holmes (propositional imagining), imagining Sherlock Holmes (objectual imagining), and imagining hearing Sherlock Holmes (experiential imagining).

Another way to group this is to say that while experiential imaginings are from within, propositional imaginings are from without. Importantly, an imagining is not made from within just because it is *about* oneself as when I imagine propositionally *that* I am rich or when I imagine objectually *myself*. What makes it from within, instead, is that it is imagining oneself *experiencing* as when I am imagining being rich, marvelling at how many zeros I have on my account, basking in the confidence that I can do virtually everything I want, etc.

Imagining can be further elucidated by distinguishing it from various (folk) psychology phenomena. One crucial point of distinction is that of propositional imaginings from belief and disbelief. Belief, disbelief, and imagination certainly all have in common that they are attitudes towards relevant propositions. In other words, they are all attitudes which may but need not be taken once the proposition is represented (typically through comprehension of its meaning). But they also differ. Belief is a mental representation which commits the one holding that what she is representing is true. If a person believes that Jack Nicholson is a multiple Oscar-winner, she holds that it is true that Nicholson won multiple Oscars. Disbelief, conversely, is a mental representation which commits oneself to rejecting the truth of the content of that representation. If a person is in disbelief that Lilly Gladstone lost the 2024 Oscar to Emma Stone, then they are mentally rejecting that the results of the 2024 Oscars in

Best Actress in a Leading Role are true. But to imagine that Nicholson is a multiple Oscar-winner or that in 2024 Gladstone did not get an Oscar involves no commitment about whether these propositions are true or not but entail instead an as-if attitude towards them.

This distinction also explains why describing engagement with fiction (film) in terms of Samuel Taylor Coleridge's (1817) formula of 'willing suspension of disbelief' misdescribes the phenomenology of that engagement. When watching *Breaking Bad* (AMC, 2009–14) audiences do not, among other things, first commit themselves to rejecting that there is a chemistry teacher called Walter White who has lung cancer and then willingly suspend that rejection. (Notice that both disbeliefs here pertain to propositions.) Rather, audiences imagine a chemistry teacher called Walter White (objectually) and that he has lung cancer (propositionally).

A further distinction from belief relates to entailment and action potential. Beliefs usually entail other beliefs. If we believe that humans have one heart and if we believe that Martin Scorsese is a human, then we also believe that Scorsese has one heart. The same does not hold for imagination. If we imagine that humans have one heart and imagine Scorsese is a human, we do not necessarily need to imagine that Scorsese has one heart. We can imagine that he has no or more hearts than one. Admittedly, entailment does not extend to all beliefs we hold because it is certainly possible to hold contradictory beliefs. We can believe that conspiracy theories are silly and not to be trusted but at the same time believe that the Moon landing was faked. But entailment in belief still has a wider scope than in imagination and it can at least in principle lead to updating beliefs. Over time we may come to believe that there is good reason to describe claims about faking the Moon landing as conspiracies and we may eventually stop believing it was faked. Entailment in imagining has no such scope or power.

When it comes to action potential, whereas beliefs are causally connected to potential actions, imaginings are generally not. If I believe that I have a ticket for the premiere of the latest film by Kathryn Bigelow I will go to the show. Of course, I will not go necessarily, but if I do go, believing that I have the ticket will be a part of the causal motivation for going. If I only imagine that I have the ticket, by contrast, I will not head out. Or if I do, imagining that I have the ticket will not be a part of the causal chain. It is true that some imaginings generate behavioural reactions. It is well known, for instance, that sexual imaginings or fantasies lead to bodily arousal which may lead to further actions. While we could still say that here the action is generated by the behavioural reaction rather than imagining itself, even if we conceded that the distinction in terms of potential for generating actions between belief and imagining is not absolute, we can still insist it is a matter of considerable degree.

While propositional imagining is contrasted to beliefs, a type of imagining bridging objectual and experiential imagining – perceptual imagining – is contrasted to perception. At the very least, imagining a silver apple involves imagining the shape of an apple and silver as its colour making it a perceptual imagining. Similarly, imagining Maria (Julie Andrews) singing the titular song in the *Sound of Music* (Robert Wise, 1959) involves auditorily imagining its pitch and the rhythm among other sound properties. Perceptual imaginings, then, are imaginings involving one or more sensory domains such as visual, auditory, olfactory, gustatory, tactile, equilibrioception, etc. Put differently, these imaginings necessarily involve mental imagery in one or more sensory domains. Unlike perception, however, perceptual imagining can be produced at will. While I cannot make myself see a silver apple or hear a tune when there are none, I can will myself to perceptually imagine the two at a moment's notice.[4]

It is important to note that not all imagination involves mental imagery (cf. Nichols, 2006).[5] It is certainly possible to include perceptual imaginings in propositional imagining. Imagining that Thatcher was the first female UK prime minister may involve conjuring the image of her face and hair or the sound of her voice. But in its minimal form it need not. We may simply imagine the proposition that Thatcher was the first female UK prime minister without any mental imagery. I will refer to this type of propositional imagining as minimal imagining and speak of it in more detail in the next chapter on imaginative resistance. Put differently, while all mental images are imaginings, there are other types of imaginings as well – viz. propositional imaginings.

Imagining can also be distinguished from other mental phenomena. For instance, imagination differs from memory insofar the existence of the latter for the person remembering implies that the content of the mental representation took place. If one remembers their first skinny dipping as an adolescent, they normally also assume that the nude swimming in question took place. By contrast, experientially imagining one's own first skinny dipping as a teenager does not imply that any such event ever occurred.

It has also been suggested that what has been referred to in psychological literature as transportation should be thought of as imagination (Matravers, 2014: 78).

> [Transportation] goes a long way toward capturing one of the most prominent phenomenological aspects of the experience of narrative worlds. Readers become "lost in a book"; moviegoers are surprised when the lights come back up; television viewers care desperately about the fates of soap opera characters; [. . .] In each case, a narrative serves to transport an experiencer away from the here and now.
>
> (quoted in Matravers, 2014: 77–8)

While it is likely that in engaging narratives, vivid imaginative participation is a key component in transportation the two cannot be the same. Audiences can engage in a much more minimal fashion, imagining only what happens and when without being swept away. Imagining a short sentence-long narrative certainly does not end up in transportation. In narrative engagements, at best, transportation describes the intensity of the relative focus on the imaginary project as opposed to the perception of the immediate surrounding. In fact, given the focus on being lost from the 'here and now' transportation is better understood as a subclass of immersion. And one can be immersed in things (a view) or actions (running) entailing no imagination.

Imagination relevant for fiction cannot be explained solely in terms of simulation as Gregory Currie (1995) suggests either. Simulation, according to Currie, enables us to take other people's perspectives and understand their behaviours. This involves taking their beliefs and desires as inputs and determining what their mental states and behavioural outputs might be. The difference is that we process these inputs as imaginings or offline beliefs and desires which give us outputs decoupled from our own action-motor system. The details do not matter for our purposes much; what is important is that these imaginings construed as offline beliefs and desires are pretend beliefs and pretend desires. In our vocabulary, these are propositional and experiential imaginings.[6] But there are other types of imaginings important for fiction – objectual imaginings – which are not covered by simulation. It is unclear what objectual imagining could be an offline simulation of. It does not help much to phrase it in terms of pretend thinking about objects either. At the same time, there must be more to engagement with fiction than simulation because while a recent meta-analysis of persuasive effects of fiction shows that fictions do not influence beliefs, they are good in eliciting both desires and behaviours (Braddock and Dillard 2016). In other words, the process is not as offline as the simulation proposal would have it.

Lastly, it is also worth differentiating imagination from pretence as another adjacent faculty especially given Currie's terminology and everyday language remarks like fiction is pretence. Already a quick ordinary language analysis evinces a difference: while we can imagine/believe/disbelieve/remember that Sherlock Holmes exists, Sherlock Holmes, and hearing Sherlock Holmes we can pretend only propositions about Sherlock Holmes and experiences about Sherlock Holmes. We cannot pretend Sherlock Holmes, i.e. pretend objectually. Moreover, while imagining experientially necessarily involves a mental component pretending experientially need not. It is possible to pretend hearing Sherlock Holmes without having any phenomenological auditory experience. What is more important for pretence is whether the pretender's behaviour matches the expectations about the content of pretence. In other words, to pretend hearing somebody we may only need to make an attentive-looking face expression or offer up words that were pretend-heard.

The nature of film imagination

Literary and film imagination

Now that we have made some key clarifications about the types of imagination and how it differs from related mental phenomena, let us turn to the discussion of imagination in film. In describing the experience of going to the movies it is common to report that when watching, for instance, *Dune: Part I* (Denis Villeneuve, 2021) we see and hear Paul Atreides. But in relating the experience of reading Frank Herbert's *Dune* novel it is generally inappropriate to use the verbs of perception to describe our imaginative relationship with Paul. One way to understand the way 'see' and 'hear' are used above is to start with the remark that unlike literary fiction which dominantly mandates propositional imagining, fiction films regularly mandate propositional and perceptual imaginings. Consider the following brief paragraph from *Dune*:

> "Now, *you* come here". The command whipped out at him. Paul found himself obeying [Reverand Mother] before he could think about it. *Using the Voice on me*, he thought. He stopped at her gesture standing beside her knees.
>
> (Herbert, 1966/2005: 7–8, italics in the original)

The reader is mandated imagining propositionally, among other things, *that* the Reverand Mother used the Voice on Paul saying the exact words 'Now, *you* come here', *that* the command whipped at him, *that* he found himself obeying before he could think about it, etc. Certainly, one could imagine Paul objectually according to the features described earlier on:

> [his] face [was] oval like Jessica's, but strong bones … hair: the Duke's dark-dark but with browline of the maternal grandfather who cannot be named, and that thin, disdainful nose; shape of directly staring green eyes.
>
> (Herbert, 1966/2005: 7)

But this is not mandated. There is no requirement to imagine Paul's oval face like Jessica's, strong bones, dark-dark hair, thin nose, and staring green eyes. The mandate is merely to imagine *that* his face is oval like Jessica's, hair dark-dark, nose thin and disdainful, and green eyes staring. Again, readers are not prohibited from imagining Paul objectually and some may and, indeed, that might be their preferred mode of engagement with literary fiction. But exactly because some readers do imagine this while others do not, or more precisely, because all readers playing the game of make-believe appropriately would agree *that* Paul looks as described above while disagreeing on the need to *visualize* Paul looking as above, the safe assumption is that only the baseline propositional imagining or minimal imagining is mandated here.

This is not to say that literary fiction cannot mandate other types of imagining. Here are the opening lines from *Trainspotting*: 'The sweat wis lashing oafay Sick Boy; he wis trembling. Ah wis jist sitting thair, focusing oan the telly, tryin no tae notice the cunt. He wis bringing me doon' (Welsh, 1993/2013: 3). Next to imagining *that* Sick Boy was trembling and bringing the narrator down we are not only supposed to imagine *that* the narrator has a Scottish accent because of the novel's orthography but also auditorily imagine the narrator *sounding Scottish*. This is so because the *form* in which propositions to be imagined are delivered sometime also influences the *content* of the proposition. Because the writing style in *Dune* is self-effacing, the form does not add to the content to be imagined. In fact, that a formal strategy is needed to imagine the narrator *sounding* a certain way is further proof that standard writing does not mandate perceptual or experiential imaginings because there is no similar imagining that the narrator of *Dune* is American although the book was written in American English.[7]

This is different in fiction films. In the matching scene in *Dune: Part 1* the mandated imagining is richer in the sense that it covers multiple domains. We certainly need to imagine *that* Reverand Mother has used the Voice on Paul, *that* he found himself obeying, etc. But we are mandated to imagine in visual and aural domains as well. The Voice, for instance, sounds a particular way – it is *this* deep, *this* distorted, *this* overlapping – and we are supposed to imagine both propositionally *that* it sounds that way and auditorily *sounding this deep, this distorted and this overlapping.* There is also a plethora of visual information – the room where Reverand Mother and Paul are is *this shade of* dark, they are both dressed in *this and that* black, Paul's hair is *this* curly, etc. – all of which are to be imagined both propositionally *and* visually (Figure 1).

FIGURE 1 ***Perceptual information is a part of the fictional world of*** **Dune: Part I *(Denis Villeneuve, 2021).***

It could be suggested that this need not be the case. According to one proposal, the audiences simply see and hear the images and sounds on the screen and then use those sights and sounds to imagine the story.[8] In other words, even here imagining is essentially only propositional (and there is no need to imagine anything visually and aurally because everything relevant for imagining the *story* is already seen and heard). But this does not capture the fictional content of the world mandated through images and sounds. In the world of *Dune: Part 1* it is not only *that* the Voice sounds deep, distorted, and overlapping but it also sounds precisely how it sounds when heard in the cinema, i.e. there is an aural qualitative nature to it. And this fictional truth is captured in the mandate to auditorily imagine it sounding as it does. The same holds for visual information. It is not only *that* Reverand Mother's face is covered with a black laced veil but there is also a visual quality to it that cannot be exhausted in a propositional account no matter what its length is. And again, this is captured in the mandate to visually imagine Reverand Mother's veil looking as it is shown on screen.

A further way to spell out the difference between propositional and perceptual imagining is to articulate the distinction between linguistic and perceptual information (cf. Currie, 1995: 181–5). Linguistic descriptions are discrete and abstract in the sense that they specify perceptual features one by one and do so with a relatively broad scope. As we have seen in the above example of Paul's description, each part of his appearance – the shape of his face, the colour of his hair, etc. – is addressed by separate words and phrases. A detailed linguistic account of a face would require a considerable word-count. And even then, a linguistic description could not be as precise as a perceptual one. This is because the specific reference of linguistic descriptions is more abstract than perceptual information. Terms like 'oval' and 'dark-dark' can be instantiated in more than one oval shape and dark-dark hair hue. But perceptual information specifies *this* oval shape and *that* dark-dark shade. Perceptual information, furthermore, comes in bundles, i.e. information about colour is not discrete as in linguistic descriptions but comes together with other bits of perceptual information such as shape, size, etc. An image of Paul's face instantaneously informs not only about the shape of his face and colour of his hair but also about the colour of his face and shape of his hair and many other things. In literary fiction, then, we are typically mandated only to imagine linguistic information, while in fiction film we are regularly mandated to imagine perceptual information.[9]

Imagining perceptually versus imagining perceiving

Having ascertained that mandates for film fiction are rich in the sense they involve different sensory domains of imaginings, we can now articulate in more detail the mandated imaginative relationship we hold to the image and the sound on screen. For while I have spoken about these imaginings as visual and aural, I have not articulated what precisely we imagine about ourselves in relation to these sensory imaginings nor have I been clear enough about whether the imagining here is objectual or experiential. In other words, there are two questions here. The first is: are audiences mandated to imagine *visually and aurally* (perceptually) or are they mandated to imagine *seeing and hearing* (perceiving)? The second is: are audiences mandated to imagine to be in any spatial position in relation to their imaginings?

Concerning the former, at first inspection it might seem that there is no difference between imagining visually and aurally and imagining seeing and hearing. It could be argued that if I have a sensory image in my mind, say, of a metronome, then I, in a sense, see and hear that metronome. Yes, but only in a sense and not in the sense of imagining *seeing* or *hearing*. We say that we see and hear these things because they have a visual and an auditory quality, but we see and hear them only in our mind's eye (and ear). We see and hear them only in the sense that we can 'see' and 'hear' memories. This is not the sense in which we see and hear objects with our eyes and ears, and this is to see and hear them as part of visual and aural field. The notion of field is crucial here. When we see objects, they are a part of a larger field, there is always something around them. Imagining visually, by contrast, singles out that object in a visual vacuum. It is just the object and nothing else. A partial analogy would be the contrast between a photograph of an apple on a table and a computer-generated image of an apple in a blank space (though, strictly speaking, blank space here is not visual vacuum but just a representation of it).

The situation with sound is somewhat more complicated because while aural perceptual phenomena are also part of an aural field there is a neutral aural field – silence – which allows for singling out of a specific sound. That is why there are occasions where imagining aurally and imagining hearing are phenomenologically indistinguishable. But in general, hearing is accompanied by other sounds in the sense auditorily imagining is not making imagining aurally and imagining hearing distinct as well. Crucially, because there is no analogous neutral visual field – darkness does not single out an object in the way silence does because darkness remains a part of the visual field – imagining visually is always phenomenologically distinguishable from imagining seeing.

It might be objected that I have not compared the relevant activities above. I have contrasted visual/aural imagining with seeing/hearing and because these differ, I have wrongly concluded that visual/aural imagining and *imagining* seeing/hearing differ as well. But it may be the case that imagining seeing/hearing singles out visual/auditory objects in the sense that visual/aural imagining does. After all, to successfully imagine experientially it is not necessary to imagine the whole experience. For instance, when imagining running I could only imagine the fast movement of my legs without, say, imagining the sense of balance which would normally accompany running and that would still count as imagining running. There seems to be some core of experience that it is sufficient to imagine for it to count as imagining that experience. Perhaps the core of seeing/hearing is the visual/aural singling out of objects. Perhaps, but imagining seeing/hearing an object in a visual/aural field would still count as imagining seeing/hearing while including that visual/aural field in imagining visually/aurally would no longer be a visual/aural imagining of that *object* but a visual/aural imagining of that *object and the field*.

Another way to flesh out the difference is in terms of imagining from within and from without. Even in 'core' imagining seeing/hearing I am imagining *myself* seeing/hearing, not some subjectless seeing/hearing. When imagining visually/aurally, I am just imagining sights/sounds. I am not imagining anything like *myself* having visual/aural experiences. In other words, I am imagining from without.

Yet another way to think about the difference is in terms of spatial relations. Imagining visually/auditorily does not establish any imaginary spatial relationships to the object. Imagining seeing/hearing, by contrast, may. If visual/aural field is included in imagining seeing/hearing, then the sight/sound is imagined seen/heard from a certain vantage point. This opens a path to imagining inhabiting that vantage point which is not a part of imagining visually/auditorily. And this raises the questions about fiction film experience: are audiences mandated to imagine objectually from without (visually/auditorily) or experientially from within (seeing/hearing)?[10] And if the latter, what is the imagined spatial relationship to these sights/sounds?

The mandate for imagining perceptual information in fiction film

Existing proposals

In film scholarship the traditional response to the above questions has been staked by Pudovkin who has argued that through camera positioning, editing, and sound the director establishes an 'imaginary observer' or 'an observer ideally mobile in space and time' (1958: 71, 254). In fact, the view has arguably already been the guiding principle in the establishment of the classical Hollywood style as can be seen in this early 1910s trade press demand: 'the film must create the impression among the audience that they are witnessing the three elements of the action, unknown to the characters of the play. They should be put in the position of being at the "knot hole in the fence" at every stage in the play' (Bathbun, 1913: 471, cf. Bordwell, Staiger, and Thompson 1985: 330–1). While the postclassical theoretical era had very different priorities it still echoed this position, most notably through the notion of 'primary identification' as espoused by Christian Metz: 'as he identifies with himself as look, the spectator can do no other than identify with the camera' (1982: 56, 49). Ordinary descriptions of shot changes among film viewers in terms of 'we jump from one location to another' seem to be another version of this idea. While in all these accounts there is a slippage between the illusion of seeing and the imagination of seeing, under a more charitable reading they can be construed in terms of what has in the analytic philosophy tradition been dubbed the face-to-face imagined seeing thesis.[11] The thesis is best pithily captured as follows: 'When the audience watches a fiction film, they are prompted to imagine that they are seeing the story events by standing face-to-face with them' (Wilson, 2011: 36).

Philosophers, with George Wilson (1997, 2011) leading the charge among them and writing the most on the subject, have also produced two more variants of the imagined seeing dubbed modest and mediated, respectively. In the modest version the audiences are mandated to imagine seeing the events but espouse no specific spatial relation to them. It is simply indeterminate what the spatial relation is (Wilson, 2011: 78–88). In the mediated version the audiences are mandated to imagine seeing the events through images of these events. These images are much like film images and while they derive from the fictional world they are derived in an indeterminate way (Wilson, 2011: 88–105).

Briefly, the main positions are as follows (cf. Curran 2016, 2019, Terrone 2020b). Scholars working in film departments generally tacitly agree with the face-to-face version (cf. Morgan and Schonig, 2023). But they have not found it necessary to defend the face-to-face thesis since critiques of it by philosophers started in the 1990s (Currie, 1995 and Wilson, 1997). Philosophers generally dismiss face-to-face imagined seeing. Some argue there is only propositional imagining because we actually perceive everything relevant (McGinn, 2005 and Carroll, 2009). Others like Currie (1995) favour perceptual imagining because they hold that imagined seeing entails problematic and contradictory imaginings. Wilson (2011) accepts that some entailed imaginings are problematic but argues that the mediated version of imagined seeing avoids these issues so there is no need to turn to perceptual imagining for explanation. I will argue that face-to-face imagined seeing is far more robust than philosophers have claimed. While it eventually fails it is not because of some problematic entailed imaginings but rather because for some types of shots (e.g. durable shot transitions and split screens) the imagined thesis simply does not clarify what to imagine. The mediated version, in turn, fails because the proposed mandate is too contrived. Instead, I will advocate for perceptual imagining because it easily handles all cases that different versions of imagined seeing cannot and because as a form of imagining it is fundamental to all versions of imagining perceiving.

Phenomenology of viewing versus mandate to imagine

In my previous work I have shown on the example of early cinema that (at least some of) these views – viz. face-to-face and modest imagined seeing – are not merely technical philosophical constructs but that they fit neatly with how historical audiences described their viewing experiences (Slugan, 2019a: 93–8). Concerning the modest version, for instance, when in the late nineteenth-century train films were briefly treated as fictions, they were essentially treated as fictions of a certain imaginary experience of and relationship with the train. These films were both advertised and received as prompting imaginings about seeing the onrushing train but without leading the audiences to imagine that they were anywhere *within* the image screened. Instead, the main mandate expressed through formulations such as 'as if' and 'as though' in the promotion and reception of films was to imagine that the train is going to jump outside of the picture and into the auditorium where the viewers are. Here is Maxim Gorky as a young journalist in 1896 just having seen *The Arrival of a Train* (Lumière brothers, 1895–7): 'It speeds right at you – watch out! It seems as though it will plunge into the darkness in which you sit' (quoted in Bottomore, 1999: 213).

The face-to-face version can be identified already in the contemporary ads and reviews of phantom rides like *The Haverstraw Tunnel* (American Mutoscope and Biograph, 1897):

> If you desire a novel experience go to the Palace Theatre any evening at a quarter to ten and travel (in imagination) on the cow-catcher of the locomotive of a West Shore (American) Express through the Haverstraw Tunnel. [...] You are supposed to witness the surrounding imposing scenery while you are seated on the express train in question.
>
> (quoted in Niver, 1971: 35, 36)

These were also fictions of imaginary experience of and relationship with the train, but now, it was one of travelling *on* the train and seeing the sights from *within* the locale depicted.

I have also argued that this interaction between promotional strategies and reception practices (as well as film style and exhibition patterns) is what constitutes whether mandates will get off the ground in the first place or not. In other words, such negotiations establish whether in a given timeframe a work is fictional or not. If that is true, why not perform a similar analysis of paratextual information to establish whether present-day audiences are mandated to imagine perceptually or imagine perceiving and, if the latter, what they are supposed to imagine their spatial relationship to be?

The reason is that such an analysis can be effectively conducted only for the baseline mandate – the mandate to *primarily* imagine. This core mandate initiates the whole game of make-believe in the first place, i.e. it establishes that the work is a prop for imaginative engagement. In the case of train films and phantom rides, it just so happened that various forms of imagining seeing were the baseline of what those fictions were about – the fictions of experience of and relationship to different vehicles. In later film fictions, imagining perceptual information is only a part of the fiction which makes such an analysis far more contestable. Looking at the reception, we would be learning more about varied phenomenological experiences, and less about whether these imaginative practices are mandated. Investigating promotion, similarly, would be more indicative of producers' intentions about mandates and not whether they were actually established. Or, to put it differently, why the analysis of baseline mandate works is because the promotional strategies and reception patterns relating to these are less expressions of (intended) phenomenology and more articulations of mandate as a norm that the audience *should* follow and the responses to that norm-making. Given the novelty of the medium and the genre, when the American Mutoscope and Bioscope cites the contemporary reviews in its promotional bulletins, it is telling the audiences what they *should* imagine, i.e. what the mandated way of engaging the work is. When Gorky and the anonymous reviewer write, they are not only describing their experiences they are also promoting their imaginative experience as normative, i.e. the one which other audiences *should* share.

In the end, then, specific mandates are a normative category, some of which are more agreed upon and others less. At the former end of the spectrum there are explicit elements of the story and audiovisual facts explained above on the example of *Dune: Part One*. At the latter end there are contested implicit elements of the story (e.g. what happens to Tony Soprano in the black screen finale of *The Sopranos* [HBO, 1999–2006]) and arguably questions about imagined perception and perceiving that we are asking here.[12] Even if we somehow managed to get a representative sample of audiences writing in a perfectly clear language which distinguishes between different ways of talking about seeing/hearing along our categories this would not resolve whether we are mandated to imagine perceptually or imagine perceiving (and, if the latter, how), any more than if there was a majority view on what happened to Tony would resolve the matter one way or another.

This does not mean that we cannot solve the issue or at least make significant headway. There are at least two approaches that we can combine. One is, of course, testing the internal coherence of the views presented and this is what will constitute the bulk of the remainder of the discussion. Here it can also help to look at mandates from adjacent cultural series like video games and virtual reality devices to grasp the situation in fiction film better. Another is to argue that while the everyday accounts of seeing and hearing fictional characters are compatible with both imagining perceptually and all the versions of imagined perceiving, among these we can identify one view that is basic to all in the sense that all other types of proposed mandated imagining incorporate it. And because this form of imagination is fundamental it is safest to assume that it is the mandated one because everybody is supposed to at least imagine that.

The ideal observer, or face-to-face imagined seeing

Given that it has had the most traction in film scholarship and film press and that it circulates widely in public discourse, let us address the imagined seeing thesis and its face-to-face version first. Here the conversation will narrow to the visual aspect of the thesis given that the debates predominantly leave out the audio aspects. But essentially the same points will apply to the theses' aural versions.

Over the years, analytic philosophers have criticized the face-to-face proposal extensively. Currie (1995: 171–7) has argued that it fails because such imagining would require us to imagine that we are in some kind of magical, invisible, and massless capsule which explains how we move around and in POV shots that we are doing and feeling whatever the character is doing and feeling; it is incompatible with selective soundtrack such as when a long shot is accompanied by crystal clear dialogue of people in the shot, the fact that we cannot move for a better view during deliberately obstructive camera blocking, or that it undermines the truth of the fiction in such cases where we witness a murder that is otherwise presented as unseen by anybody in the story world. Carroll (2009) has added that in watching action sequences we should also imagine ourselves in danger. The key problem for Currie (1995: 177) and Carroll (2009: 199) is that it is unlikely that anybody imagines such things.

Addressing the last point quickly: strictly speaking, Currie and Carroll are conflating the actual experience or the phenomenology of viewing with the mandate. If a viewer does not imagine something, it does not mean that they are not supposed to imagine it. If my experience is at all representative, it is unlikely that audiences actually imagine much in the active sense of perceptually imagining while watching films. While I am supposed to imagine that Paul looks and sounds so and so I am happy not to, because I have seen how he looks like and sounds. In fact, as Enrico Terrone (2020b: f6) points out, there is empirical evidence that it is difficult to see and visually imagine at the same time because brain areas related to vision and visual imagery overlap significantly. It does not seem to be much different in literary fiction. Again, I suspect that once the initial imaginative framework has been established it moves to the back of our mind and we read fictions as factual reports in the sense that we build a model of the world being presented without actively propositionally imagining every and each claim. But, of course, we are aware that the work does mandate us to imagine each and every claim.

The more relevant critique of Currie and Carroll is that all their objections rest on the idea of entailment, i.e. that imagining one thing necessarily means having to imagine something else because in the real world that entailment would hold. But we have seen above that that is not the case. We are not forced to imagine any such things. If we are mandated to imagine seeing face-to-face, this does not mean that we are also mandated to give an explanation in imagination for how we move around. It is simply fictionally indeterminate how we jump from one place to another. It does not follow that we are supposed to imagine sharing the characters' non-visual experiences during POV shots either. We are only supposed to imagine sharing their visual experiences. Nor does face-to-face imagining entail being unable to imagine hearing from a closer position while presented with selective sounds. We are just supposed to imagine seeing from one perspective and hearing the conversation perfectly well regardless. We do not have to imagine ourselves being frustrated with not moving for a better view during camera blocking or being threatened in action scenes either. In the former case, we are just supposed to imagine that we have no agency in the fictional world. In the latter, we are merely supposed to imagine ourselves as a disembodied presence. Lastly, if we are mandated to imagine face-to-face a murder that has been specified as unseen in the story world, imagining seeing does not mandate us to imagine that the murder has now been seen in the story world. Rather, given that it is possible to imagine contradictions, it is sufficient to imagine that the unseen murder has been seen by me and that it remains unseen in the story world. This is because, again, I am merely supposed to imagining myself as a disembodied presence without any agency, 'a knot hole in the fence'.[13]

Despite this, Wilson (2011), the key proponent of the imagined seeing approach rejects its face-to-face version. For him, face-to-face variant fails because while it is true that in fiction film imagining seeing a fictional situation means imagining seeing *from a certain specific vantage point* it does not follow from that that imagining seeing also means imagining seeing from a certain specific vantage point *which one inhabits*. In other words, imagining seeing does not necessarily entail anything about one's spatial position to what is imagined seen. This version of imagined seeing is known as the modest variant.

Currie (1995), by contrast, argues that imagining seeing from a certain specific vantage point *necessarily* entails imagining seeing from a certain specific vantage point which one inhabits. Put in another way, Currie accepts that entailments of belief are not as robust or as far-reaching as entailments of imagining. But he still insists that there are stronger bonds than entailment – call it necessary entailment – that must hold even in imagining. For instance, if one imagines seeing, then, unless it is explicitly specified otherwise in the story, one also imagines having a visual experience. That is simply what (a part of) imagining seeing is, i.e. what the concept means. The disagreement with Wilson is that for Currie part of what imagined seeing is, is imagining seeing face-to-face, whereas for Wilson imagining oneself positioned in fictional space at the vantage point of seeing is not a part of what imaged seeing is.

Here I agree with Wilson, for three reasons. First, there are instances of actual seeing such as seeing objects in photographs or on screens which do not involve positioning oneself face-to-face to the relevant vantage point. In, say, *Lunch atop a Skyscraper* (1932) photograph, we see the workers (or representations thereof) from the vantage point of the camera. But we are clearly not positioned on that skyscraper ourselves. Rather, we are somewhere in front of the photograph. Admittedly, if we instead spoke of the *photograph* as an object, we would have to say that we are seeing it from the vantage point where we are positioned, say, a gallery in which the photograph is exhibited. Yet the point remains that there are legitimate instances of seeing entities (or representations thereof), where the vantage point of seeing and the position occupied do not coincide.[14]

The second reason is that the historical reception I have cited earlier also articulates imagined seeing in which there is a disconnect between the imaginary vantage point and the imaginary occupied position. In films like *The Arrival of a Train* the turn-of-the-nineteenth-century audiences reported imagining seeing the train from the position in the *auditorium*, not in the locale depicted on screen. Consider another account, this time by George Méliès: ' … the train dashes towards us, as if about to leave the screen and land in the hall' (quoted in Bottomore, 1999: 194). Analogous to the above example, when watching these films audiences have imagined seeing the train from the position of the camera on the train station but have imagined themselves remaining in the auditorium. Admittedly, once the train is imagined jumping out of the screen the face-to-face position is established where the vantage point and the position occupied coincide in the spectator's seat. But before that imagining seeing did not entail imagining being on the train station depicted.

Last, POV shots allow for a phenomenology of imagined seeing where a viewer imagines sharing the visual experiences of the character from the character's vantage point without necessarily imagining herself occupying the exact position where the character is. Importantly, this does not resolve the question of what the actual mandate is because this is what *can* be imagined, and not what should be imagined. But the fact that it is possible is sufficient to disarm Currie's remarks about necessary entailment.

However, that I agree with Wilson on this, is not to agree with him that this is a sufficient reason to dismiss the face-to-face thesis. Even if there is no necessary entailment from imagining seeing from a vantage point to imagining seeing occupying that vantage point this does not invalidate the face-to-face thesis.[15] This is because the mandate for face-to-face imagined seeing, if there is one, does not derive from a mandate to imagine seeing *and* whatever necessarily follows from imagining seeing but from the mandate to imagine seeing '*from a knot hole in the fence*'. In other words, the core mandate is imagining seeing from an occupied vantage point, not merely imagining seeing.

Face-to-face imagined seeing also appears to withstand scrutiny when compared to other audiovisual screen media and genre which undeniably authorize imagining seeing face-to-face. This is so because while there is a clear difference between mandates in standard fiction films and the following examples in video games, VR presentations, and modern-day phantom rides, the difference can be explained away by appealing to some *additional* core mandates that are present in these media and genres and absent in fiction film.

There is a whole genre of video games inaugurated by *Wolfenstein 3D* (1992) and *Doom* (1993) called first-person shooters which uncontroversially mandate imagining seeing face-to-face. A critic of the face-to-face thesis in fiction film could say that because the mandate in these video games is clearly different from that in standard fiction films it cannot be the case that imagining seeing face-to-face is mandated in fiction film. The problem with this critique is that there is much more to the mandate in such video games because first-person shooters also mandate being an *active* agent in the fictional world who controls where to go and how to fight the enemies. So, it could be argued that the noticeable difference in mandates between the two media boils down to the difference in the mandate about active participation.

Turning to VR presentations which mandate only imagining seeing face-to-face without active participation in the fictional world does not seem to work either. Numerous flight presentations mandate the viewer to imagine themselves flying (in a plane or 'magically') and imagine inhabiting the position of the presented vantage point.[16] And this mandate is obviously different from the one in a typical fiction film. But even here the proponent of the face-to-face thesis can claim that because standard films involve editing, the difference stems from discrete dislocations that are mandated in fiction films, whereas VR provides a mandate for continuous movement.

To eliminate potential differences in mandates stemming from editing, a better comparison would be between VR presentations and single-shot films like *1917* (Sam Mendes, 2019). True enough, it seems that the audiences would agree that, as far as imagining seeing is concerned, the mandates are different even here. But the advocate of the face-to-face thesis might again object that the difference stems from the fact that VR presentations allow for moving the headset. So, at the very least they mandate imagining being able to look around from a fixed position and explore the sights from a given vantage point in a 360-degree fashion. This is what explains the noticeable difference in the mandates from VR presentations and even films like *1917* where audiences are mandated not to be able to move their head and look around while at a fixed position.

One last option is to consider a *recording* of such a VR presentation which eliminates the 360-degree exploration in question.[17] We are dealing here with a present-day update of a phantom ride. Arguably, much like the turn-of-the-nineteenth-century *The Haverstraw Tunnel* audiences were mandated to imagine themselves travelling on the rail track and seeing within the locale depicted that is how we are supposed to imagine ourselves flying and imagine seeing the surrounding buildings. It is true in the fiction of this VR presentation that I am flying and seeing the sights face-to-face. By contrast, it does not seem to be straightforwardly true in the fiction of *1917* that I am moving and witnessing the events of the story face-to-face. Yet again, the proponent of the face-to-face thesis might claim that the difference in mandates stems not from the difference between face-to-face imagining and another type of imagining but from an additional mandate next to face-to-face imagining seeing present in our examples and absent from a film like *1917*. In the (recording of) VR presentations, first-person shooters, and phantom rides (and train films) alike there is also the mandate to imagine oneself bodily present in the sense that if one imagines swerving close enough to a building, they should also imagine themselves in danger of hitting the building. That is why historical articulations of mandates in train films and phantom rides regularly refer to the possibility and consequences of a crash. Gorky continues his warning about the onrushing train – it will 'turn[] you into a ripped sack full of lacerated flesh and splintered bones' (quoted in Bottomore, 1999: 213). In fiction films, by contrast, the mandate is to imagine oneself being present face-to-face in a disembodied fashion impervious to surrounding. It is to imagine oneself being only an eye (and an ear) without bodily presence.

There is arguably one more avenue open to the critic of the face-to-face thesis in fiction film. Consider a phantom ride which eliminates the mandate for bodily presence by eliminating potential dangers. The phantom ride depicts smooth sailing on the sea or peaceful gliding through a space nebula.[18] Is there a difference in mandates when it comes to imagining seeing between this and *1917*? Cleary, different things are imagined being seen and there is a different dynamism to imagining changing the position but is there a difference in the *core* mandate? The critic might say, and I would agree, that there is. And yet, I would argue that the proponent of the face-to-face thesis has run out of *additional core* mandates to explain the difference. I suggest that the difference is that in the space phantom ride we imagine *ourselves* seeing that whereas in *1917* we simply imagine *perceptually*. Of course, the proponent of the face-to-face thesis might respond that now I am confusing my own preferred phenomenology of imaginative engagement with mandates. The proponent could simply say that I am only insisting that there is a difference in core mandates between space phantom ride and *1917* but that my insistence is based only on what I think I am supposed to imagine and/or what I do imagine. My claim that there is a difference is not substantiated at all, it is merely an intuition stemming from how I usually imaginatively engage such works. Moreover, the proponent could just say that given that they think they should imagine *themselves* seeing in both cases we have not resolved the matter one way or another. In other words, even considerations of what should be imagined as opposed to what is actually imagined eventually hit a point where there is disagreement in what different viewers think should be imagined. There was agreement that there were noticeable core mandate differences up to phantom rides of corporal imagining but no further. Point taken.

What is instead necessary to reject the face-to-face imagined seeing is that the mandate runs into conceptual problems when applied to less standard types of film shots. Imagining seeing face-to-face arguably works well for different shots like objective and authorial shots. There the audiences are mandated to imagine seeing from and inhabiting the given vantage point. And on this account, it also works for POV shots where the audiences are mandated to imagine seeing from the position of the character in a disembodied fashion. But face-to-face imagining seeing stumbles with a range of transitions and split screens. It is not that there is some entailment here that it is problematic. Rather, it is conceptually unclear what the mandate is to begin with. Take, for instance, a transition where one shot fades into another through superposition. What are we supposed to imagine in terms of our position when at the end of *Psycho* (Alfred Hitchcock, 1960) the face of Norman Bates transitions into the image of a car being pulled out of the swamp (not to mention the split-second of a skull superimposed over his face)? Somehow transitioning between the jail where Bates is and where the car is being dragged out? Or consider wipes. What are the audiences mandated to imagine about their spatial relations to the two scenes they see concurrently in *Star Wars: Episode VI – A New Hope* (George Lucas, 1977) when in the middle of a wipe we see Luc Skywalker in an exterior on the left and at another place in an interior on the right (Figure 2)? Are they supposed to imagine themselves seeing both from a position in the desert and from a position of an interior at the same time? Or just in one of those? And if so, which one? The problem is not that it is impossible to imagine either of these things, including being in two places at the same time. The issue is that the mandate as it stands does not clarify *what* should be imagined. An even more complicated version of this is the split screen. When watching a film like *Timecode* (Mike Figgis, 2000) where four different screens run simultaneously for the duration of the movie are we supposed to imagine to be in four positions at once? Only one of them but if so, which one? Or should we imagine ourselves to be in front of some overall screen which shows these four different split screens?

This is the reason why face-to-face thesis should be dismissed. It is simply conceptually unclear what it means to imagine seeing face-to-face in these examples, i.e. what is to be imagined. And this is also the reason why the modest version of imagined seeing does not work either. Admittedly,

FIGURE 2 *Face-to-face imagined seeing thesis does not specify what is to be imagined during shot transitions like in* Star Wars: Episode IV – A New Hope *(George Lucas, 1977).*

the problem is not with the imagined position because this position is indeterminate under the modest version. The issue, instead, is that this version defines imagining seeing from a singular vantage point: 'If movie viewers imagine seeing a fictional situation in a given shot, then these viewers imagine seeing that fictional situation from a certain determinate visual perspective' (Wilson, 2011: 79). Because the above examples have multiple vantage points, it is again conceptually unclear from which of the vantage points should the audiences imagine seeing.

Modest and mediated imagined seeing

Wilson still believes that the imagined seeing thesis can be salvaged. This is why he develops the mediated version according to which viewers are mandated to imagine seeing moving images of fictional events (Wilson, 2011: 88–9). Crucially, while these moving images are derived from the fictional world, the exact way in which they are derived is left indeterminate. In other words, much like in *Cloverfield* (Matt Reeves, 2008) we are mandated to imagine that the film coincides with the moving images that have been derived from the fictional world, this is how every fiction film mandates imagining seeing moving images from its relevant world. The only difference is that in standard films as opposed to found footage films (where the images were usually made by protagonists themselves filming) the precise way in which these images were filmed is indeterminate.

Interestingly, the reason why Wilson dismisses the modest version is not the specific shot transitions and split screens I introduce but the broader distinction between diegetic and nondiegetic visual elements (Wilson, 2011: 92–9). He claims that the modest version (and, by extension, the face-to-face one as well) cannot handle examples like nondiegetic words 'Phoenix, Arizona' imprinted over the opening shots of *Psycho* because it would require of us imagining these words as floating somewhere in the story world's fictional space. According to him, only the mediated version explains how we readily distinguish between diegetic and nondiegetic elements. This is because we imagine seeing a sort of a recording of Marion and Sam meeting in a hotel onto which the words 'Phoenix, Arizona' have been inscribed. But this misconstrues what the other two types of imagined seeing are about. Both face-to-face and modest imagined seeing can handle (most of) nondiegetic visual elements, including black-and-white photography, atypical focus, slow/fast motion, etc., because it is clear to standard viewers that these are not elements which determine how the fictional world visually looks like. The two theses' mandate at no point implies that there should be a complete visual coincidence of the image and the visual properties of fictional events and objects to be imagined. These imagined seeing variants are primarily about singular vantage points and positions occupied, respectively, which is why they cannot handle various forms of split screens.

Regardless of Wilson's motivation it is still the case that the mediated version easily accommodates different shot transitions and split screens because the mandate is to imagine seeing moving images of the fictional world which, obviously, can be manipulated in all ways actual moving images can. But this is no reason to accept the modest thesis. Importantly, Wilson himself admits that subjective shots are an exception and that they should not be imagined as derived from the fictional world (Wilson, 2011: 89). That is a huge caveat for, arguably, there should be a single mandate which is applicable to all types of shots. After all, Wilson dismisses other versions of imagined seeing precisely because they cannot handle all types of shots. The second and more important reason is that, as we have seen, there are films like found footage films which mandate imagining that the film text coincides with the fictional footage, but these mandates are noticeably different from the mandates in standard fiction films to think that the same mandates apply.[19]

The found footage genre is identifiable precisely in this opposition to what is mandated in terms of how the fictional world is mediated in other fiction films. *The Blair Witch Project* (Daniel Myrick and Eduardo Sánchez, 1999) which essentially established the genre as discussed in the previous chapter was innovative precisely because it, among other things, contributed to establishing the mandates to imagine that the film coincides with the moving images made within the story world. One of the key differences from non-found footage films including *Psycho* is that there is no such mandate outside the genre. Following the line of argumentation in the discussion of first-person shooters, VR, and contemporary rides Wilson might suggest that the difference can be explained by the fact that in found footage films the image is derived in a determinate fashion – it is usually protagonists or their cameras that shoot (parts) of the film in one way or another. In other films, under his proposal, this is, by contrast, indeterminate. But this does not seem to be the relevant difference. The determinacy of moving images to be imagined is not an *additional core* mandate in the way active movement in first-person shooters is or bodily positioning in contemporary phantom rides. It is just what is true in the fictional world which will always vary from film to film.

But even if determinacy were an additional core mandate, there are examples of indeterminate moving images to be imagined that Wilson himself invokes to explain his idea, but which inadvertently end up showing how the mandate to imagine them differs from mandates in standard fiction films. The first is from *Flash Gordon* (Mike Hodges, 1980). There it is fictional in the story that photograph-like images from anywhere in the universe can be thrown on a screen while it is left completely indeterminate how this is done. But precisely because *Flash Gordon* needs to explicitly introduce these images and what they are, it becomes clear that no comparable mandate about film coinciding with such photograph-like images of the world can operate implicitly. It is just too convoluted for anybody to think they should imagine seeing something like such moving images when watching a typical fiction film. The other example is *Caché* (Michael Haneke, 2005) whose strength, as Wilson (2011: 101–2, f26) points out, rests in good part on the questions it raises about which shots of the film coincide with the surveillance recordings from within the fictional world and which do not. But the fact that the film is innovative precisely because it raises the question of what moving images we are mandated to imagine as deriving from the fictional world and which do not, demonstrates that there is no implicit mandate to imagine moving images deriving from the story world in typical films. Moreover, if mediated imagined seeing was correct *Caché* could hardly ask such questions because under Wilson's proposal all shots are by definition derived from the fictional world which would dismantle the whole mystery.[20]

The case for perceptual imagining

None of the versions of imagined seeing thesis, then, captures what we are supposed to imagine when watching fiction films. The last standing alternative is perceptual imagining. As I argued, perceptual imagining means we use the images and sounds as props to imagine fictional entities and events visually and aurally. We are not mandated to imagine any spatial relationship to these entities and events. Nor are we mandated to imagine *perceiving* them from any specific vantage point. This is not to say that we are *prohibited* from imagining them *perceptually* from a singular vantage point and for visually imagining events it is probably easiest to imagine them from the vantage point provided by the camera. Instead, we form mental and aural images of these entities and events in our mind's eye (and ear). And indeed, perceptual imagining can handle all the problems faced by its competitors.

Special transitions and split screens pose no problems because imagining perceptually does not involve imagining occupying any vantage point or *perceiving* from that vantage point. Unlike with face-to-face and modest imagined seeing there is nothing unclear about what we are supposed to do, which position of vantage point to choose. We should just take sights and sounds from each of the split screens to form perceptual imaginings about the relevant entities and events. And we could even imagine each of them from the vantage points provided by each of the screens without running into conceptual problems facing face-to-face and modest imagined seeing.[21] Nondiegetic elements pose no issues either because we simply bracket off these elements when imagining relevant entities and events. Contrary to the modest version of imagined seeing, there is no mandate to imagine these elements to begin with.

A comparison with literary fiction can give us another reason why perceptual imagining rather than imagining perceiving is what is mandated in fiction films. In novels it is usually indeterminate how the words and sentences making up the work are fictionally presented or accessed. This issue is distinct from whether there is a fictional narrator or not.[22] Even when there certainly is one, it is usually left fictionally indeterminate whether the words conveyed are spoken, written, thought, or delivered in some other form. And there is also regularly no mandate to imagine we are hearing, reading, mind-reading, etc., these words. Because there is usually no mandate to imagine we are *experiencing* access to the words in literary fiction, it is safe to assume that there is similarly no mandate to imagine we are experiencing access – seeing and hearing – in film fiction either. And even when literary fiction specifies how the words are delivered as is, for instance, the case with epistolary novels like *Dracula* (Bram Stoker, 1897) where the texts are written extracts from diaries, letters, press, etc., it is not necessarily the case that we need to imagine ourselves reading just because we need to imagine that the words have been written down. We are simply mandated to imagine the content of these words propositionally without imagining we are experiencing access to them through perceiving. After all, that *Ulysses* (James Joyce, 1919) mandates imagining that words in the final chapter are Molly's stream of consciousness does not mean it mandates us to imagine that we are mind-reading them.

One last way to argue the case for perceptual imagining as the one mandated by film fiction is to evince that perceptual imagining is the imagining that is fundamental to all other competing imaginings discussed here. If all competing imaginings involve perceptual imagining, then we need to agree that at the very least the mandate in fiction film is perceptual imagining. Given that a lot of philosophical discussion on the subject slides between phenomenology and mandate often invoking what audiences do or do not imagine as proof in favour or against mandates, I suggest that advocates of different theses are actually presenting their own preferred phenomenological imaginative engagement as mandated. I have tried to dispel accusations of the same for my proposal by distinguishing between variable phenomenology and normative mandates. But even if I am guilty of this, the proposal here still has the advantage of being fundamental to all other types of advocated mandates. If other commentators still insist on their versions of imagining, they can be explained away by appeal to phenomenology of actual imaginative engagement. Perceptual imagining cannot and must not be explained away by appeal to phenomenological experience because it is fundamental to all other competing imaginings.

This point can also be articulated from the perspective of what Walton (1990) calls work fiction as opposed to game fiction. According to Walton, something is work fictional if all audience members are supposed to imagine it. It is game fictional otherwise. For Walton, it is work fictional that Rachel and Deckard are romantically involved, but it is game fictional that George, while watching *Blade Runner*, is imagining making love to Rachel, if he is. In that same way I suggest that perceptual imagining in film is work fictional, while other forms of imagining perceiving are game fictional. They are not prohibited but they are not mandated either.

In the comparison of face-to-face thesis to imaginings in other media and genre I have already pointed out how the face-to-face imagined seeing is fundamental because the latter involved *additional core* imaginings such as imagination of active participation, head movement, bodily presence, etc (Figure 3). In the same sense all forms of imagined seeing presented here involve core imaginings additional to imagining perceptually. Face-to-face and mediated imagining each have modest imagined seeing at their base, while modest imagined seeing has perceptual imagining at its foundation. Face-to-face imagined seeing adds disembodied presence at a vantage point to modest imagined seeing. Mediated imagined seeing introduces photograph-like pictures to modest imagined seeing. Modest imagined seeing, in turn, combines imagining seeing from within and imagining from a vantage point with perceptual imagining making perceptual imagining the most fundamental.

I have mentioned that there is a basic form of imagining seeing which eliminates the visual field and as such is different from imagining visually only in that it is imagining from within whereas imagining visually is from without.[23] Perhaps this could be a better proposal for what is mandated about perceptual information in fiction film than perceptual imagining? Like visual imagining, basic imagined seeing passes every hurdle that trips up other forms of imagined seeing. There is, however, one drawback that can be fleshed out through comparison with literary fiction.

As I argued above, we are not required to imagine how we are accessing the fictional words and sentences that make up the novels, i.e. we are not mandated

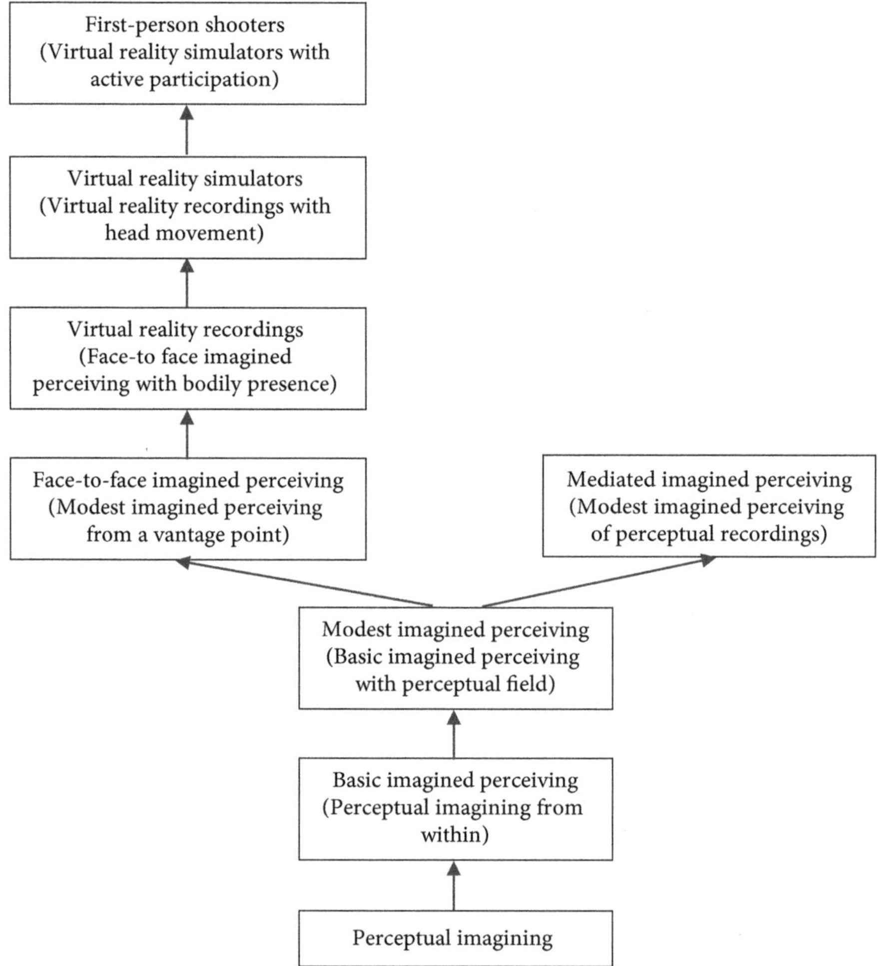

FIGURE 3 ***Relations between different forms of imagining perceptual information.***

to imagine that we are reading, hearing, etc., these linguistic components. I would suggest that the same holds for other art forms as well. In theatre, we are also not required to imagine anything about whether and how we have access to the fictional world. In non-first-person video games alike, it is generally left fictionally indeterminate whether and how we access the fictional world.[24] In fact, even in some epistolary novels which determine the words and sentences as coinciding with fictional writing like *Dracula*, we are not mandated to imagine *reading* the fictional text.[25] This means that in all these examples we are not required to imagine anything about ourselves experiencing something. In fact, even films like *The Blair Witch Project* do not necessarily mandate anything about the viewers' fictional access to the fictional footage. Certainly, the actual film coincides with the fictional footage, but this does not mean we need to necessarily imagine *seeing* that fictional footage and imagine oneself as *having* perceptual experiences.[26] After all, even in the actual world in the same way that something is written does not entail that it is read so is it that something that is recorded does not entail that it is seen.

This is the reason why ultimately perceptual imagining is the best candidate for how we are mandated to imagine perceptual information in film. It is the imagining that is fundamental to all other competing imaginings. Unlike these other imaginings perceptual imagining can accommodate all types of shots. And in not involving any imaginings about oneself experiencing something it is consistent with the mandates in other media as well.

PART THREE

IMAGINATION AND THE EFFECTS OF FICTION

5

Imaginative resistance and the richness of imagining

Part Two has focused on fiction as *primarily mandated* imagining and primarily *mandated imagining*, respectively. The previous chapter, more specifically, discussed how the audiences are mandated to imagine perceptual information typical of fiction film. To do that, I had to differentiate the normative demands of mandates from the actual phenomenology of viewership. In this chapter, which opens the monograph's third part focusing on actual responses to film fiction, I will concentrate further on the phenomenology of imaginative engagement. But there is no need to rehash the discussion of imagining perceptual information here because in explicating perceptual imagining and different forms of imagining perceiving and determining which one of these is mandated, I already described the phenomenology of these different forms of imagining. Instead, I will turn to the puzzle of imaginative resistance, or imaginative resistance for short.

One of the key debates among scholars interested in the relationship of fiction to imagining has been on this topic. In fact, imaginative resistance has since Richard Moran's (1994) and Kendall Walton's (1994) seminal papers generated so much discussion in the last three decades that it has even secured a separate chapter in a companion to fiction (Gendler and Liao, 2016) and a stand-alone entry in Stanford Encyclopaedia of Philosophy (Tuna, 2020). The original articulation of the puzzle has been traced to David Hume (1757/1875) who remarked that while it is easy to engage works whose worlds factually diverge from our own, works whose worlds are morally deviant from ours make this engagement very difficult. Providing what would become a classic example, Walton (1994) has argued that a story such as 'In killing her baby, Giselda did the right thing; after all, it was a girl' elicits imaginative resistance that Hume had in mind.

Most of the debate has revolved around these and similar examples of moral deviation precisely because, as Hume originally framed it, it was perceived that there was something special about the moral world when engaging fiction. But, as already Walton (1994) proposed, there appear to be examples of nonmoral divergence which arguably elicit imaginative resistance as well. Consider the following very short story: 'Jake delivered the most hilarious joke ever told: "A maple leaf fell from the tree"'. Given that the joke is obviously not funny, it seems to be difficult to *imagine* it is funny, let alone 'the most hilarious joke ever told'.

Interestingly, the debate has had little to no traction in film studies which, on first inspection, is not surprising since the examples have been almost exclusively from literary fiction.[1] But this is a missed opportunity because even a quick look at online fora reveals that movie viewers regularly report having issues imagining what they are supposed to. Typical cases involve problems with imagining the depicted entities in poorly made horror films like *Plan 9 from Outer Space* (Ed Wood, 1959) as gory or characters in teenage dramas like *Beverly Hills, 90210* (Spelling Television, 1990–2000) played by older actors as young. And again, these examples are nonmoral.

In what remains, I will focus on nonmoral deviations for a couple of reasons. First, the debate hitherto has been far too categorical and reliant on personal intuitions and philosophers' own preferred phenomenological engagement as guides for whether an example will evoke imaginative resistance or not in general audiences. Second, audience reports paired with recent empirical evidence evince that imaginative resistance covers not only the nonmoral examples but often those explicitly denied by philosophers such as contradictions suggesting that there is considerable individual variation in the phenomenology of imaginative resistance. Third, moving images afford types of nonmoral deviations which arguably entail resistance, but which have not been discussed in the literature, viz., as I explain above, instances where visual representations clash with what is supposed to be visually imagined. Fourth, visual representations allow us to address the key, often unexplored, problem behind the discussions of imaginative resistance and that is whether the imagining that is mandated is minimal or involves a richer activity. Fifth, the solutions offered for the puzzle of imaginative resistance revolve around propositional imagining while visual representations force us to tackle objectual imaginings as well. In short, I will argue that imaginative resistance depends to a great extent on how richly the imaginers (think they need to) imagine, i.e. on variations in the phenomenology of imaginative engagement.

To set the terms of debate for those less familiar with it, I will first briefly outline what distinguishes imaginative puzzle from related fictional, phenomenological, and aesthetic puzzles. I will concisely address the fictional puzzle because it is together with the imaginative puzzle the most closely related to the mandate. While the fictional puzzle is about the discrepancy between identifying the mandate and questioning whether it has been successfully established, the imaginative puzzle concerns the difficulty with imagining the identified mandate.

In the second section, I will draw on experimental findings to put pressure on armchair philosophical approaches. Results from a string of recent experiments suggest that there is nothing special about moral examples and that, contrary to philosophical intuitions, nonmoral logical contradictions are the most difficult examples to imagine. Crucially, there is a considerable individual variability in how much imaginative resistance all the examples cause, if any. What remains open in these experiments, though, is the possibility that the subjects interpreted the instruction to imagine differently. In the vocabulary from Chapter Four, the subjects could have imagined minimally but they could have also imagined richly.

I turn to fiction film and online fora commentaries in the next section to propose another form of nonmoral examples which lead to imaginative resistance but have not generated much discussion – occasions where audiences are mandated to imagine objectually based on a faulty prop. For instance, when audiences are mandated to visually imagine characters as young using images of considerably older actors as props, they are supposed to imagine the characters both perceptually and experientially. This is so because to *visually* imagine somebody as young necessarily entails imagining them experientially *as young*. These are cases of objectual-effectual imagining.

In section four, I elaborate further on minimal and rich imagining. I suggest that richness should be understood multi-dimensionally. Horizontal richness is the amount of detail of imagining within a domain. Vertical richness relates to the number of domains in which one imagines. In this sense, mandated film imagining is vertically rich by definition. I also return to my proposal that mandated imagining in literary fiction is minimally propositional in the vertical sense and propose an empirical test for the claim. At this point, I propose that imaginative resistance is proportional to the richness of imagining. Some imaginative resistance is a direct consequence of the mandate because of prescription for vertical richness whereas the other is a matter of personal imaginary engagement strategies where audiences indulge in additional horizontal and/or vertical richness beyond the minimally propositional mandate.

I discuss horizontal richness further in the fifth section. I draw on existing experimental results to suggest that the influence of genre and text length on imaginative resistance is due to how the two promote or alleviate the audiences' need for horizontally rich imagining. I also suggest how horizontal richness can explain the experimental findings that even SF and fantasy films cause imaginative resistance. I propose that the concern over factual inaccuracies should be treated as a form of imaginative resistance.

I conclude with how my solution to the imaginative puzzle relates to the three existing general solutions to the puzzle – eliminativist, cantian, and wontian. While context plays a role, eliminitavism cannot be completely right because it cannot explain away all imaginatively puzzling examples, especially film ones. The underlying difficulty in imagining is imagining contradictions but this is not an absolute impossibility as some cantians have suggested; rather it is a matter of degree. Lastly, some audience members clearly refuse to imagine in line with wontian explanations, but this cannot be the whole picture either. Most importantly, imaginative puzzle is only a puzzle when the mandate demands rich imaginings – oftentimes the resistance is just a consequence of preferred reading and viewing strategies.

Different puzzles

It is generally accepted that the puzzle of imaginative resistance involves at least four distinct puzzles – imaginative, fictional, phenomenological, and aesthetic (Weatherson, 2004). Imaginative puzzle is the one we have addressed as it relates to issues audiences have with imagining what is mandated. Why is it, if indeed it is, difficult to imagine that Jake's joke is hilarious? Fictional puzzle concerns the perceived failure of generating fictional truths. Why is it difficult to accept that in Jake's world the above joke is the funniest ever? Phenomenological puzzle relates to the jarring impression the audiences get when asked to imagine the joke's hilariousness. Why are they jolted? Aesthetic puzzle, finally, concerns the perception that the work is aesthetically compromised because of this request. Why do the audiences perceive the mandate to imagine so as the work's failing? While in this chapter I will mostly be talking about the imaginative puzzle because it has commanded the most attention, it is important to address the fictional puzzle first briefly because, within the framework presented in this book, it is essentially understood as a perceived failure of mandate. I will not offer a solution to it, but I will provide film examples not discussed in philosophical literature to get a better handle on its variants.

According to Walton and Weatherson, it is not only that audiences experience issues when imagining that Giselda's female infanticide was morally right, but that they cannot accept that it is fictionally true that in Giselda's world such moral deviance obtains. In a Waltonian framework, the fictional puzzle means that the audiences cannot accept that they are *mandated* or *supposed* to imagine this moral deviation. This means that, while otherwise mandates are prescribed, there are certain mandates which fail to be prescribed or to be taken up.[2] This, crucially, is different from having difficulties with imagining what we are mandated to imagine. The first, to put it in intentionalist terms, is a matter of intentions which, while still recognizable, have fallen flat. Not everything can be mandated by fiat. The second is about taking the mandate at face value and experiencing difficulties in responding imaginatively to the letter of it.

Whatever the solution to the puzzle is, it is difficult to deny its existence. Some like Kathleen Stock (2017) have, of course, tried by claiming that there is no fictional puzzle because what is true in fiction is determined by authorial intentions alone. But this cannot be the whole story. Some things are more difficult to establish fictionally than others. These include examples with moral and humour deviances. The *Monty Phyton* sketch about the funniest joke ever written (which kills everybody from laughter on the spot) is aware of this and never divulges the joke. So is the Tenacious D when the duo sings a song which is merely the Tribute to the Greatest Song in the World that they performed for the Devil and which they no longer remember.[3]

It is also unclear whether explaining the limits of authorial authority can be pursued solely in terms of whether lower-level truths have been established in virtue of which higher-level truths obtain (cf. Weatherson, 2004). *Stage Fright* (Alfred Hitchcock, 1950) is usually cited as a work in which the author cheated in the sense that he did what he was not allowed to (cf. Bogdanovich, 1963). Therein the flashback in which the protagonist professes his innocence turns out to be a lie. At the time, the flashback was assumed to be fictionally true, so the breaking of the norm caused considerable complaints. But if this is an example of the fictional puzzle, then it has nothing to do with lower-level truths but rather with flaunting the convention of flashback use.

It could be retorted that *Stage Fright* caused only aesthetic and phenomenological resistance. Complaints about cheating mentioned by Hitchcock in an interview almost more than a decade after the film came out, not even corroborated by contemporary reviews, do not necessarily amount to issues with accepting the mandate. But even if we conceded here, there are examples where at least parts of audiences have clearly rejected the mandate for certain fictional content. Considerable uproar about the inclusion of black stormtroopers in *Star Wars VII: The Force Awakens* (J.J. Abrams, 2015) is a case in point. While the objectors have articulated their rejection in terms of internal inconsistencies of the world, cultural commentators have tried to explain it with recourse to racism and adherence to canonical fidelity, respectively (Proctor, 2018). We need not decide between the proposed accounts here. What is important is that none of them can be articulated in terms of the relationship between lower-level and higher-level truths. Racism, on the one hand, is clearly a separate matter. On the other, debates about what constitutes the canon and the ensuing internal incoherences are a question of resisting the introduction of a deliberate contradiction. But Walton (1994: 47), Weatherson (2004: 8), and Yablo (2008: 143) are all clear that deliberate contradictions do not introduce the fictional puzzle.

The lesson from this brief discussion is twofold. First, fictional puzzle appears to be more varied than assumed. Second, there also appears to be considerable individual variability among audiences – for some a work of fiction causes fictional resistance while for others it does not. These two points will inform the discussion of imaginative resistance as well.

False certitude of intuitions and their empirical correctives

Taking lessons from the previous section to heart, we should be also sceptical about the general status of the imaginative puzzle because of generalizations that have been made about what are essentially individual and varied responses. Consider the level of certitude that philosophers exhibit when discussing their examples. 'I am sceptical-sceptical about whether fictional worlds can ever differ morally from the real world' (Walton, 1994: 37). 'The sunset's aesthetic properties ["The scene was marred only by the awkwardly setting sun"] are not up to her [the author]' (Yablo, 2008: 143). 'There are science fiction stories, especially time-travel stories, that are clearly impossible [*Back to the Future* (Robert Zemeckis, 1985)] but do not generate resistance' (Weatherson, 2004: 8). Key figures in this debate, claim, in turn, that, among other things, imaginative (and fictional) puzzles obtain for every fictional world like Giselda's and for every fictional world where sunset is not pleasing to behold. By contrast, conceptual contradictions in fictional worlds in which, say, a time-travelling character prevents themselves from being born produce none of these puzzles. These scholars are categorical (something either is puzzling or is not) and very certain that their intuitions are correct.

But, of course, intuitions differ. I, for instance, have no difficulty imagining (or accepting) a world in which Giselda's action is morally right. (Honestly, I am surprised that Walton et al. do, given the great variation of moral systems that exist and the still widespread occurrence of female infanticide.) If anything, it is more difficult for me to imagine that Jake's joke is funny, let alone the most hilarious thing ever, given its wording. Does that prove that there is no such thing as imaginative puzzle? Of course not. But it does evince that categorical statements are misplaced when we are dealing with reception-dependent phenomena. Moreover, such variations also pave the way for questions of whether imaginative resistance is a matter of ability or willingness. Most importantly for this section, these differences in reception raise the question of what a typical response to such examples is. Perhaps I'm an outlier here. Perhaps it is Walton et al. who are outliers. And perhaps we are all outliers but on different ends of the spectrum. Luckily, we can move beyond the bulk of discussion on the phenomenon which essentially turns on theoretical justification of competing intuitions and consider the experimental studies on imaginative resistance which have started to appear in the last decade.

It is Jennifer Barnes and Jessica Black (2016, 2017, 2023) who have done the most extensive experimental work on the topic. The core model of their studies is to present the subjects with fictional examples drawn from the philosophical debate and ask how easy it is for the participants to imagine the scenario in question using the scale from 0 ('I absolutely cannot imagine such a world') to 100 ('I can very easily imagine such a world'). Their results provide a considerable correction to the armchair debate.

Perhaps the most important result is that there is substantial individual variation. Irrespective of the example investigated, there were always some participants who rated its imaginability with 0 and others who rated it with 100 (Barnes and Black 2016, 2023). In other words, imaginative resistance ultimately depends on the audience members. Categorical statements that something causes resistance while something else does not should have no place in the debate. Or, to put it in yet another way, commentators would profit from checking their intuitions against these empirical results.

Another key finding considers the types of deviations that cause the most resistance. The earliest empirical study (Liao et al., 2014) assumed that moral deviation is the basic form of resistance and explored variations within it, i.e. how genre contextualization influences the level of resistance. Barnes and Black

(2016, 2023), by contrast, were interested in whether different types of non-moral deviations might cause more resistance than moral ones. They grouped their examples into three categories – morally deviant, factually unlikely, and conceptually contradictory. Morally deviant examples included the Giselda case. Factually unlikely cases involved short dystopian stories like the ones in which wolves have taken over English towns. Conceptually contradictory, finally, involved tales such as Tamara Gendler's (2000) yarn in which 12 both is and is not a sum of 7 and 5. Crucially, it was conceptually contradictory stories that were found to be the most difficult to imagine, followed by morally deviant ones. In other words, while morally deviant stories on average produce imaginative resistance, they are no more special than contradictory ones. Moreover, it is contradictory stories – ones that are in theoretical literature typically presented as unproblematic (Gendler, 2000, 2006, Yablo 2008) – that empirical studies demonstrate to be the most problematic.

One last result that is worth addressing and that even Barnes and Black do not seem to emphasize is that *all* categories of stories on average cause at least some resistance. To put some numbers on it, in their first study contradictory fictions had the mean result of 40.23, morally deviant ones 55.56, while unlikely scenarios scored 67.66 (Barnes and Black 2016). This means that even fictions that virtually never appear in theoretical literature as problematic (fantasy, SF, horror, etc.) still cause some troubles for imaginers. 67.66 is some way from 100 or the standard ease with which the philosophical literature assumes these stories are imagined. It might be responded that we are not attentive enough to the scale and that 67.66 does not really demonstrate resistance for we can think of 50 as a situation in which it is neither difficult nor easy to imagine something. So, scores over 50 are just a matter of how *easy* it is to imagine something. It is only under 50 that the real resistance shows for here we are talking about how *difficult* it is to imagine something. But if that is the case, then morally deviant examples also do not evince imaginative resistance, for they are at 55.56. Depending on the interpretation of the scale then, it is either that only conceptual contradiction causes genuine resistance or that all types of stories cause contradiction.[4]

Once we start thinking about what the scale means, the question also arises what precisely the prompt *imagine* means to the participants. Barnes and Black (2016) have astutely recognized that the prompt might mean different things to different test subjects. To some it might simply mean imagine in a minimal sense like suppose the scenario whereas for others it might mean imagine in a more fleshed out sense of a more complex mental model of the same scenario. The sliding scale from 0 to 100 certainly suggests that there are levels of richness in how one might go about imagining what they are prompted to imagine. This richness may be within a domain or across domains. In the first case, it is about the level of propositional detail going into imagination such as drawing out the implications (e.g. Giselda might have felt badly despite it being the right thing to do) or filling out the gaps with background knowledge (e.g. this must be some historical world where female infanticide is morally right). Call this horizontal richness. In the latter case, it concerns marshalling imaginings from other non-propositional domains, forming mental images of characters and situations, the gory sight of infanticide, the dreadful growl of wolves, etc. This I have referred to as vertical richness. And, of course, within different perceptual domains there can be different levels of horizontal richness. While singling out the problem of what the prompt is taken to mean as in need of future research, Barnes and Black have unfortunately not returned to the question.

This might be perceived to open the way for criticism of empirical results by those who claim that imagining involved in fiction is not minimal but rich in both ways (e.g. Walton 1994, Gendler 2000, Weatherson 2004). Perhaps they would argue that participants imagined only minimally so the results are not representative of how it is if one imagines richly. Notice, however, that these same authors claim that not only that the audiences should imagine richly when engaging fiction but that they normally do. If their view of imagining fiction is true, that would mean that participants did imagine richly undermining the potential criticism. While this preserves Barnes and Black's findings if standard imagining in engaging fiction is rich, it does not necessarily invalidate them in the minimal case either because the typical imagining could also be minimal, and the participants could have imagined what they were asked to imagine only minimally. In other words, we are still left with the question of whether we imagine minimally or richly when imagining fiction. Moving away from literary examples will help us in resolving the problem.

Minimal, rich and objectual imagining

All the examples discussed up until now have been propositional. They have mandated imagining *that* something is the case. But as discussed in the previous chapter, there are other types of imaginings and cinema regularly mandates us to imagine in these other domains. *Alien* (Ridley Scott, 1979), for instance, mandates us to imagine not only propositionally – say, that the xenomorph has a tail and a mouth within a mouth and that it hisses and screeches – but also perceptually – we are supposed to visually imagine how this tail and mouths look on the basis of the images on the screen and we are supposed to aurally imagine how these hisses and screeches sound based on the sounds we hear from the screen. Because moving images regularly mandate perceptual imaginings on top of propositional ones, I will say that at least in one sense – vertical one – they regularly demand richer imaginings which move beyond minimal propositional imagining.

Now, perceptual imaginings should not necessarily be perceptually indistinguishable from their props – the images and sounds on the screen – though in films which generally aim for photographic verisimilitude the props should be a good guide for imagining. Here, photographic verisimilitude should be understood as a style of representation where if the entity depicted existed in the real world and were to be captured on camera (and microphone), it would look (and sound) very much like the visual (and aural) representation offered on screen (cf. Gaut, 2010). So, while we might recognize that the images of the spaceship Nostromo in *Alien* are recordings of a scale model, they are still a very good guide for imagining the vessel.

I want to suggest that in films aiming for photographic verisimilitude, there are occasions of imaginative resistance. One class of examples includes bad props. Consider *Plan 9 from Outer Space* and the scene in which Inspector Daniel Clay (Tor Johnson) comments on the two corpses they just found: 'finding a mess like this ought to make anyone frightened'. The trouble is that the 'mess' on screen is just two mannequins lying face down in a ditch donned with some clothes. Arguably, using these props it is difficult to imagine that the corpses are scary (Figure 4).

FIGURE 4 ***Visually imagining the scene as scary in* Plan 9 from Outer Space *(Ed Wood, 1959) leads to imaginative resistance.***

Another example concerns a different type of mismatch between the prop and the imagining which could be broadly described as unconvincing but is certainly not bad in the photorealistic sense above. Take a show like *Beverly Hills, 90210* in which, at least in the early seasons, teenagers were played by adult actors, including 29-year-old Gabrielle Carteris portraying 14-year-old Andrea Zuckerman and 26-year-old Ian Ziering embodying 14-year-old Steve Sanders. Imaginative issues start, I suggest, once their images on screen are used as props for imagining 9th graders. Another example of this type is from films like *She's All That* (Robert Iscove, 1999) where the heroine Laney (Rachel Leigh Cook) is transformed from an unattractive ugly duckling into a stunning swan. The problem is, of course, that whatever kind of make-up the actress sports to make her look unattractive at the beginning her physical appeal shines through regardless (Figure 5).[5] The underlying trouble here is somewhat different from *Plan 9 from Outer Space*. There the prop is unconvincing because it is badly made but here the prop is unconvincing because we are mandated to imagine that how the actors are shown on screen is precisely how the characters look like – like young adults and physically attractive, respectively – yet the characters are also early teenagers and unattractive.

FIGURE 5 *Visually imagining Laney (Rachel Leigh Cook) as ugly in* She's All That *(Robert Iscrove, 1999) leads to imaginative resistance.*

Unfortunately, I cannot back my claims that the above is a prevalent phenomenon with experimental evidence, but my claims do not rest simply on my intuitions either. *Plan 9 from Outer Space* is widely discussed as one of the worst movies ever made, arguably because it fails in making the audience imagine what they are mandated to, or, as *Rotten Tomatoes* critical consensus puts it: 'The epitome of so-bad-it's-good cinema, *Plan 9 from Outer Space* is an unintentionally hilarious sci-fi "thriller" from anti-genius Ed Wood that is justly celebrated for its staggering ineptitude'.[6] In the case of object-prop mismatch there are numerous discussion threads on Quora which express that there is something wrong with older actors playing younger characters.[7] While the posts do not necessarily articulate it in terms of imaginative resistance, they certainly do point out that something is off here, and I take it as reasonable to assume that (at least part of) the problem is imaginative resistance. In fact, in cases of un/attractiveness, there is an explicit comment about Rachel Leigh Cook's character Laney in the unattractive phase which, if we take 'believe' to actually mean 'imagine', does articulate the problem precisely along our lines: 'Who would believe this girl is so ugly no boy would approach her.'[8] Or consider the obverse for Maggie Gyllenhaal in *The Dark Knight*: 'She's a fine talented actress, but the other characters in the film refer to her as a stunning beauty and it kind of takes you out of the movie. Had to suspend disbelief with Joker's line: "Well hello, beautiful! You must be Harvey's squeeze, hm? And you are beautiful".'[9] At the very least, this demonstrates that I am not alone here in my intuitions.

At the core of these examples, there appears to be some kind of discrepancy between the prop and the imagining mandated by the prop – call this object-prop incongruence. However, it is not only the *content* of the imagining that is incongruent with its prop, but the *effect* as well. As Ronald de Sosa (2010) explains, there is a difference between the content of imagining and the effect of that imagining, as in experiencing disgust (effect) when imagining oneself as old and feeble (content). But there is more here. The effect that de Sosa refers to is actual, i.e. it is not what one imagines, although it is a consequence of imagining. In my film examples the effect is also to be imagined. In the case of *Plan 9 from Outer Space*, we are mandated to imagine perceptually not only two corpses but to imagine them perceptually as *scary looking*. Yet the poorly arranged mannequins hardly evoke any fright and are more likely to garner chuckles. In *She's All That*, the mandate is to visually imagine both that Laney looks like Leigh Cook and to imagine her as *unattractive*. But Leigh Cook, as the Quora commentator conveys, hardly looks unattractive to heterosexual men. In other words, in these cases we are supposed to experientially imagine effects as well.

It could be retorted that in these object-prop incongruence examples, there is no imaginative puzzle because there is no need to imagine perceptually in the first place.[10] Audiovisual stimuli are merely used for propositional imagining so any incongruence there is, is about actual perception and not imaginative one. I have already shown in the previous chapter that there is a need to imagine perceptually in engaging fiction film if the need is understood as mandate. The content of the fictional world presented cannot be exhausted in propositional translations of perceptual information. Certainly, the need to imagine can also be construed as whether the audiences need to actually imagine perceptually to understand the film. I agree that they do not.[11] In this sense, the overall imaginative stance that the perceptual representations stand not for the profilmic, but the fictional world is enough.

This, however, is also the reason why the incongruence cannot be on the level of perception and the resistance must be imaginative. On the profilmic level, the actors are not made to look younger than they are, they simply look their own age. It is only in the fictional world that we are supposed to imagine them visually as young. So, the incongruence must be between imagining the characters visually as looking like they do on the profilmic level but also imagining them as younger than they are on the profilmic level.

As I stressed earlier, I am not claiming that the audiences need to imagine perceptually to understand the fictional world. Global propositional imaginative attitude suffices for that. But because there is a mandate to do so and because in this case there is a specific discrepancy between the perceptual aspects of the profilmic and what is to be perceptually imagined, they are likelier to pursue this imagining either spontaneously or deliberately and end up with clashing of the content and the effect of imagining than if there was no discrepancy.

The classic example that object-prop incongruence is the closest to is Walton's joke because there is an incongruence with the effect there as well (but only in de Sosa's sense). (This would also explain why these examples are particularly problematic for me to imagine as opposed to moral deviations.) 'A maple leaf fell from the tree' does not come across as funny. Yet we are supposed to imagine it being extremely funny and, in fact, the most hilarious ever.[12] But there is a subtle yet, I will argue, important difference from film examples. In Walton's example we are only required to imagine propositionally, i.e. *that* the joke is extremely funny. Strictly speaking, we are not requested to imagine the joke perceptually and experientially *as* extremely funny. And this seems to be the consequence of the fact that the imagining is propositional.[13]

In films, because we imagine perceptually, on occasions we are also supposed to imagine at least some of the effects of imaginings or imagine them experientially as well. Because we imagine perceptually and experientially (next to propositionally), there is a vertical level of richness to the imagining that is missing from propositional imagining. When imagining Laney, we are supposed to imagine her visually and visually as looking like Leigh Cook. When also mandated to imagine her as unattractive in the first part of the movie, because we are dealing with a film, we are mandated to imagine her *visually* as unattractive. And to imagine her visually as unattractive requires we also include experiential imaginings into perceptual ones, i.e. to imagine experiencing her appearance as unattractive. In other words, there are occasions when objectual imagining combines perceptual and experiential imagining. Put in yet another way, the mandate of increased vertical richness may mandate even more vertical richness. To use the vocabulary from Chapter Four there is something necessarily entailed by some imaginings. It is a part of imagining somebody *visually* as unattractive to involve the imaginative *experience* of finding them unattractive. Imagining somebody propositionally as unattractive does not necessarily entail this.

It might be objected that in Chapter Four I implied that objectual imagining cannot be experiential. The point there was to use objectual imagining to distinguish perceptual imagining from imagining perceiving. More precisely, the goal was to differentiate visual imagining from imagining seeing by pointing out that imagining seeing, unlike visual imagining, necessarily involves experiential imagining which is about oneself, i.e. about how one is imaginarily accessing visual information. I stand by the claim that the examples of objectual imagining I discussed there were indeed not experiential in this sense. Objectually imagining a silver apple does not necessarily entail imagining experiencing anything. It is just a visual imagining of a silver apple.

But this does not mean there are no occasions where films also mandate embedding perceptual effects as experiential imaginings into imaginings about objects. This is in line with the claim I made in the same chapter that perceptual imagining bridges objectual and experiential imagining. And it still coheres with the distinction between visual imagining and imagining seeing because the imaginary experiential difference there is about how access to the visual information is given, whereas here the experiential imagining refers to the effect of an object imagined perceptually. Early seasons of *Beverly Hills, 90210*, for instance, mandate both propositionally that the protagonists are underage and perceptually them as *very young*. Yet in using adult actors as visual props according to the demands of photographic realism, audiences end up imagining them as *older*. Because 'very young looking' and 'older looking' are essentially evaluations or effects of how perceptual phenomena appear, much like 'un/attractive looking' in *She's All That* or 'scary/funny looking' in *Plan 9 from Outer Space* are, these cases introduce experiential imaginings into objectual imaginings. We can call such objectual imaginings effect-objectual imaginings to distinguish them from objectual imaginings in general.

Why mandated literary imagining is vertically minimal

Walton might respond that the difference between propositional and such objectual imagining is far less relevant in this context than I make it to be. In his framework, we are in any case supposed to imagine more richly beyond propositions even in literary texts. For him, in the joke example, we are supposed to imagine 'a way of thinking about it in which it would strike one as funny' and 'imagine finding it funny' (Walton, 1994: 48). In other words, for Walton we are supposed to flesh out our imaginings beyond minimal imagining to include experiential imaginings in examples like these. At this point, I could stick to my guns and insist, well no, read the props, all they provide is a mandate that this joke 'A maple leaf fell from the true' is the most hilarious ever. You are certainly free to imagine more richly and imagine in what conditions it could be funny for you if any, but you are not *mandated* to do so.

Another way to think about is on the example of sexual fantasies about movie stars. Casting Rudolf Valentino or Channing Tatum in films like *The Sheik* (George Melford, 1921) or *Magic Mike* (Steven Soderbergh, 2012) plays to (at least) heterosexual female and homosexual male fantasies. If a viewer is a member of these groups, the fantasies usually involve some degree of sexual imaginings about Valentino and Tatum. The imaginings are not mandated because it is not what every audience member is supposed to imagine. But they are not completely free either because Valentino's or Tatum's sexual appeal is a part of the film design. Though it is not a perfect analogy (because the target groups are not defined as well in Walton's example), I suggest that in this sense while not everybody is supposed to imagine the experiential effects of Walton's joke, the example is designed to elicit the effect contradictory to how it is described in the text and, for some, to elicit imagining that effect.

But I do not think this will do because what we are essentially arguing about is preferred personal engagement with fictional literary texts, or, what I see as preferred engagement Walton sees as mandated and vice versa. There is, however, another way to resolve the disagreement or at least suggest how to do so. For this, let me spell out my position first.

My view is that the mandated imagining in literary texts is one of merely supposing what is offered, i.e. that propositional imagining is minimal. The reason is because we all seem to manage to have conversations about conceptual impossibilities such as the sum of 5 and 7 is and is not 12, while only some report imaginative resistance here. I am not denying Barnes and Black's (2016, 2023) results that these examples cause the most imaginative resistance, merely that for participants even to report on their experiences in imagining they need to have had some tentative grasp on what they were asked to do, and arguably this grasp is accomplished through minimal imagining.[14] It seems to me that imaginative resistance is proportional to how richly we imagine when confronted with an effect-clashing or conceptually contradictory mandate. In other words, I suggest that individual variation in imaginative resistance is in large part due to a person's preferred phenomenological engagement with literary texts in terms of richness of imagining. (This phenomenological engagement may be further modified by contextual factors such as genre or length.)

This is why Walton et al. report imaginative resistance where I do not. They feel forced to flesh out in imagination how female infanticide could be morally right. I do not because the contemporary existence of alternative moral systems and of the practice allows me not to pursue the matter further imaginatively beyond simply supposing what is mandated. I have more difficulty imagining the joke example because the joke does not have any humorous effect on me.

Because, unlike in the moral example, I am not aware of an alternative system of humour where this is funny, I seem to be coaxed towards thinking and, in turn, imagining how this could be funny. I do not consider this nudge to be a mandate proper, but it is certainly a valid reading strategy. In the film example, however, I am supposed to imagine effect-objectually corpses as scary, Steve Sanders as teenage young, and Laney as unattractive which causes me imaginative resistance.

If Walton's view is correct – call it rich imagining – then there should be no difference in the level of imaginative resistance when confronted with examples whose content is the same across different media. So, a literary version of *She's All That* should instil as much imaginative resistance as the film example. Now, we might disagree on what amounts to equivalent literary content, but I would argue something like this should do: 'Laney looked exactly like the actress Rachel Leigh Cook with big glasses. Oh boy, was Laney unattractive'. Under my view – call it minimal imagining – an experimental test should evince that the imaginative resistance with the literary version is significantly lower than the imaginative resistance in the film example. (Another way to test whether engaging fiction entails minimal or rich imagining would be to repeat the Barnes and Black 2016 studies but with two groups of participants where one is asked to 'merely suppose' and the other to 'imagine' the provided scenarios. My theory predicts that the levels of imaginative resistance would drop in the 'merely suppose' group.)

I concede that my proposal for a literary version of *She's All That* is not well suited for experimental testing. For one, all the participants in the literary condition would have to have a very clear mental image of how Rachel Leigh Cook looks like, and they almost certainly will not. But we can take another example from the debate and transform that one into a film example. Walton's joke example will not do because we need a case in which the effect and the experiential imagining of this effect are a consequence of perceptual imagining. In a film, the joke would certainly have to be delivered in a certain way by the actor playing Jake, but its prosodic and/or performative qualities are in the end not that which make the joke funny or not. This is dissimilar from how properties of Leigh Cook's face determine whether Laney is experientially attractive or not.

A better example is Yablo's (2008: 143) scenario in which children are playing a game wherein to win, it only remains to find an oval-shaped leaf. At that point, Sally grabs a five-fingered maple leaf and the game finishes: 'Here was the oval they needed!' Walton (2006: f13) seems to agree with Yablo that this is an instance of imaginative resistance. I am less convinced for three reasons. First, because I am imagining minimally, I am not forced to imagine objectually how a five-fingered maple leaf can be oval. Second, even if I am to flesh out this imagining it seems to me it is not too difficult. What comes to mind is a five-fingered maple leaf mutant whose lowest pair of leaves bend parabolically towards the bigger pair which bend even more tightly towards the central leaf making the whole thing kind of oval-looking. Last, Barnes and Black (2023) have found that this example does not evoke that much imaginative resistance scoring at 62. But regardless of how easily I engage the written story and what Barnes and Black have found, my theory predicts that the film version of the story should generate more resistance. In the film version, we see Sally grabbing a five-fingered maple leaf and cut to black with intertitles 'Here was the oval they needed!' Also, to guard against my second objection we modify the story to specify *Canadian* five-fingered maple leaf and have Sally grabbing a *Canadian* five-fingered maple leaf in the film.

The richness of imagining and the drive to flesh out imagining

The two main points that I have made in this chapter are: (1) contrary to classic philosophical intuitions on the subject there is considerable individual variation in imaginative resistance and (2) the richness of imagining plays a key role in this variation. I am not claiming, however, that this is the whole explanation. Black and Barnes (2017), for instance, suggest that other factors such as the ease of imagining, fear of generalizing about morality from either authors or characters, political orientation, and concerns about moral purity play a role. But I am claiming that all other things being equal, richness of imagining pushes imaginers towards imaginative resistance. This demands some more clarification, however.

One way I have spoken of richness is in terms of numbers of domains in which one imagines – joint propositional and experiential imagining that I have dubbed effect-objectual imagining is richer than only propositional imagining; joint perceptual, experiential, and propositional imagining that is typical of film is richer than joint perceptual and experiential imagining. This I termed vertical richness. I am not saying that in itself it is more difficult to imagine a film than it is to imagine a written story just because the film standardly mandates imagining in more domains.[15] I am only saying that vertical richness of imagining opens more possibilities for clashes because there are more domains. In the joke example, the clash was between the *effect* of mandated propositional imagining (joke is not funny) and the *content* of mandated propositional imagining (joke is funny). In film examples, the clash was between experiential imagining as a necessary entailment of mandated perceptual imagining due to photographic realism (attractive/not scary/older because how props look) and experiential imagining as a necessary entailment of mandated perceptual fictional content (unattractive/scary/young because it is stipulated in the story). These clashes potentially arise only when fiction diverges (substantially) from what is believed (to be important) to hold in the real world.

Next to richness across domains or vertical richness, I have also spoken of richness within domains or horizontal richness. This is a matter of detail or how much content within a domain – in this case propositional one – the imaginer imagines beyond the minimal mandate. For instance, it has been argued based on experimental findings that genre as context modifies the level of imaginative resistance (Liao et al., 2014). Framing Giselda's story as an Aztec myth causes less imaginative resistance than when it is framed as a contemporary detective tale. From the perspective of richness of propositional detail this is so because the myth genre background that is introduced suggests to readers that this is also a world of alternative morality and allows them not to pursue imaginative fleshing out as much as they do in the contemporary detective story case.

Moreover, I propose that the reason why even literary time-travel stories, or for that matter, fantastical, SF, or dystopian stories are found problematic to an extent (Barnes and Black, 2016, 2023) is because some people try to flesh out the conceptual or physical impossibilities there in detail and find themselves that they cannot. Some might simply find it difficult to imagine the exact nuts and bolts and cause-effect conundrums of Marty McFly's time-traveller paradox in *Back to the Future* (Robert Zemeckis, 1985) (if Marty stopped his parents from meeting how exactly was he born in the first place to stop his parents from meeting?). I also suspect that if in an episode of *Star Trek: The Next Generation* (Paramount, 1987–94) commander Data started explicitly specifying real-world physics (where travelling faster than the speed of light is impossible because as an object accelerates its mass increases to the point that it would have an infinite mass if it were to reach the speed of light) more people would report imaginative resistance with Warp travel then they currently do. This is because here the added mandated imaginings are more suggestive of thinking about the paradox of travelling faster than light and therefore imagining solutions to it.[16]

In fact, there is good reason to believe that for some audiences, factual inaccuracies cause imaginative resistance as well. I suggest that the concern about what is referred to as 'errors' in public and fan criticism on online fora such as Quora or Reddit is another subclass of imaginative resistance.[17] One film that has been repeatedly chastised for its supposed errors is *Gravity*

(Alfonso Cuarón, 2013). Among other things, jumping between different space stations that are key for the story is not possible in the real world because they are not even remotely close to each other, and using a fire extinguisher to propel oneself through space would, given real-world physics, only ends up in spinning around. As one commentator puts it, 'OK, I understand it's a movie, and I did enjoy it. Am I such a geek for noticing hundreds of technical inaccuracies and having that REALLY bother me?'[18] That these examples are still construed as errors despite them also being recognized as deliberate creative decisions typical of SF genre where real-world physics regularly takes a back seat to dramatic effect suggests that the commentators do not deny they are supposed to imagine this – therefore, this is not an articulation of the fictional puzzle – but find it difficult to do so.[19] (These same statements also seem to express the phenomenological and aesthetic puzzle.) While empirical studies have not addressed such examples explicitly, I also predict that these and similar audiences would, unlike Walton et al. deem fictional works with plot holes difficult to imagine. The reason, again, is that they would feel impelled to imaginatively fill out the holes, though not necessarily mandated to do so.

The main thing to remember then is that minimal imagining is, under this model, the best recipe for avoiding imaginative resistance. This is because richer forms of imagining are more likely to have to address clashes. And imagining phenomena that are impossible or unlikely is more difficult to imagine the richer one is supposed to imagine. Moving away from written examples to film ones is key to grasping this.

Imaginative resistance in literary texts, by contrast, is only a puzzle if the mandated imagining is rich. Under the framework proposed here, it is not a puzzle because imagining minimally allows us to engage in literary fiction without running into conceptual or experiential contradictions. This is not to say that imaginative resistance does not exist – it is just that it is not puzzling in the sense that it derives from imaginings that we are *supposed* to do. The resistance derives, instead, because of the preferred (or, perhaps, even somewhat compulsive?) individual reading strategies which involve fleshing out prescribed imaginings – fleshing out which is, strictly speaking, not mandated. In the film examples provided, by contrast, imaginative resistance is a puzzle in the sense that it is a direct consequence of what we are supposed to imagine.

It is true that numerous studies of engagement with literary narratives argue that one of the key components in transportation is mental imagery (Green and Brock, 2000, van Laer et al., 2014). In other words, such engagement involves both vertically and horizontally rich imagining. But even so, this type of engagement does not evince a mandate to imagine richly. The studies only tell us about the phenomenology of narrative engagement. Moreover, it is not contradictory that increased richness of imagining leads to both increased transportation and increased imaginative resistance. The other key factor to consider is the text itself – whether it introduces potentially difficult mandates or not.

Other solutions

It remains to say a few words about how my proposal relates to other general solutions to the puzzle – eliminitavist, wontian and cantian. In short, eliminitavists argue that the puzzle is an artefact of highly artificial examples in the philosophical literature and that it disappears if the examples are provided with sufficient context. Wontians propose that consumers of fiction simply refuse to imagine what is requested of them. Cantians, finally, contend that imaginative resistance is due to the genuine inability of audiences to imagine what is mandated (cf. Tuna, 2020).

If the main eliminitavist claim is that the imaginative puzzle disappears when an appropriate context which allows it for the consumers to imagine what is mandated is provided, I share the view only to an extent. While context does play a role in the sense that it can diminish imaginative resistance as we have seen with genre and expanding the story (putting the Giselda story into an Aztec myth framework), a change of genre and an increase in length can also add to imaginative resistance (putting the same story into a contemporary detective genre). Moreover, *She's All That* and similar films are full-fledged non-artificial examples of fiction that we find circulating widely outside of specialist philosophical literature and arguably cause imaginative resistance if viewer reports are to be believed. It is difficult to think of any context which could disarm such examples and the burden of proof at this point rests with the eliminitavists.

I have spoken about difficulties stemming from imaginative resistance mostly in terms of inability to imagine what are essentially contradictory imaginings or contradictory effects and imaginings which are close to a cantian position. But this is distinct from saying that imaginative resistance is a consequence of the impossibility to imagine contradictions because I have argued that contradictions can be imagined so long as they are merely supposed without fleshing them out further and imagining them richly.

Lastly, I am not claiming that wontian unwillingness can never play a role in the phenomenon either. There are people who clearly report that they do not want to engage in certain mandated imaginings as can be seen from a response by a participant in one experiment using the Giselda example: 'I don't want to think about a young girl being killed' (Barnes and Black, 2023: 199). It is also possible that in being impelled to imagine in more detail, i.e. to flesh out one's imagining, this might lead to a reaction of unwillingness because of the realization that the process is cognitively taxing or time-consuming. In fact, inability and unwillingness might combine and the former might be confused for the latter. This is similar to when people are faced with a task which they might think that they do not have the ability to solve so they refrain from expending the energy to solve it, though in reality they could solve it if they tried hard enough.

But to return to an earlier point, all this should be understood in the context of the level or richness of imagining which, I propose, is a key, yet hitherto overlooked aspect to explaining the hitherto insufficiently addressed variability of imaginative resistance among audience members. And, as I argued, while in literary fiction the level of richness depends on preferred phenomenological reading strategies, in fiction film it is embedded in the mandate for imagining that may involve a combination of perceptual and experiential imagining dubbed effect-objectual imagining.

6

Imagination and emotional engagement with characters

In the previous chapter, I have started the exploration of the phenomenology of imaginative engagement with fiction film by taking the puzzle of imaginative resistance as its case study and focusing on imagining specific objects and their effects. Some of these effects have included emotions – viz. the mandate to imagine the poorly made corpse mannequins in *Plan 9 from Outer Space* (Ed Wood, 1959) as scary-looking. Here I will continue the discussion of emotions elicited by works of fiction in the context of paradox of fiction as initially introduced by Colin Radford (1975) and Kendall Walton (1978).

While in the account of imaginative resistance I downplayed the importance of moral examples, this chapter proposes that the existing debates overlook the paradox's moral dimension. Focusing either on its descriptive or normative aspects, commentators have had little to say about why consumers of fiction are regularly more emotionally involved with or care more for fictional characters than for real-life people. Formulated in this way, the moral problem of fiction is linked to the paradox of fiction insofar as they both assume that fictional entities cause genuine emotions. Building on (counter)factualist solutions to the paradox of fiction, and contrary to the jointly most commonly accepted proposals involving quasi-emotions (Walton, 1978) or thought theory (Carroll, 1990b), I suggest that the best way to proceed is to deny (in most but not all cases) the assumption that *fictional entities* are the cause of emotions (be they genuine or quasi). Where I part ways from (counter)factualists, however, is in identifying the objects and causes of emotions. Whereas (counter)factualists claim that we react emotionally to entities who are or could be like the fictional entities depicted, I suggest that we emotionally react to real-life structures such as implausible yet logical possibilities, appearance, representational techniques, investment, and expectations. I conclude with a proposal that there are some emotions that fictional entities do cause – viz. sympathy and antipathy – but that these emotions are characterized by the absence of clearly associated actions.

As originally formulated, the paradox of fiction involves three assertions. Separately they all appear intuitively correct but taken together they cannot hold simultaneously: (1) fictional entities (characters, objects, events, etc.) cause genuine emotions, (2) only entities which we believe truly exist can cause genuine emotions, (3) we do not believe that fictional entities truly exist. The dominant view is that the paradox is not really a paradox, i.e. the proposition (2) is seen as false (Stecker 2011, Friend 2017, Konrad, Petraschka and Werner 2018). In other words, the generally accepted solution – dubbed the 'thought theory' – is that there are numerous objects and events in whose existence we do not believe but which do cause genuine emotions (Carroll, 1990b and Gendler, 2008). One example includes sexual fantasies which lead to actual emotional arousal. In the case of horror, then, we actually fear the fictional monster lurking in the shadows.

There are, of course, other ways to defuse the paradox.[1] Some scholars deny (3). Samuel Taylor Coleridge (1817) proposed that consumers willingly suspend their disbelief when engaging fictional entities. More recently, David B. Suits (2006) has argued that because it is possible to believe both *p* and not-*p*, it is also possible to believe in fictional objects and events while at the same time also not believing in them. A larger minority reject (1). Walton (1978, 1990, 1997), most notably, maintains that fictional objects and events cause only make-believe or quasi emotions which should be characterized as distinct from emotions that we experience in real-life situations. Regardless of the solution to the paradox, the underlying concern for most of those engaged in the debate is that in our engagement with fiction the fictional entities (whether we believe in them or not) do cause emotions of one type or another (genuine or quasi). But what if, as the (counter)factualists have suggested, it is not fictional entities that cause these emotions, or, at the very least they do so in far more limited cases than previously thought? And, even more importantly, what if the focus on the epistemological aspect of the paradox precludes us from recognizing its more pressing moral dimension?

In the first section, therefore, I outline the moral version of the paradox of fiction – viz. how do we square the moral demand for emotional investment in real-life people with the common phenomenon that audiences regularly care more for fictional characters than actual people? Using *The Game of Thrones* (HBO, 2011–19) as an example, I suggest the strategy is to deny that we are invested in fictional characters and that we are actually responding to what I refer to as real-life structures – time commitment, emotional expectations, qualities of props, formal strategies, etc.

I develop this strategy further on the example of fear and horror films in section two. I propose that in monster horror films all three main fear-inducing strategies – suspense, surprise, and appearance – capitalize on real-life elements rather than mandated imaginings. Suspense coaxes (but not mandates) the audiences into thinking and imagining the implausible but not impossible existence of monsters in question. Surprise is usually a matter of formal techniques such as jump scares. Appearance, finally, rests on how the profilmic prop looks and what its actual emotional effect is rather than on what one is supposed to imagine. I conclude with the claim that my proposal is to be preferred over competing ones because they only tackle appearance.

In the last section, I discuss whether the solution can be generalized, and emotions articulated in terms of real-life structures. In the classic case of pity and Anna Karenina, I propose that to pity Anna is to pity somebody (who might be) like her. This, however, can only go so far. There are emotions like sympathy and antipathy whose objects appear to be fictional characters and not some possible real-life equivalents. But we should not treat this as proposal's failure. Rather, it makes sense that, if fictions are generally less likely to lead to behavioural reactions than real-life structures, only emotions which have clearly associated behavioural actions (e.g. fear with fight or flight, pity with helping) would be caused by real-life structures while those without such associated actions (e.g. sympathy and antipathy) would be generated by fictional entities.

The moral dimension of the paradox of fiction

It is undeniable that morality comes into play in discussions of puzzles and paradoxes of imagination and the arts. The puzzle of imaginative resistance discussed in Chapter Five often revolves around the difficulty to imagine 'morally deviant' fictional worlds such as the one in which female infanticide is the right thing to do (Hume, 1757/1875 and Weatherson, 2004). There also exists a large literature on the role of imagination and the arts in moral persuasion (for overviews see Eaton 2015, Liao and Gendler 2019). It discusses why we sympathize with morally otiose characters such as Tony Soprano (James Gandolfini) from *The Sopranos* (HBO, 1999–2007) when in real life such characters would be deplored has also been discussed at length (Carroll, 2004, Smith, 2011, Slugan, 2019c). But when it comes to the paradox of fiction, scholars identify only its descriptive and normative dimension (cf. Friend, 2017). Whereas the descriptive question asks whether emotions induced by fictional entities are of the same type as those elicited by real-life structures, the normative concern relates to whether emotions induced by fictional entities are somehow inappropriate.

Importantly, neither the descriptive nor the normative question has a moral dimension. Descriptive concerns, clearly, deal only with categorization. But even the normative question understands the (in)appropriateness in terms of subjective rationality or justification (Radford, 1975), rather than morality. Under this framework, an emotion is justified if it is appropriate to the evidence of the situation. If I have good reason to believe that my friend has betrayed me, my anger is justified. But if it turns out that there was no betrayal, I would no longer be justified in being angry at her. Similarly, if a colleague tells me a tragic story of his sister and elicits my pity, but then reveals that in fact he does not have a sister, I would be unjustified in pitying his sister because she does not exist. According to Radford, emotions induced by fictional entities are precisely of this type – unjustified – because they do not have an appropriate object.

I propose that there is a moral dimension to the paradox which has garnered virtually no attention in these discussions. I refer to the phenomenon where consumers of fictions appear to care about fictional entities far more deeply than about real-life people and events. A cursory online search of the subject reveals numerous threads on online fora such as Quora or Reddit which tackle questions such as 'why do I prefer fictional characters over real people?', 'why do I have no empathy for real people only fictional characters?', and 'does anyone else feel empathy for fictional characters but practically zero for people?'[2] The widely reported teen infatuation with the vampire protagonist of *The Twilight Saga* (2008–12), Edward Cullen, also fits this bill.

To get a better understanding of how deep these emotions can run and how much more involving they can be than engagement with real-life tragedies, I wish to first offer my own experience of watching *Game of Thrones* as anecdotal evidence.[3] In episode 8 of season 4 – 'Mountain and the Viper' – Tyrion Lannister (Peter Dinklage) awaits trial by combat after Oberyn Martell, known as the Viper (Pedro Pascal), has volunteered to serve as his champion against Lord Gregor, the titular Mountain (Hafþór Júlíus Björnsson). Oberyn has the upper hand throughout the combat but, once he knocks out Gregor, instead of finishing him off he demands a confession for a previous crime. Gregor uses this opportunity to get a hold of Oberyn and crushes Oberyn's skull with his bare hands. Tyrion, in turn, is sentenced to death and the episode ends.

I remember I was so upset about this turn of events that I could not come to grips with what had happened for a whole week (until the next episode when the narrative took a different turn). And I recollect trying to come to terms with how shaken up I was – for I could not recall the last time something had unnerved me this much. Crucially, this 'something' involved real-life events. Certainly, not even reports about Daesh's war crimes at the time of the episode's original screening – the summer of 2014 – came close to disturbing me as much. In this context, the problem is surely primarily moral rather than epistemological – how can I be so disturbed by this fictional event and yet care so little about factual contemporary atrocities by comparison?

Now, the example is clearly anecdotal and could be dismissed merely as evidence of an antisocial personality disorder. Yet, I would argue that being afflicted by the suffering of fictional characters more than by that of flesh and blood people is a regular occurrence. Consider the fate of your favourite fictional character and compare the intensity of your resulting emotion to what you feel when you, say, meet a homeless person on the street. Or think of how often you have cried about some news report as opposed to when watching your favourite melodrama. That you have cried even once over a fictional fate such as the perishing of Lee's (Casey Affleck) children in a fire due to his negligence in *Manchester by the Sea* (Kenneth Lonergan, 2016) while having not cried a single time when you see reports of real-life tragic losses of life in the Mediterranean Sea or Gaza should be enough to raise the moral dimension of the paradox. It should also discount the talk of antisocial personality disorder in my anecdotal case or, alternatively, indicate that all who standardly engage with fiction suffer from it.

Phrased in a more formal way and building on premise 1): x) most consumers of fiction have at least once had an intensive emotional response (hatred, infatuation, crying, etc.) to a fictional entity, y) most consumers of fiction have at least once *not* had an intensive emotional response to real-life people facing tragedies, z) it follows that some consumers of fiction are sometimes more emotionally involved with fictional entities than with real-life people.

The problem which I dub the moral problem of fiction (MPF henceforth) can be formulated as follows:

(A) We should be more emotionally invested in real-life entities than fictional ones.

(B) We are regularly more emotionally invested in fictional entities than real-life ones.

As we can see the MPF takes a different slant than the normative aspect of the paradox of fiction. The MPF is not about the justification of emotions but about the comparison to real-life emotional responses. Whereas in the discussion of normativity the emotional response appears to be irrational, in the MPF the emotion's intensity trumps what would be fitting for an emotional response to a real-life entity. In the MPF, it is not that the emotional response is inappropriate in Radford's sense but that it is scandalous that there is an emotional response for a fictional entity (Lee's children) when there is little or none for a comparable real-life entity (actual child victims of fires).[4] In other words, to defuse this problem it will not help us to argue contra Radford by identifying how emotional responses to fictional entities might be rational after all or how different justifications might apply to fictional as opposed to real-life emotions (for overviews see Friend, 2017, Liao and Gendler, 2019). Rather, I propose that the solution is to deny (B). Allow me to sketch out the idea on the *Game of Thrones* example first.

It was clear to me that I was not concerned with Oberyn's fate: it was the effect that his death had on Tyrion – the fact that this amounts to his death sentence – that had me all up in knots. But then I started wondering: is it really Tyrion that I fear for, or is something else bothering me here? Tyrion was clearly my favourite character in the show and with him out of the picture I would no longer enjoy the show nearly as much. His jokes and cynical remarks, such as 'All dwarfs are bastards in their fathers' eyes', were a constant source of delight and amusement. From this perspective, what is really making an emotional effect on me is the possibility that I will no longer derive pleasure from the show – for there will no longer be a vehicle for delivering lines of the above type – rather than fretting for a fictional character's life. Similarly, I have also invested a substantial amount of time in the show for it not to keep paying off. The fact that I have recast my emotional engagement in this way – as an investment of time and an expectation of a specific type of pleasure – disarms the MPF because I am not actually emotionally involved with the fictional Tyrion, but with real-life structures.

The general idea of this chapter, then, is that it is possible to take the above line of reasoning and apply it to the paradox of fiction. In other words, it is possible to circumvent the classic solution to the paradox of fiction – denying (2) – in such a way that what our emotions pertain to are not fictional characters but real-life structures, including the investment of time or narrative expectations. Moreover, once we recognize the existence of the MPF we have a novel (and more pressing) incentive to solve the paradox of fiction which goes beyond epistemological concerns. At the same time, my position differs from that of the (counter)factualists who claim that there are no occasions when we emotionally engage fictional entities (Weston, 1975, Paskins, 1977, Charlton 1984, 1986, McCormick, 1988). In other words, what I do claim is that numerous classic examples in these discussions can be rearticulated as pertaining to different real-life structures. In other words, this is more about arguing that the paradox of fiction can oftentimes be sidestepped than about arguing what the solution to the paradox is. Put in yet another way, I am more interested in trying to articulate the phenomenological experience of the varied causes and objects of emotions in engaging fiction and the accompanying moral problem (after all, the personal anecdotal evidence I return to so much has been the original impetus for this chapter), than in proceeding by way of eliminating specific premises constituting the paradox of fiction (1, 2, or 3).

Not fearing fictions

Kendall Walton's slime and Charles, its fearful spectator, offers itself as the first case study on which to test the idea.[5] According to Walton's famous example, when Charles, a stand-in for the standard spectator, watches a horror film and is faced with a green slime on screen, he fears the monster: 'His muscles are tensed, he clutches his chair, his pulse quickens, his adrenalin flows. Let us call this physiological/psychological state "quasi-fear"' (1978: 6). The fact that Walton speaks of quasi-emotions, as explained above, and denies (1) rather than (2), should not worry us because the point here is to sidestep the paradox rather than to probe its standard solutions. In other words, I propose that Charles does not fear the slime at all (genuinely or quasi) but a real-life structure instead. Interestingly, Walton briefly addresses the possibility that Charles's fear is about real-life matters and not of the slime:

> If Charles is a child, the movie may make him wonder whether there might not be real slimes or other exotic horrors like the one depicted in the movie, even if he fully realizes that the movie-slime itself is not real. Charles may well fear these suspected actual dangers; he might have nightmares about them for days afterwards (*Jaws* caused a lot of people to fear sharks which they thought might really exist. But whether they were afraid of the fictional sharks in the movie is another question).
>
> (Walton, 1978: 10)

This is his only reference to the solution and Walton dismisses the option as quickly as he introduces it. I, however, do not think that he is right in eliminating the explanation as a fringe phenomenon or as relating to a different matter. In fact, it seems to me that standard monster horror films, the subgenre from which Walton takes his example, hinge precisely on this type of reaction for their emotional effects. Consider the subgenre's typical bipartite structure – before and after the monster's full reveal – and the three broad ways – suspense, surprise, and appearance – in which the fear of the monster may be generated.[6]

The structural pivot around which most monster horrors revolve is usually what Carroll (1990b) refers to as onset while I prefer to call it the full reveal of the monster.[7] The first part usually rests on building up suspense and fearful expectations in preparation for the revelation of the monster by showing the signs of the monster here and there. This can be done by a range of techniques – use of negative space, character blocking, underexposure, shadows, atypical movement, tight framing, camera movement, shot prolongation, ominous sounds and music, infrasound, etc. Crucially, the monster will eventually be revealed in full. As guides for writing horror films suggest (Blake and Bailey 2013 and Bell 2020), once the monster has finally fully revealed itself, precisely because the spectator now knows what the monster she was fearing is and how it looks and sounds, the general fear levels seem to drop off and different fear-inducing strategies need to be deployed in the subsequent part of the film. Building suspense at this point can only go so far and strategies usually change to eliciting fear by surprise or by appearance (visual and audio alike).[8]

To flesh out this bipartite structure and the threefold fear-inducing strategy, let us briefly consider the short film *Lights Out* (David F. Sandberg, 2013).[9] In the first part of the film, the protagonist turns the light on and off a couple of times because each time it is off, a silhouette appears at the end of her corridor. She stops this when, in a partially revealing jump scare (followed by a discordant sound to keep the unease), the being abruptly appears only a foot away from her but now with its back turned to the camera. Once the protagonist retires to bed (with her corridor and bed light on), the suspense continues with the play of approaching off-screen sounds, the switching off of the light in the corridor, her bedroom doors creaking, and her bed light slowly losing power. Trembling, she manages to fix the bed light, the light returns to the corridor as well, and she sighs with relief, but it is all just to make the finale more potent – a jump scare cut to a close-up of the fully revealed monster with the light switch in its fingers. Again, the discordant sound plays, and the light goes out …

I propose that until the full reveal, the fear elicited is not of some fictional monster partially visible only in the dark but rather of an implausible yet logical possibility that something like this might be lurking somewhere in the real world. That monsters might indeed exist. That something horrendous like this might happen. That one day we might be in a situation of this sort. What films of this sort do is, I suggest, to tap into a scientifically irrational, but strictly speaking not illogical fear that there are dark stones left unturned. Suspense of the reveal, then, is really about the minuscule possibility that the world is not free of monsters after all. In the end, there is no logical reason why something like the being from *Lights Out* could not exist in the real world. Perhaps we have simply not come across it hitherto.

To put it in terms of mandates and phenomenology of imaginative engagement, and to expand on a line of thinking about fleshing out imaginings from the previous chapter, the film does not mandate imagining anything of the above, but it does provide an opportunity to pursue imaginings of this type. In other words, not only do horror films stimulate lines of thought about all types of potential monsters that may yet exist they also provide fertile ground for fleshing out those thoughts in imaginings. But as I argued earlier, these are suggestions rather than mandates proper.

Once the monster in *Lights Out* is fully revealed, the object of fear is again better described as one of real-life structures rather than that of the fictional monster. First, the reveal itself is frightening precisely because it hinges on the representational suddenness of the jump scare rather than on the nature of the fictional being. There is a loud noise, something jumps onto the screen.

As numerous horrors demonstrate, the subject of the jump scare need not be frightening in itself. So long as it is unexpected it will work. This is the shock quality of the manner of representation rather than of what is represented.

Of course, in this particular instance the shot is a reveal of the monster – the camera lingers on for a moment and allows us to take in its visual appearance, a woman-like figure with blank eyes where pupil and iris should be, wide open mouth, and sharp teeth (Figure 6). As such, it is precisely what Walton had in mind when discussing the slime – the moment the spectator faces the frightful being. But again, there is no reason to say that what is frightening is the fictional monster. Rather, we can say that what is frightening is primarily what Walton (1990) would call the prop in the game of make-believe that is fiction. We are afraid of the *appearance* of the person made up to look like they have blank eyes and sharp-looking teeth – the prop – rather than of the make-believe monster who is about to murder its victim. In this case, our fear arises from the uneasy feeling that something is almost human but not quite (certainly the case in contemporary zombie films). Many times, fictions can also capitalize on other hardwired phobias such as those of snakes and spiders or, in the audio domain, of shrieking sounds.

Does this not contradict what I have been claiming in the previous chapter? There I have argued that imaginative resistance is due to rich imagining of clashing effects including experiential imagining. More specifically, I proposed that perceptual imagining sometimes necessarily entails experiential imagining as in the case when we are mandated to imagine certain fictional entities as scary. If that is the case, are we also not supposed to imagine experientially the *Lights Out* monster as scary? And is this not essentially the same as imagining being afraid meaning that we are afraid of the fictional monster after all?

It is true that we are mandated to imagine being afraid, but the mandate does not necessarily mean that the viewer will actually imagine what she is mandated to imagine. And this is not meant in the sense of resistance, but

FIGURE 6 ***It is the prop in* Lights Out *(David F. Sandberg, 2013) rather than the imagined fictional monster that is frightening.***

simply in the sense explained in Chapters Two and Four that there is no need to imagine perceptually and experientially to understand the film. Moreover, imagining being scared and being scared are two different things. It is possible that the former, if rich enough, may lead to the latter. We may imagine the blank eyes and the sharp-looking teeth in detail and shiver in response. But in principle the two are distinct. More importantly, there already is something that is scary-looking – and that is the prop.

Why not say that both play a role in eliciting fear – both the actual effect of the prop and the imagining of being afraid? Taking the lesson from the previous chapter about individual variability in imaginative engagement to heart I do not wish to categorically deny this possibility. But the response to the prop must still be the dominant cause for a number of reasons. The prop functions at the level of fundamental understanding of the image – to recognize the prop on the profilmic level is also to recognize its scary-looking features and have an emotional reaction to them. This happens automatically. Moreover, precisely because there is no clash between the demands of photographic verisimilitude and the content of the story as far as the mandated perceptual and entailed experiential imagining of the monster is concerned, there is no need to pursue the mandate and even less to flesh it out in horizontal detail.

What is the upshot of arguing that we fear real-life structures rather than fictional entities beyond sidestepping the paradox of fiction and not running afoul of the MPF? First, the offered explanation deals with at least three types of the *fear of* in monster horrors – what is coming next (suspense), jump scares (surprise), and props (appearance). By contrast, Walton (and most of the participants in the debate) tackle only the appearance type of *fear of*. (In fact, as can be seen from the discussion of Tyrion, my explanation also covers *fear for* a fictional character.) Moreover, Walton would not deny that the jump scares work on the level of how something is represented rather than what is represented. And there are also techniques such as shrieking sounds which elicit immediate fear responses. So, if there is at least one type of *fear of* in monster horrors which is undeniably due to real-life structures, I propose that an account which rests solely on real-life structures is theoretically simpler and more elegant than the one which needs to deal with fictional entities.

Admittedly, I have explained the suspense type of *fear of* with recourse to implausible yet logical hypotheticals – what if something like the depicted monster actually exists? Although I have referred to this in terms of real-life structures, hypotheticals are imaginings as much as imaginings involved in fictional engagement. In other words, why prefer one solution over the other if both involve imaginings? Because this is a better description of what the phenomenological experience of the object of fear is in monster horror than the one offered by Walton. This brings me to the second upshot of this analysis. It reveals that the essence of monster horrors is not the fear of fictional monsters but the irrational fear for oneself. Irrational here is meant not in Radford's sense of normativity, but in the sense that contrary to standard evidence we still cling on to the implausible yet logical possibility, dramatized by horrors, that monsters might exist and that we might encounter them. After all, why are people afraid to turn the lights off even after the monster film has ended? They must be afraid of some horrific real-life possibility rather than the fictional monster from the film.

The last upshot of this account is that it explains the structure of the monster horror genre. If we feared the monster because of its fictional nature rather than its prop-like qualities, then once the monster is fully revealed – as a slime, ghost nun, zombie, etc. – it is reasonable to assume that we should fear it even more given that now we fully know its horrifying nature and what it is capable of. But that does not seem to be the case. Usually, the moment of unveiling is as anticlimactic as it is climactic precisely because thereafter, we know what it is that we were anticipating. Once the focus shifts from the monster to the protagonist after the full reveal, and what Carroll refers to as confrontation is being set up, we do not fear the monster during that period. But arguably, we are still supposed to imagine a monster on the loose and, given its nature, we should still be afraid of it even if the film is presently not focused either on it or its signs. If it were the nature of the monster that frightens us, simply entertaining in imagination that it has proved itself threatening should keep us scared. But in the absence of screen time, i.e. where fear-generating strategies are missing, make-believing the monster alone does not suffice to scare us. This demonstrates that it is not the fictional entity that we fear but real-life structures evoked by the aforementioned strategies.[10] This is also why looking away and shutting our eyes during the projection temporarily rids us of fear.

It is worth pausing here for a moment and articulating this further with the help of Carroll's definition of art-horror. According to him, we are art-horrified by a monster if and only if our state of agitation has been caused by the thought that the monster is possible and that it is threatening and impure (Carroll, 1990b: 27). Given that art-horror is different from fear for Carroll and that for horror impurity plays a vital role, we can bracket off the notions of art-horror and impurity. This allows us to say that we fear a fictional monster if and only if our state of agitation has been caused by the thought that the monster is possible and that it is threatening. My point is that following the full reveal we keep imagining (a subset of thinking) the monster's possibility and its threatening nature, yet this does not cause us to fear. This suggests that it is not the fictional monster that is scaring us but the fear-inducing strategies. Crucially, these strategies – suspense, surprise, and appearance – all boil down to real-life structures.

If we disregard the cases when mandated experiential imaginings are taken up and fleshed out, we can formalize the argument as follows:

1) The fictional monster in horror is a specific content of mandated imagination,

2) The fictional monster in horror either causes quasi-fear (Walton, 1978) or fear (Carroll, 1990b),

3) From 1) and 2) it follows that in horror it is the specific content of mandated imagination that causes either quasi-fear or fear,

4) Yet, in horror, the specific content of mandated imagination on its own typically neither causes quasi-fear nor fear,

5) From 3) and 4) it follows that the fictional monster in horror neither causes quasi-fear nor-fear,

6) Yet, horror causes either quasi-fear or fear,

7) In horror it is either the fictional monster that causes quasi-fear or fear or it is the real-life structures (suspense, surprise, and appearance) that cause fear,

8) From 6), 7), and 8) it follows that in horror it is typically the real-life structures that cause fear.

Generalizations and their limits

Can these claims about real-life structures as both causes and objects of emotions be applied more generally outside of horror and the emotion of fear?

The example that has commanded the most attention in discussions of this sort is, of course, Anna Karenina. Although the majority view today is that we do feel for the fictional character Anna, in the past it has been argued that we feel for some real-life structures instead. Barrie Paskins (1977) and William Charlton (1984, 1986) proposed that we have feelings towards people who are or could be like Anna. Michael Weston (1975) and Peter McCormick (1988) suggested variants of the view that feelings are due to general truths about life that issue from the works. These views purport to be general solutions to the paradox of fiction so only one counterexample is enough to disqualify them (cf. Yanal, 1999). Indeed, sympathy with Tony Soprano undermines Paskins' and Charlton's position because were there somebody like Tony Soprano in real life, we would not sympathize with him. The issue here is that the emotions towards the fictional Tony and the hypothetical real-life Tony are quite different – sympathy and opprobrium, respectively. Sympathy for the fictional Tony is also a problem for Weston and McCormick because this sympathy can hardly be because of some general truth *The Sopranos* conveys, whatever that might be. In fact, my analysis of fear also presents a challenge to their formulations. Fearing surprises like jump scares and appearances like props is neither to do with people who are or could be like the green slime, nor about general truths. And fearing for Tyrion is about something else altogether: expectations and time investment.

Although (counter)factualists' claims cannot be generalized to all fictional emotions, this does not mean that (counter)factualists are incorrect when it comes to examples like Anna's. Radford's insistence that it is *her* that we pity and not somebody else (who might be) like her is not a problem because, under Paskins's account, to pity *Anna* is precisely to pity somebody (who might be) like her. The same logic also applies well to the already mentioned infatuation with Edward Cullen. Being smitten by a character like him, I propose, is accurately described as obsessing about, however far-fetched, the possibility that somebody as good-looking and gentle, yet at the same time exciting and dangerous might come into one's teenage life. Like above, the real-life truth here is that there could be somebody (who might be) like Edward.[11]

But despite my best efforts to the contrary, it remains the case that it is difficult to completely deny proposition (1) in the paradox of fiction. Sympathy and antipathy towards fictional characters are emotions which are difficult to rearticulate as real-life structures. In other words, on top of wise-cracking remarks which can be enjoyed on the level of their non-fictional content, as demonstrated by their publication in an illustrated book form as *The Wit & Wisdom of Tyrion Lannister*, I think it is correct to say that I was genuinely harbouring positive emotional dispositions towards Tyrion as a fictional character, i.e. as a make-believe structure. Although I was not genuinely afraid *for* Tyrion or upset that *he* might die, I think it is fair to say that I like *Tyrion*.

Something similar holds for Anna and Edward. While it is possible to rearticulate the pity and infatuation towards them as a pity and infatuation towards somebody who is like them, the same does not seem to work for sympathy (or for those who are annoyed with them, antipathy) towards them. We seem to dis/like this specific Anna and this specific Edward. Although we have provided a more precise account of the object of emotions in Charles's and some other key cases, the paradox of fiction appears to persist.

But this does not mean there has not been any headway on the matter. There is something in common among the emotions whose objects we have identified as real-life structures as opposed to the ones whose objects remain fictional entities – the existence of clearly associated actions, i.e. behavioural responses. In real-life contexts, whereas emotions regularly involve objects (cf. Friend,

2017), only some emotions entail typical actions.[12] Fear, for instance, entails flight (from the object) or fight (with the object). Pitying somebody regularly generates helping him or her. Aggressive behaviour towards the object typically accompanies hatred. Standard action accompanying infatuation is seeking closeness to the object. By contrast, sympathy and antipathy lack clearly associated actions. The emotions entail feeling generally positively or negatively inclined towards the object, respectively, but do not specify a clear action issuing therefrom. We may give a person who we sympathize with a thumbs up or frown at the person we feel antipathy for, but these are hardly clearly defined action types as above. Moreover, in cases of sympathy and antipathy, no action at all is also a perfectly typical behavioural response.

We might say, then, that the emotions elicited by real-life structures, unlike the ones induced by fictional entities, have a strong and clear action potential insofar they have a clearly associated behavioural reaction with them. This chimes well with one of the main traits of fictional entities – their general dissociation from behavioural effects. If fictional entities generally do not have behavioural effects, it is reasonable that fictional entities would only generate emotions which have no clearly associated actions. Conversely, it would also make sense that fictional entities do not generate emotions which have clearly associated actions. Similarly, only real-life structures should generate emotions which have clear behavioural reactions (although they can also generate emotions without clearly associated actions).[13] And this is precisely the result that the above analysis of fictional monsters and characters produces. In other words, we could hypothesize that fictions generate only a subclass of emotions related to real-life structures – those without clearly associated actions.

What remains is the status of the MPF. The emotions elicited by real-life structures identified here – fear, infatuation, hatred, pity – are also of higher intensity than those elicited by fictional entities – sympathy and antipathy. This looks promising for the MPF for it is how *much* we care that is at stake. At the same time, both sympathy and antipathy might be said to cause the MPF if emotions towards real-life people are of lower intensity or non-existent. It is possible to have more sympathy for Tyrion than for, say, a deserving local troubled youngster. In this case we might want to say that the problem is not really MPF but a *pathological* issue in the sense that our normal reaction to *real-life people* should be stronger. The MPF is really about the fact that even when we *normally* react to real-life structures, it is still the case that the *normal* reaction to fiction is more intense than to real-life structures, which seems scandalous. Whatever its solution might be, I hope the chapter has demonstrated that the MPF is ripe for exploration and that it may also help us rethink the paradox of fiction.

7

Fiction, belief and knowledge acquisition

In the first two chapters of Part Three I have focused on the relationship between mandated imaginings, actual imaginative engagement, and the effects of fictional works. The last effect that I will address is belief acquisition. This is both due to the importance that the distinction between imagination and belief has played in the definitions of fiction (mine included) and the key assumption in film studies that fiction film influences real-life beliefs. I will place this discussion in the broader framework of knowledge acquisition and aesthetic cognitivism.

The debate about the potential value of art can be tracked to at least Plato's banning of artists from his ideal *Republic* for misrepresenting the world and thereby corrupting its citizens (Plato, 1997). In doing so, Plato also set the terms of the debate which has since mostly revolved around whether art can be a source of epistemological and/or ethical knowledge (Aristotle, 1987, Horace, 1990, Boileau, 1674, Schiller, 1794, Spivak, 2012). Put differently, the value of art has traditionally been construed in terms of the potential, on the one hand, for conveying truths about the world (Walsh, 1969, Lamarque and Olsen, 1994) and, on the other, in promoting ethical development (Shelley, 1891, Levinson, 1998). While in its broader sense, aesthetic cognitivism may be said to cover both these claims, in this chapter I want to investigate only the former given the traditional link between justified true belief and knowledge. I will refer to this as aesthetic cognitivism narrowly understood.

It is important to keep in mind that aesthetic cognitivism in all its form is an optimistic take on the debate. Insofar, aesthetic cognitivists follow Aristotle's lead in arguing about the benefits of art. Aristotle, of course, was responding to Plato who staked out the pessimist position by arguing that art has negative impact. Film studies have traditionally espoused the pessimist outlook on film fiction. Where optimists purport that art expresses truth, pessimists insist that it peddles in lies. Where optimists argue that art can justify the truths it conveys, pessimists respond that it capitalizes on various illusionistic strategies meant to lower our critical skills. But regardless of their differences, both optimists and pessimists agree that art influences real-life beliefs. That the former claim that art instils justified true beliefs, while the latter see imprinting of unjustified false beliefs, does not change the underlying agreement about the power of art to impart beliefs. And this agreement is what this chapter seeks to challenge by arguing that fiction films are not effective in instilling real-life beliefs. In other words, while the chapter focuses on narrow aesthetic cognitivists or the optimistic side of the debate, the core of the argument – that belief acquisition is far less prevalent than assumed by either optimists or pessimists – is directed against both camps.

In what remains, I will argue that, while narrow aesthetic cognitivism and the pessimistic epistemic claims of film studies as its flipside are certainly a possibility, as it stands philosophers and film scholars subscribing to their respective views have not produced convincing arguments in favour of their core claim about imparting beliefs. That is because they have primarily engaged in theoretical debates rather than in discussions of existing empirical literature on the subject. To make my case, in the first section I distinguish between weak, narrow and broad aesthetic cognitivism. I argue that the debates about aesthetic cognitivism are not really about art in general but about fictional works instead.

I will then propose that the scope of the narrow claim needs to be quantified with more care than has been hitherto. To do so, I focus on the types of fictional works, potential benefactors, and type of knowledge relevant for the debate. I suggest that the real focus is on highbrow and middlebrow works, audiences instead of fiction makers, truths about the non-aesthetic world rather than the aesthetic one, and truths conveyed by the works qua fictions as opposed to works qua texts. Specifically, I investigate claims to propositional truth because the acquisition of these appears to be the simplest to prove for the narrow aesthetic cognitivist.

The next three sections survey three types of arguments in favour of the narrow claim and demonstrate that they fail to accomplish what they set out to do. The first which purports that fictional work sometimes expresses truths is found lacking because for the work to impart knowledge it must justify this truth. Even instances of conceptual knowledge need to justify that the concepts developed in a work are applicable outside the world of fiction. Knowledge conferred about possibilities, finally, is essentially trivial.

I tackle the argument that fictional works do justify their truths or, more precisely, that their justification is no different than that of truths in nonfictional works in section four. I concede that in the end the justification of truths in both types of works rests on the experiences outside of the text. But we should not forget that the institution of fiction operates with a significantly different tacit agreement than the institutions of history or science. While the latter ask the audiences to believe, the former primarily mandates them to imagine. This means that regardless of whether truths conveyed are justified or not it is an empirical question of whether they end up being believed or not.

Section five addresses narrow aesthetic cognitivists who appeal to empirical studies to support their claims. I argue that while there certainly exist studies which show that engagement with fictional works leads to acquisition of real-life beliefs, the most recent meta-analysis on the subject evinces that overall fictional works are not an effective means for imparting beliefs about the non-aesthetic world. I also discuss how this finding undermines a string of proposals from psychology and philosophy about the mechanisms of belief acquisition.

If belief acquisition is far less prevalent than thought, I tackle the question of why the idea to the contrary is so widespread in the chapter's last section. Among the potential reasons I discuss are the long traditions of the idea in different cultures, the long history of censorship, anecdotal evidence, and the demands of academic disciplines to keep their subject matter relevant.

Weak, broad and narrow aesthetic cognitivism

Here is a sample of explicit articulations of aesthetic cognitivism.

> Aesthetic cognitivism may be said to be the view that art at its best is a form of understanding and as such, though it differs greatly in other respects, is to be accorded the same evaluative status as science, a status which its undoubted capacity to entertain and give us pleasure could not justify.
>
> (Graham, 1996: 1)

> Aesthetic cognitivism […] is best thought of as conjunction of two claims: first, that art can give us (non-trivial) knowledge, and second, that the capacity of art to give us (non-trivial) knowledge (partly) determines its value *qua* art, i.e. its aesthetic value.
>
> (Gaut, 2005: 437)

> Aesthetic cognitivism and aesthetic anti-cognitivism can be defined as opposing responses to two questions: (1) Can art provide knowledge? And, if it can, (2) how is this aesthetically relevant?
>
> (Thomson-Jones, 2005: 376)

> [T]he claim that narrative art is a source of truth, capable of transferring knowledge and other cognitively relevant states (aesthetic cognitivism)
>
> (Vidmar Jovanović 2019a)

> One possibility is that art can promote new knowledge and understanding, a notion referred to as *aesthetic cognitivism*.
>
> (Christensen, Cardillo, and Chatterjee, 2025: 1)

As we can see the claims are both quite broad and quite weak. In the former case, Gaut and Thomson-Jones point out that the key component of aesthetic cognitivism is not only the epistemic import of art but that this epistemic payoff is also a key part of the aesthetic value of art. Concerning the latter, their proponents explicitly state than only some art conveys knowledge or that art can on occasions be of epistemic value by conveying knowledge.

Here, I will be focusing exclusively on the question of epistemic value without exploring whether or how it relates to the problem of aesthetic value. But I want to be even narrower than that. I also want to delimit 'knowledge' that I will be addressing from those more broadly understood 'form[s] of understanding' and 'other cognitively relevant states'. Here I am discounting potential wider cognitive benefits such as the positive impact of art on imagination, emotions, curiosity, reasoning, etc. I will also not be addressing the debate on whether art conveys moral knowledge (Nussbaum, 1990, Gaut, 2005, Plantinga, 2018). For one, a recent research project led by Iris Vidmar Jovanović explicitly treats moral knowledge under a banner distinct from aesthetic cognitivism which she refers to as aesthetic education: 'the exploration of the transformative power of aesthetic experience with respect to one's ethical development' (2019a).[1] The other reason is that scepticism of moral knowledge is far more prevalent than scepticism about traditional knowledge making the debate potentially moot (Campbell, 2019). Instead, I am zeroing in on less controversial forms of knowledge usually captured under the banners of *know that*, *know how*, and *know what it is like* that I will outline in the next section.

The second point I want to address pertains to the 'weakness' of the claim. In the forms expressed above, it is hard to deny that art *can* and does convey knowledge. Religious art regularly conveys religious truths. Michelangelo's *Sistine Chapel Ceiling* (1508–12) imparts, among other things, the knowledge that in the Christian tradition God created Adam. Calvary paintings standardly inform the viewer that in the same tradition Jesus was crucified and died on the cross. Portraiture usually provides information about how the subject looked. Jacques-Louis David's painting *Portrait of Pope Pius VII* (1805) tells us a lot about the facial features of the eponymous sitter at the time the painting was made. Eddie Adams's photograph *Execution of Nguyễn Văn Lém* (1968) informs us not only about the appearance of both the victim and his executioner but also about a number of things about the act of killing (type of gun, place, its summary nature, etc.) as well as of the emotions of the two people at the fateful moment. *Grizzly Bear* (2005), a documentary by Werner Herzog, imparts next to, again, a range of visual information (about how its protagonist Timothy Treadwell looked like or the places he visited), also the information about Treadwell's life, such as his enthusiasm for grizzlies and eventually death at the hands of one. Truman Capote's 1966 nonfiction novel *In Cold Blood* teaches the readers about the particularly gruesome murders that took place in Holcomb, Kansas in 1959. Under this analysis, the weak version of aesthetic cognitivism is trivial, and the underlying claim must be stronger.

That this is the case and that the quoted general formulations are somewhat disingenuous is evinced by the fact that the discussions that follow regularly turn to fictional narrative arts such as literature and film. Graham (1996) immediately turns to literary fiction as does Gaut (2005) and Vidmar Jovanović's team is explicit that they are concerned with narrative art and in practice tackle fictional narratives.[2] In other words, the non-trivial discussions about whether art imparts traditional forms of knowledge are really about whether fictional works of art do so. In the first instance, therefore, I take (non-trivial) narrow aesthetic cognitivism to mean something like fictional works convey knowledge.[3]

Narrow aesthetic cognitivism

In the previous section the problem of quantification already arose, but there I discussed it in terms of the claims' 'weakness'. While modals and quantifiers are not the same thing, the way in which proponents of narrow aesthetic cognitivism articulated in terms of 'can' proceeded to evince their position was to find examples of at least *some* fictional works which convey knowledge. This is why I also framed my discussion as a list of examples vindicating the weak thesis. And while I have avoided modals in my formulation of narrow aesthetic cognitivism, the problem remains. Would one fictional work of art suffice to evince narrow aesthetic cognitivism? Would one person learning something be sufficient? Who is this person who acquires knowledge? How much knowledge? And what is the relevant type of knowledge that should be acquired here? Let us address these questions in turn.

Fictional works

Proponents of narrow aesthetic cognitivism do not usually explicitly address what subset of fiction is relevant. One option is that the discussion here is really about high fiction. The examples that reappear in the discussions such as Tolstoy and Dickens are certainly consistent with this version. However, when narrow aesthetic cognitivists address other media more middlebrow examples start appearing including *Mission Impossible* and *Alien* series as well as *Game of Thrones*. This suggests that the implicit relevant subset is at least something like high- and middlebrow fiction. Importantly, we are talking about fiction *stories.* When in the rest of the chapter I write something like fiction imparts knowledge I take this to mean a significant subset of fiction stories of at least high- and middlebrow nature imparts knowledge.

Beneficiaries

The statement that fiction confers knowledge does not specify who the beneficiaries are. I suggest that we should be interested here more in the audiences than in the makers of fiction because it is uncontroversial that making a fiction involves a more sustained engagement than reading, watching, or listening to it. For instance, writers regularly learn about the subject of their writing. It is hard to deny that in writing three books about Thomas Cromwell, Hillary Mantel acquired substantial knowledge about her protagonist and sixteenth-century England. The same holds for directors and screenwriters. In making *Oppenheimer* (2023), Christopher Nolan must have learned a lot about the eponymous physicist's life. In bringing characters to life through performance, actors learn about the people they portray. Through filming *The Iron Lady* (Phyllida Lloyd, 2011), Meryl Streep acquired, among other things, knowledge of both how Margaret Thatcher's movements look and how her voice sounds as well as how to imitate them.

It might be objected that it is not really fiction making that confers knowledge here but the *preparation* for the production of an artwork, i.e. the research that precedes it is the relevant process. On this account, Mantel learns about Cromwell and his times not by writing proper but through reading the books about the man and the period which she only later applies to writing. The same holds for Nolan and other biopic makers. And for Streep, similarly, it is watching and listening to the tapes of Thatcher that secures the actor's knowledge about her subject, not the performance itself.

The objection holds only under an improperly limited understanding of what it means to make fictional works. This cannot exclusively refer to the acts of putting certain words on paper, instructing the film crew what to do, or making certain bodily movements in front of the camera. Making fiction also entails researching one's subject, thinking about how to execute one's craft, drafting, and redrafting what has been done with reference to previous research and attempts, etc. This is no different from producing an academic piece – in writing this chapter I have learned a lot about aesthetic cognitivism. But on the limited view of academic writing which entails only the typing of the words and leaves out the preceding research I would have acquired no knowledge. Moreover, even this limited view which considers writing only to be the act of putting words on paper must admit that this act of writing is not merely the movement of hands but also involves a lot of mental processing such as organizing of thoughts and articulation of those thoughts in words. Similarly, the very act of executing one's craft, be it novelists' and scriptwriters' writing, instructing the film crew, or moving for the camera, also brings clarity to the ideas that one has about the subject of that craft. So even in putting the words on paper and formulating her sentences Mantel must have formed new connections and gained a clearer picture of Cromwell and early modern England. In instructing Cillian Murphy on how to perform, Nolan must have arrived at a firmer grasp of Oppenheimer and his motives. In performing for the camera through multiple takes Streep must have developed her knowledge of how to sound and move more like Thatcher.[4]

Therefore, it is hard to deny that fiction regularly confers knowledge to its makers. The more controversial question – and certainly the one that has garnered more attention but remains underspecified in the definitions of aesthetic cognitivism – is whether fiction conveys knowledge *to its audiences*.

Once this is determined, we also need to ask what the size of the effect is. In other words, what subsets of audiences should gain knowledge for narrow aesthetic cognitivism to hold? There appears to be agreement that the audiences who will profit are those who are sufficiently attentive. Gregory Currie, for instance, talks about 'suitably prepared readers' (2020: 158).

Vidmar Jovanović has in mind 'an active, reflective reader' (2019b: 366). Stacie Friend, similarly, argues that all audiences are expert audiences for at least some genre (2014: 244). At the same time, narrow aesthetic cognitivists would also probably allow that fiction imparts knowledge of the aesthetic world more easily than knowledge of the non-aesthetic one. Put differently, while these attentive audiences will regularly gain knowledge about the story-world, this will be less frequent for knowledge about the actual world. Put in yet another way, under this view learning from fiction is something like learning through classroom lectures – some students will be able to say what the lecture was about and others not, and a subset of the first will also have learned about some claims made in the lecture while another subset of the same will not. When I write that fiction imparts knowledge from hereon, then, this is shorthand for saying that a subset of fiction stories of at least high- and middlebrow nature imparts knowledge to a significant subset of audiences.

Knowledge

It is also uncontroversial to say that all fiction conveys knowledge, if we do not specify what kind of knowledge we are interested in. Put otherwise, if we take knowledge simply to mean some form of justified true belief, then fictions regularly convey knowledge about what is true in the world of fiction. Upon reading *Anna Karenina* audiences learn, among many other things, that Tolstoy's heroine killed herself by jumping in front of a train. Furthermore, audiences regularly acquire knowledge of genre conventions by consuming fiction. After a certain number of contemporary zombie horror films, audiences recognize that in these films humans are oftentimes a greater danger to protagonists than the zombies. Having seen a sufficient string of whodunnits, audiences will know that the convention of the genre is an elaborate revelation of how the crime was committed and by whom in the last act by the protagonist. By engaging with an artform, the audiences will also gain knowledge of the stylistic features and narrative structure of that artform such as that the events depicted through parallel editing usually take place at the same time or that there is a certain class of narrators who are not to be trusted. While the knowledge about the fictional story might be trivial, the ensuing examples become less and less so, essentially moving into some basic, but crucial, territory of formal analysis and narratology. Yet, I suggest, because the acquisition of such knowledge is not controversial and/or because all these types of knowledge are about a specific work of fiction or fiction in general, discussion of narrow aesthetic cognitivism has mostly skirted the subject.[5] Put differently, narrow aesthetic cognitivism is dominantly interested in whether fiction conveys *non-aesthetic knowledge* to its audiences, i.e. the knowledge of the world (minus the world of art).

But I should be more precise and list at least some of the relevant types of knowledge that narrow aesthetic cognitivism is interested in within that non-aesthetic brand. These are: perceptual, propositional, experiential, social and how to knowledge.[6]

Perceptual knowledge relates to how something appears to the senses: how it looks, sounds, smells, feels, or tastes. At present, fiction standardly conveys only visual and sound information. As such, we may, for instance, be interested in whether *Jurassic Park* (Steven Spielberg, 1993) conveys knowledge about how Tyrannosaurus Rex looked and sounded, or, to use the above example, how Margaret Thatcher appeared, moved, and spoke. But there are some relevant examples of knowledge import which are difficult to deny. For instance, *Vertigo* (Alfred Hitchcock, 1958) confers, among other things, knowledge of how James Stewart and Kim Novak looked at the time of the shooting, as well as of what the appearance of different places in San Francisco was at the same time. More generally, every photographic fiction film conveys a plethora of historical information on the visual aspects of various entities including the actors, locations, and whatever was in front of the camera at that moment.[7]

Does this not mean that narrow aesthetic cognitivism is vindicated for there is a significant subset of fiction – namely photographic film fiction – which provides nontrivial non-aesthetic knowledge to its audiences? I suggest this depends on what aspect of fiction narrow aesthetic cognitivism takes to be important for conferring knowledge. The absence of discussions about the above point suggests that narrow aesthetic cognitivism is not really interested in this type of knowledge. I assume this is because the reason behind the imparting of knowledge in this case is medium properties – the photographic nature of traditional fiction film – rather than fiction *qua* fiction. The perceptual knowledge is conferred because conventionally photographic fiction film hinges on verisimilar photography. Except for, perhaps, radio drama there is no equivalent of imparting perceptual knowledge among other fictions.[8] Were the acquisition of knowledge due to aspects different than basic medium properties, I assume those debating narrow aesthetic cognitivism would have taken more interest. Instead, the implicit demands seem to be that the imparting of the knowledge should come through fiction qua *fictional representation.*

What certainly commands considerable if not the most interest in these debates is propositional knowledge of the form knowing that *p* (Stolnitz, 1992, Gaut, 2005, Gibson, Huemer, Pocci, 2007, Vidmar Jovanović, 2019b, McGregor, 2021a, Slugan, 2021a). Here the discussion is most often about statements about the world as it is. The question here is, do audiences, by reading Mantel's trilogy about Cromwell and watching Nolan's film about Oppenheimer acquire knowledge about these and related historical persons. When reading the sentence from the second instalment *Bring Up the Bodies* (2012) – '"Cromwell has the skin of a lily", the king pronounces' – do audiences learn something propositional about Cromwell or Henry VIII such as the shade of Cromwell's skin and/or his king's opinions about it? When watching the opening of *Oppenheimer* and seeing the titular character read the statement at a hearing do audiences learn something specific about the theoretical physicist such as the exact words that he said at the time in question or how he felt when saying them? Propositions can, of course, be broader and relate to general social and human condition such as the opening sentences of *Anna Karenina* – 'All happy families are alike; each unhappy family is unhappy in its own way' – raising the question of whether novels impart such lessons. And propositions need not be explicit but may be implicitly conveyed through fiction such as 'drug crime is a structural problem' that is generally agreed to be articulated in *The Wire* (HBO, 2002–8). In the next section, when we discuss strategies for answering these questions, we will see that the crucial thing to remember here is that audiences need to learn from fiction unlike makers who learn from the process of making fiction based on research.[9]

An important subclass of propositional knowledge is the knowledge of possibilities, hypotheticals, and counterfactuals. In this case, it has been debated whether fiction confers knowledge of what might happen and what could have happened (Putnam, 1978, Gaut, 2005, McGregor, 2021a). Does, for instance, Dora Lessing's *The Golden Notebook* (1966) account of her heroine impart knowledge of a possible person in a specific historical period? Does Marlon James's *A Brief History of Seven Killings* (2014) confer CIA as a possible cause of crime and social harm in 1970s Jamaica?

Another type of knowledge relevant for narrow aesthetic cognitivism is experiential or phenomenal knowledge, a knowledge equivalent to experiential imagining. This is the knowledge of what it is to have experiences more complex than perceptual ones such as what is to be in love, what is to be in mourning, as well as, less dramatically, how is it to ride a horse or go deep diving (Walsh, 1969, Putnam, 1978, Gaut, 2005, McGregor, 2021a, Slugan, 2021a).[10] This type of knowledge also covers a particularly valued knowledge among aesthetic cognitivists of how it is to be in somebody else's shoes (Smith, 2017). One question, for instance, might be: does *Memento* (Nolan, 2000) teach audiences how it is to have anterograde amnesia? Another: does *Requiem for a Dream* (Darren Aronofsky, 2000) confer how the high of using controlled substances feels like?

The last type of knowledge falling under narrow aesthetic cognitivism I will address is how-to or practical knowledge. This knowledge type involves non-propositional knowledge of how to undertake certain activities such as how to type with all ten fingers, how to play the guitar, how to tie a tie, how to score a penalty or how to dance. While it is not impossible that this type of knowledge could be articulated in propositional terms, it is often the case that the people who possess it are unable to do so. From the perspective of this knowledge, perhaps one can learn how to fight by watching kung fu films or how to dance and sing by watching musicals.

There is, admittedly, at least one other form of knowledge which bridges the propositional and practical type and generally refers to the domain of social relations. These include knowledge about human motivation and folk psychology more generally, knowledge of societal norms, how to behave in certain situations, and consequences of not doing so, knowledge about what it means to be a good parent or spouse, etc. It has been argued among those interested in evolutionary aspects of narrative and fiction that these are the reasons why the capacity to tell narratives and convey fictions evolved in the first place (Gottschall, 2008, Hutto, 2012, Boyd, 2018).

I will focus on the acquisition of propositional knowledge as this type is most often debated in literature and arguably the easiest to demonstrate. To do so, I will discuss the general structure of the argument in favour of narrow aesthetic cognitivism and argue that what they present as evidence of the claim is invalid. Many only argue that fiction expresses truth. This fails because for knowledge to be obtained it also needs to be justified. Some also address the issue of justification. But even they regularly assume that justified truth will be automatically believed by the audiences. There is an even smaller group that addresses potential mechanisms of belief acquisition. However, the empirical evidence they cite is selective and leaves out the most recent meta-analysis of the problem, which contradicts their argument. In other words, to argue that fiction confers knowledge to its audiences, one needs to argue that it expresses truth, justifies the truth it conveys, and instils belief in this justified truth.

Does fiction express truth?

In a recent contribution to aesthetic cognitivism, Rafe McGregor (2021a) has argued that fiction imparts at least three types of knowledge about causes of crime and harm – phenomenological, mimetic, and counterfactual. In my typology, McGregor's phenomenological knowledge (e.g. what is it like to live in a war zone through a graphic novel *The Sheriff of Babylon* [Tom King and Mitch Gerard, 2018]) corresponds to experiential knowledge, mimetic or knowledge of everyday reality (e.g. the resources at the disposal of criminal cartels and their appearance via *Miami Vice* [Michael Mann, 2005]) to a combination of perceptual and propositional knowledge, and counterfactual knowledge (e.g. CIA as a possible counterfactual cause of crime in Jamaica in the 1970s through *A Brief History of Seven Killings*) to a subtype of propositional knowledge.[11] While it is certainly possible that all these fictional representations are true, McGregor is generally uninterested in demonstrating the way in which fiction justifies its truth. *Miami Vice*, undeniably, depicts in a rich perceptual way a range of material resources at the cartel's disposal – from motorcades transporting new hires through mobile jammers to hundred-metre killing fields. But given that the audiences are watching a *fiction* film, what is to *justify* them in believing that what is depicted is the case in the real world? McGregor does not tackle the question. Yet, if knowledge is some form of justified true belief, proponents of narrow aesthetic cognitivism need to address the question of how fiction justifies its truths.[12]

A critic of the idea that the discussion of propositional knowledge necessarily needs to involve a discussion of justification, might point out that conceptual knowledge also falls under the banner of propositional knowledge. The critic will point out that this type of knowledge requires no justification through empirical investigation of reality. Gaut (2005), for instance, argues that the knowledge of a definition of a term is conceptual knowledge. If we have been acquainted with the articulation of, say, the notion of 'crystallization' that Stendhal proposes and elaborates upon in his *On Love* (1822) we get to know what crystallization is (Gaut, 2005). While this is true in non-aesthetic settings like the nonfictional treatise *On Love* (which articulates that love essentially rests on attribution of imaginary qualities to the object of love, qualities which are not actually possessed by it), the case is different in fiction.

If the relevant knowledge acquired here is simply what the term means, not whether the proposition the term expresses is true or not, then any instance in which a fictional work explains what a word means should under Gaut's view count as a case of acquiring conceptual knowledge. *Pulp Fiction* (Quentin Tarantino, 1994) opens with a dictionary-style definition of 'pulp'. *The Big Short* (Adam McKay, 2015) has Margo Robbie explain what 'subprime mortgages' are and what 'shorting' means. However, that Gaut (2005: 441) continues his discussion of the defence of conceptual knowledge by saying that the defence may go too far suggests that the truth of the matter is relevant after all. He talks about how the defence fails when applied to know-how and instances in which it turns out that a detailed fictional account of plumbing is completely inaccurate and causes a flood when 'lessons' learned are applied in one's real home. From this perspective, conceptual knowledge can also fail when applied to the real world. It is true that it does not fail in Tarantino and McKay, but that is only accidental. The definitions provided could well have been inaccurate. And given that they occur in fiction, it is a reasonable possibility that they are. In fact, the definitions could also refer to phenomena which are non-existent. Stanisław Lem, for instance, develops a term 'solaristics' – a scientific discipline focusing on the planet Solaris – in his eponymous 1961 novel, but the concept has no real-world equivalent. In other words, learning about the meaning of solaristics does not teach us anything about the non-aesthetic world.

But even if Gaut is correct that there is no need for justification of conceptual knowledge, the question of whether audiences reading *On Love* acquire knowledge of crystallization and whether audiences engaging fictions acquire any knowledge in general is empirical. And rarely has it been tackled by philosophers in a sustained manner as we will see in the section after next.

Before proceeding, a word or two about knowledge of possibilities as a subset of propositional knowledge. Like conceptual knowledge, it could be said that a knowledge of possibility only requires acquaintance with the possibility given that the space of possibilities is much wider than what is actually the case. And fiction excels in conveying detailed stories which are possible, be it very probable historical accounts, plausible gangster and romantic narratives, or improbable but not impossible horror, fantasy, and science fiction tales. On this account, by reading *A History of Seven Killings* audiences become acquainted with a possible history in which the CIA supplied weapons for the assassination attempt on Bob Marley. Two points should be made here.

First, as discussed in Chapter Five, there is much fiction which conveys impossible worlds, be it logically or against the laws of physics. Science fiction often involves travel at or higher than the speed of light which is not allowed by laws of physics. Other fictions involve stories which are logically inconsistent either by mistake or design. Acquaintance with such stories could bring no knowledge of possibilities because what is depicted is impossible. Moreover, if the idea is that acquaintance with fiction in general leads to knowledge of possibilities, then there will be many fictions which form inaccurate beliefs about what is possible.

Second and more importantly, knowledge of possibilities is arguably considerably less weighty than that of what actually is the case and is in a sense trivial. Certainly, upon reading James's novel audiences might arrive at the knowledge that it is possible that the CIA was involved in Marley's assassination attempt. But so could have KGB, MI5, or any other intelligence service for that matter. If a fictional work about a game of dice specifies that the sequence was 3–4–3–2, this does not seem to impart any special knowledge because audiences generally know that any sequence is possible in such a game. It might be retorted that the value is in the level of detail with which this sequence has been represented, how much the players bet, how they felt when betting, what the win or loss meant for them. But that does not change the fact that what is reported is a space of possibilities of human action and sentiment and that this space of possibilities is in a good sense already known.

Lastly, proponents of narrow aesthetic cognitivism also usually focus on propositional cases which are plausibly true but, as mentioned earlier, there is another tradition, running from Plato, which argues that art regularly expresses falsities. Film studies have traditionally been interested in the ways in which films excel in misrepresentations especially when it comes to underrepresented groups and minorities (women, ethnic and sexual minorities, etc.). In other words, proponents of narrow aesthetic cognitivism who are uninterested in the way fiction justifies its truth would end up with fiction which, arguably, imparts inaccuracies more often than it does knowledge for, on average, fiction certainly involves more inventions and misinformation about the non-aesthetic world than truths.

Does fiction justify its truth?

Jerome Stolnitz (1992) has produced one of the strongest critiques of narrow aesthetic cognitivism by arguing that fiction, unlike science and history, does not have established procedures for justifying what it conveys is true. Fiction regularly mixes truth with other elements, be it inventions or inaccuracies, but for the audiences who consume it, it does not provide any tools for disentangling the two. In other words, while it is the case that fiction can convey truth it cannot convey any knowledge because whatever belief audiences acquire through their engagement with fiction, this belief is not justified. There have, of course, been responses to Stolnitz's proposal arguing that fiction does justify its truth.

One line of defence has been to argue that there are subsections of fiction which audiences can assume are truthful. Proposed candidates have included realist fiction (Gaut, 2005 and Vidmar Jovanović, 2019b) and sub-genres such as works by Dickens (Friend, 2014). Vidmar Jovanović argues, for instance, that writers committed to realism such as Austen will accurately depict social and economic relations of their time. For Friend, we can assume Dickens to be a truthful guide on social facts but less so on scientific ones (given his recourse to spontaneous self-combustion in one of his novels). In other words, membership of a specific (sub)genre is what justifies truths in these fictions. From Stolnitz's perspective, however, the problem remains because even the most realist (sub)genres involve admixtures of other elements. Despite what the opening of Dickens's *Our Mutual Friend* (1865) suggests, for instance, there was no such a thing as collector of dead bodies from the banks of Thames. Put differently, for Stolnitz no (sub)genre of fiction justifies its truth because it is a typical feature of all (sub)genres of fiction to involve inventions and inaccuracies.

Gaut has provided perhaps the strongest response to Stolnitz by arguing that while there is an institutional difference between nonfiction and fiction in terms of immediate justification, in the end the deeper justification of both nonfiction and fiction lies in one's experience. Gaut acknowledges that, unlike for fiction, nonfiction which standardly makes a claim to imparting knowledge is vetted through some kind of expert process. In academia, for instance, this is through peer review while in journalism it is through editorial fact-checking. However, Gaut points out that there are still nonfictional works which have escaped vetting either by design (frauds like *Hitler Diaries*) or mistake (arguably, even the best history books involve some inaccuracies). And just by looking at such nonfictional work audiences cannot know whether the vetting has been effective. To ascertain that, audiences need to go outside the text, examine the conditions of its making, check its claims against other sources, i.e. appeal to experience. In that sense, there is no substantial difference with fiction because in both cases the ultimate justification lies in the appeal to experience.

While justification does ultimately lie with experience, the institutional guarantee does play an important role that is not addressed in Gaut's retort.

Justification pertains to ascertaining whether something is true or not. But knowledge also involves belief and just because a truth is justified it does not mean a belief about it will be formed. In other words, narrow aesthetic cognitivists also need to explain how audiences come to acquire beliefs and whether they do acquire them in the first place. Institutional guarantee that comes with nonfiction which is absent from fiction is arguably part of the mechanism for acquiring beliefs. Put in yet another way, the underlying contract for consuming the forms of nonfiction discussed here (e.g. history, science) is that one is supposed to believe in them. There is no similar underlying contract for fiction not even in its most realist subsets. As discussed in Chapter Two at length, the underlying contract here is primarily mandated imagining.

Does fiction impart beliefs?

A minority of proponents of narrow aesthetic cognitivism have recognized that it is also necessary to investigate how and whether fictions influence beliefs. They usually cite a selection of empirical studies and propose certain mechanisms of belief acquisition (cf. Friend, 2014 and Plantinga, 2018). The work that is usually put forward to support the idea that fictions change beliefs comes from a few psychologists including frequent collaborators Deborah Gerrig and Richard Prentice (Gerrig, 1991, Prentice et al., 1997. Prentice and Gerrig, 1999), Melanie Green and Timothy Brock (2000), and Elizabeth Marsh (Marsh et al., 2003 and Marsh and Fazio, 2006). These are usually studies of literary fiction where a general knowledge test follows the exposure to a fictional text set against a control group.

In one string of studies, one group read fictional stories with general statements about the non-aesthetic world which were either true (e.g. mental illness is not contagious) or false (e.g. mental illness is contagious). The control group read either unrelated stories or no stories at all. Those exposed to fictional texts containing the above general statements (the test group) were statistically more likely than the control group to agree with the claims in the follow-up questionnaire so long as they were consistent with the information in the text, even if the information was false (Gerrig, 1991, Prentice et al., 1997, Prentice and Gerrig, 1999). When participants read one and the same story, but one group was told the story is fictional and the other nonfictional those in the fictional group were more likely to agree with the statements they have read (Prentice and Gerrig, 1999). In another set of experiments, the general statements about the non-aesthetic world which could be either true (e.g. extant is used for navigation via stars) or false (e.g. compass is used for navigation via stars) were only peripheral or in the background of the fictional story. Much like in the previous studies, those exposed to the general statements did significantly better (in case of true statements) or worse (in case of false statements) than the control group on a follow-up general knowledge test (Marsh et al., 2003 and Marsh and Fazio, 2006). In other words, a significant subset of audiences acquires propositional beliefs from fiction. From this perspective, fiction is even more persuasive than nonfiction in imparting beliefs about propositional claims. Interestingly, even those more sceptical of knowledge acquisition like Gregory Currie have argued that '[i]t is an obvious truth that fictions affect the beliefs of those who come into contact with them' (2020: 161).

This, however, is belied by the currently most comprehensive meta-analysis of persuasive effects of fiction (Braddock and Dillard, 2016). In the last four decades, meta-analysis has become a key method of summarizing research on a given subject in various disciplines including psychology and an important way to tackle replication crisis in those disciplines (Sharpe and Poets, 2020). Meta-analysis as a method identifies different studies focusing on a similar question and statistically combines the results of these studies to compute whether there is an effect and the size of the effect (Borenstein et al., 2009). Given that the results of single studies are statistical analyses themselves based on sample sizes and quantified responses which provide values for whether there is an effect and what its size is, with right parameters and weightings these analyses can be combined into an overarching statistical analysis to ascertain whether the effect holds more broadly or not and its size if it does. As such, meta-analyses are not competing studies which look at the same question and find the effect (size) or not. They are analyses of the whole body of research on a topic of interest and their results hold more generally than any single study.

Braddock and Dillard have produced a meta-analysis of seventy-four empirical studies investigating the effects of fiction across media (visual, audio, theatre, literary) on four different aspects of persuasion – attitudes, desires, behaviours, and beliefs. For each of these aspects of persuasion, they have made a separate analysis to see whether there is a difference in how fiction and nonfiction influences a given aspect. For beliefs, they have found that 'nonfictional narrative stimuli significantly affect belief change, but fictional narrative stimuli do not' (2016: 457).[13] In other words, while about a dozen different studies that Friend et al. cite find the sought-out effect – that fictions change beliefs – the meta-analysis of seventy-four studies on the subject demonstrates that there is in fact no such effect – fiction does not change beliefs. From a statistical perspective, the reason is that the effect sizes and sample sizes in studies reported by Friend are outweighed by the lack of effect and sample sizes in the studies she does not cite. In fact, the most recent non-statistical literature review of the subject arrives at the same conclusion (Dubourg and Baumard, 2023).[14]

Moreover, Braddock and Dillard have also considered whether each of the four aspects of persuasion effects – attitudes, desires, behaviours, and beliefs – depends on the medium. They have found that '*existing data support the conclusion that medium of presentation is unimportant for inducing persuasion via narrative*' (Braddock and Dillard, 2016: 462, italics in the original). Put differently, that fictional narratives do not change beliefs cannot be explained by the claim that one type of fictional narratives, say the textual ones put forward by Friend, change beliefs whereas the others do not. In general, in the fictional case no medium type changes beliefs (in the nonfictional case they all do).

Braddock and Dillard's findings also problematize some of the proposed mechanisms of belief acquisition already mentioned at the end of Chapter One. Building on the work of Prentice and Gerrig (1999) and Gilbert (1991), Friend (2014) has advocated for scrutiny lowering – an idea that the very label 'fictional' lowers a more critical outlook on what is consumed leading to easier persuasion than in nonfiction. This, however, is contradicted by the above meta-analysis which has the opposite results of what the scrutiny-lowering theory predicts. Braddock and Dillard's findings also contradict proposals such as availability heuristic (Tversky and Kahneman, 1973) and acceptance by default (Gilbert, 1991) as both would predict that, all other things being equal, effects of fictions and nonfictions are the same.

Other mechanisms such as Currie's (2020) narrative value have different issues. While Currie is sceptical of a general belief acquisition mechanism, he still proposes a typical way in which audiences infer beliefs about the non-aesthetic world from beliefs about fiction: 'Deviations in fiction from truth are expected to be justified by their narrative payoff' (2020: 161). In other words, if information is simply in the background, then the tacit assumption is that it is true in real life. Because French interpolations by Russian aristocracy in Tolstoy's *War and Peace* (1869) are not of particular narrative importance (they could have been in, say, Italian and nothing much would change narratively speaking) but happen in the background, audiences generally infer that nineteenth-century Russian aristocracy spoke French. By contrast, because Dickens's *Our Mutual Friend* opens in a particularly dramatic fashion with a collector of dead bodies from the Thames, audiences can assume that the collector is not a historical profession. Counterexamples, however, abound. In the case of background, in historical fiction films characters regularly speak in contemporary languages rather than languages of the epoch depicted yet a diet of, say, Hollywood epics on Rome will not lead to an inference that Romans spoke English. Similarly, irrespective of their occupation, characters in American TV shows regularly look like models; yet this hardly leads to inferences that a typical policeman, doctor, or a lawyer conforms to contemporary standards of beauty much more than an average person. When it comes to the foreground, Currie himself admits that when he first read *Our Mutual Friend*, he came to mistakenly believe that there was such a profession as collector of bodies from the Thames. This means that the difference between foreground and background is much less clear than he professes it to be leading to problems in determining what to believe. There is also a matter of middle ground: what do we do with fictional truths which are neither crucial for the storyline but are at the same time not unimportant such as that Queen Anne was a lesbian (*The Favourite* [Yorgos Lanthimos, 2018]) or that the first inoculation took place on the Danish Court (*A Royal Affair* [Nikolaj Arcel, 2012])?

In short then, existing studies disprove the claim that fiction imparts beliefs making general proposals about belief acquisition moot. It is true that virtually all the studies in the meta-analysis are short-term studies in the sense that they only look for effects immediately after the exposure to fictions. But this arguably makes things even more difficult for narrow aesthetic cognitivists because it is unlikely that there would be long-term effects on beliefs without there being short-term ones. In other words, the biggest hurdle for proponents of narrow aesthetic cognitivism is that empirical findings contradict the view that fictional works impart beliefs.[15]

It is possible, however, that the proponents of narrow aesthetic cognitivism will not be persuaded by the empirical findings I cite. One objection could be that psychological studies of the type that Friend et al. refer to and that are included in the meta-analysis are simply not a good way of exploring the question that interests us – whether fiction changes beliefs. The objection broadly claims that what the cited experiments measure is not belief but something else. Therefore, it is irrelevant for the debate either way. If we think about beliefs as cognitive states which are relatively stable over time, then short-term studies deploying questionnaires only immediately after the exposure to fiction to gage beliefs stemming from that text are lacking. Such studies are not really measuring belief but some kind of acceptance or subconscious recall. What is required is a long-term study where the questionnaires are repeated after a prolonged period of several weeks or more.

In another variant of the objection what is actually studied is not beliefs derived from fiction, but beliefs formed on the basis of who presented them. When participants are provided with information in experimental conditions because the information is provided by experimenters whom participants intuitively trust to convey truths, it does not matter whether the information is labelled fiction or nonfiction. What matters is the implicit trust in the presenter of information. The conclusion of both variants is the same – short-term studies do not capture (relevant) beliefs, only long-term ones do.[16]

Tackling the second variant first, if participants generally got their beliefs from the fact that experimenters provided implicitly trustworthy information, then all the experiments in which the control group engages unrelated or no works and the test group is presented with fictional works would need to show effects because questionnaires would necessarily include references to statements in the fiction provided by experimenters. Yet clearly there are such studies which do not find an effect. Moreover, as mentioned earlier, there are studies which present one and the same text to the control and test group but label it as nonfiction and fiction, respectively (Prentice and Gerrig, 1999). According to the second variant, the result of this experiment should show no difference between the two groups (both groups are getting relevant information from the trustworthy experimenters), but the experiment reports a significant difference.

Most importantly, there is also the matter of long-term studies which invalidates both variants of the objection. While there are only a handful of such long-term studies, they do exist (cf. Strange and Leung, 1999, Brodie et al. 2001, Marsh et al., 2003, Howell, 2011, Schneider-Mayerson et al., 2020). Crucially, all but Marsh et al. (2003) report the disappearance of the effect while even Marsh et al. report a significant decrease in the effect size. In other words, even if we accept that short-term studies do not actually measure beliefs, long-term studies evince that fiction does not establish imparting or change of beliefs construed as temporally stable cognitive states.[17]

The persistence of an idea

If what I have argued is true, then why does the idea that fictional works influence beliefs persist among optimists and pessimists alike? One reason is that the idea is literally ancient. Not only is it at least two and a half millennia old, it has been documented in two very different cultural circles. Writing more than a hundred years before Plato, in *Classics of Poetry* Confucius broached remarkably similar ideas about the negative influence of misrepresentation in poetry on audiences' moral beliefs and social and political forms of life. In other words, it could be argued that one of the earliest concerns of philosophy is the impact of fiction on beliefs.

While Plato and Confucius effectively proposed theories of censorship of art, the history of the practice of censorship is a long one as well. In fact, if the biblical proscription 'Thou shalt not make any graven image' is construed as censorship of the visual arts, then this history is probably even longer than the one about the debates on the value of art. Moreover, specific to film, external censorship of the seventh art has persisted longer than that of literary arts and in some parts of the world continues to persist.[18] All this warrants even more reason for film scholars to treat their assumption about real-life beliefs as a given.

Anecdotal evidence abounds as well. Audience members regularly talk about books and films that changed their lives. This, presumably, involves changes in beliefs about the non-aesthetic world. I must admit to still being quite certain that films instilled in me the idea of an ideal romantic relationship. Less radical version of this can be found in the writings of public intellectuals like Martha Nussbaum whose pages burst with confidence that works of high art have enriched their own lives in numerous domains. And the influence of fictional narratives on people has also been a common trope in literary fiction going back to at least the beginnings of the modern novel and Don Quixote who had read one too many chivalric romances.

One last reason that coaxes confidence into the idea that fictional works lead to belief acquisition is the imperative of academic disciplines to make and keep themselves relevant. If what they study does not have influence on the non-aesthetic world then why keep studying or funding these disciplines? It is not only film studies that are invested in keeping film an important cultural artefact by investing it with power of changing people's minds. The same can be said of literary, theatre, performing arts, art history, and all other departments dealing mainly with the arts.

This attitude seems to characterize the much broader domain of academic and non-academic cultural criticism as well. The focus on representation, whose stories are being told, whose stories are being neglected, and who has the right to tell stories about whom makes sense only if the underlying assumption of such discourse is that the way people are represented matters for what we come to believe about these very people. If this were not true, much of the commentary of this sort becomes superfluous. Put succinctly, the idea is old, transcultural, practised through censorship, and serves to legitimize academic disciplines and popular forms of cultural criticism alike. It assures us that fiction (in the narrow sense) is not merely fiction (in the broad sense) and justifies the cultural and personal investment in the category.

But there is no need to appeal to belief acquisition to legitimize the existence and the power of the institution of fiction. The power of fictional works to move us should suffice as a reason for continued relevance of the institution. While the other two effects of fiction discussed in part three – imaginative resistance and belief acquisition – have their doubters, nobody denies the existence of emotional engagement. At most, there are questions about whether the effect should be classed with other emotions and whether they are rational but even then, the effect's intensity is undeniable so much so as to raise moral questions. It is no wonder so many genres are named after the emotions they are aiming to elicit. Arguably, exploring a range of experiences and emotions which the audiences might not have a chance to partake in or if they do are safely bracketed from interpersonal interactions which usually accompany them, enriches lives in a literal sense.[19]

Conclusion

I have concluded the final full-length chapter of the monograph by speaking of works of fiction as artefacts for generating emotions. But there are other effects which contribute to the importance of the institution of fiction. In their meta-analysis of experimental studies of four main aspects of narrative persuasion – beliefs, attitudes, desires, and behaviours – Kurt Braddock and James Price Dillard (2016) evince that narrative fictions are effective in influencing all but beliefs. In other words, fictional narratives are good at impacting whether we have a positive or negative stance towards represented non-aesthetic phenomena, they are efficient at instilling wants towards those same phenomena, and they are consequential in acting on those attitudes and desires. This includes as varied effects as developing negative views about religious order Opus Dei following the viewing of *Camino* (Javier Fesser, 2008) and visiting the Maya beach in Thailand made famous by *The Beach* (Danny Boyle, 2000).

With one possible non-aesthetic legitimation of the importance of the institution of fiction in place we can return to the question of belief acquisition and future direction of research on fiction more even-handedly. While the last chapter presented a dominantly sceptical view of the arguments in favour of narrow aesthetic cognitivism, I would like to start the Conclusion to the monograph with a more affirmative outlook on the programme's core claim. That the existing arguments are not solid does not mean that narrow aesthetic cognitivism is necessarily false. It may just be that the proponents have been looking in the wrong places for evidence of belief acquisition. Following the sketch of alternatives, I will discuss adjacent research avenues and the disciplinary commitments they require. I will wrap up with some thoughts on the ideal relationship between film studies and philosophy of fiction.

One obvious limitation of Braddock and Dillard's work and the experimental studies they analyse is that the empirical findings relate only to situations where audiences are exposed to a limited number of works within a short period of time. It is possible that if fiction imparts beliefs, it is not because a viewer has seen a single work at one point in time. Rather, it may be the case that beliefs accrue over time through a repeated exposure to fiction. Audiences might not pick up that the Roman Republic was run by the Senate after watching *Cleopatra* (Joseph L. Mankiewicz, 1963) once or if they do the effect might not be long-term. But they might acquire a robust belief of this after a more extensive engagement with the genre of Hollywood epics about Rome. In other words, there is much space for long-term studies investigating repeated exposure to certain types of fiction.

Another drawback of the above meta-study is that it relates only to propositional belief. As we have discussed, however, there are other types of belief that could be acquired including perceptual and experiential beliefs. In the previous chapter I have assumed that a typical fiction film is efficient in conferring perceptual beliefs because of its traditional photorealistic commitments. Presumably, many a belief about the appearance of various landmarks derives from fiction film. But even if this is not a belief imparted by the work *qua* fiction it is still an assumption which should be investigated for it may well turn out that the assumption is wrong. Moreover, given a range of styles of animation and CGI, it would be interesting to learn whether the acquisition of perceptual belief, if it takes place, is a function of the level of photorealism or not.

While studies involving perceptual beliefs could be easily implemented with general knowledge tests which include audiovisual information, those exploring whether fiction films confer experiential beliefs would require more innovative design. While I do not have the expertise to provide one, it seems to me possible to capture the acquisition of experiential beliefs in open-ended questionnaires as a function of the richness of the description of those experiences. Presumably, when prompted what it is like to drive fast, the experiment participant who goes into detail about the pull of inertia at each bend, the sound of screeching tires, and the rush of adrenaline has a clearer experiential belief than the one who offers only a couple of descriptors like 'exciting'. Whatever the eventual design turns out to be, the question is well worth exploring not least because experiential beliefs are beliefs about physical and sensory experiences, i.e. embodied states.[1]

Although I have addressed the matter only cursorily in a footnote in Chapter One, there is a substantial tradition of film scholarship which takes an embodied approach understood either phenomenologically (Williams 1991, Marks 2000, Sobchack 2004) or in terms of embodied cognition (Coëgnarts 2019). While neither has engaged explicitly in the debate about aesthetic cognitivism, their views could be construed as compatible with at least its broad version wherein fiction is seen to have general positive epistemic effects on audiences. For those working in the phenomenological tradition, fiction film may contribute to developing our skills to experience in a more fine-grained fashion and to better differentiate similar experiences. For those interested in embodied cognition, because all types of belief including propositional are grounded in physical and sensory experiences (cf. Lakoff and Johnsons, 1980) exposure to such experiences in fiction may influence those beliefs. These are certainly other research avenues to be pursued.

Others drawing on or working in the embodied cognition tradition have argued that fiction film contributes to social cognition by developing empathy through the activation of mirror neurons (Smith, 2017 and Gallese and Guerra, 2019). Originally co-discovered by Vittorio Gallese in the 1990s, mirror neurons are sets of neurons which fire both when an animal performs an action and when it perceives the same action performed by another animal. Because such neurons appear to identify gestures and behaviours with one's own gestures and behaviours it has been hypothesized that mirror neurons form the neural basis for understanding other people including the capacity for empathy. Given that a typical fiction film is photographically verisimilar, acted in a naturalistic manner, and with close-ups regularly devoted to expressions of character emotions, engagement with such films mobilizes mirror neurons and trains audiences' skills in empathizing.

Mirror neurons, however, remain controversial. The claims that they are the neural substrate of empathy, that they actually fire when the relevant action is observed, and even that they exist at all, have all been challenged (cf. Turvey, 2020). But this matters less for us because the idea that films promote social and moral understanding is not new. Appeal to mirror neurons is just its latest iteration, albeit one which makes a further claim to its neural substrate. The idea that films contribute to social and moral comprehension can be found in the works of scholars as varied as Stanley Cavell (1979), Gilles Deleuze (1983, 1986), Robert Sinnerbrink (2016), and Carl Plantinga (2023). What is more important is whether fiction films actually do promote such understanding. And this is an empirical matter. Thankfully, led by Plantinga interdisciplinary research on the subject has started by focusing on whether engagement with fictional film characters influences moral comprehension.[2]

One last aspect of broad aesthetic cognitivism I wish to address is the potential of fiction film to contribute to well-being. Although film scholars regularly recognize that film viewing is hedonically pleasurable, in the tradition of the Frankfurt School this short-term pleasure is usually seen as the main ingredient in cinema's overall negative effects. Put differently, film scholars have traditionally been very sceptical of and said even less about the potential positive effects that screen stories may have where these effects are understood not as hedonic well-being (which generally overlaps with basic short-term pleasure) but as eudaimonic well-being with long-term effects such as personal growth and realization of own potential (cf. Plantinga, 2018).

It is only lately that these possibilities have started to be systematically addressed usually by explicitly connecting the acquisition of ethical knowledge (Hjort, 2011 and Plantinga, 2018) to eudaimonic well-being. Starting from the WHO definition of health as 'a state of complete physical, mental and social well-being and not merely the absence of disease or infirmity' (n.d.) and building on the Arts Council of England policy-oriented reports on contributions of culture to society, Mette Hjort has made a strong argument that 'film's potential in connection with such public values as health and well-being is only beginning to be acknowledged' (2019: 8). She has argued that cinema can have immediate instrumental health value through filmmaking and viewing alike and in domains such as psychotherapy, alleviating symptoms of Alzheimer's and effects of medical treatment among others (2019: 8). And, following the Danish Film Institute, she has also proposed that we need 'to explore the extent to which health-related benefits can be derived from the activity of viewing quality films across an entire lifespan' (Hjort, 2022: 511) offering feel-good film genre as a leading candidate. The next step is to empirically test all these claims.

But perhaps the most important avenue to pursue because it pertains to beliefs about the social world and the roles and relations therein is the question of age. Braddock and Dillard's meta-analysis takes studies with adults as their subjects. So does the work proposed by Hjort and Plantinga. It has been recognized, however, that it is difficult to evidence this type of belief acquisition in adults because they might have already hit the ceiling having been embedded in a storytelling society from their birth (Boyd, 2018). In other words, any beliefs that might have been imparted would have been acquired at an early age. And these might be some core beliefs about how the world is and/or should be. That is why we need to turn to children and adolescents to investigate in more detail whether fiction imparts beliefs about social relations. While studies on the subject exist, they have mostly focused on literary fiction (cf. Gasser, Dammert, and Murphy, 2022) and I have not been able to identify any meta-analyses. The matter might be further complicated by the fact that it takes time for children to fully grasp the difference between fiction and nonfiction.

At the same time, what proponents of both narrow and broad aesthetic cognitivism must recognize is that fictional works in general and fiction film in particular may prove to have a net negative rather than positive epistemic outcomes. If, on average, fiction instils false beliefs more often than true beliefs, then we can hardly speak of overall knowledge acquisition. Audiences are then not learning but being misinformed. Similarly, it may turn out that fiction is not good at developing audiences' empathy or other forms of social and moral understanding and that it is a hindrance instead. The same may be true of the impact on well-being – rather than contributing to personal growth and realization of own potential, fiction may have deleterious effects on it. In other words, it is the sceptics who may be proven right. But it also may be the case that thinking of the matter in net terms conceals a more complicated picture. Some genres may have positive epistemic effects while other genres have negative ones. Or the same genres may have different valence of effects depending on the effect in question with, for instance, positive effects on well-being while imparting false beliefs.

Moving away from positive and negative impacts there is also much to learn about other phenomena explored in Part Three of the monograph. We have already seen that a potential link between emotional character engagement such as sympathy or antipathy and moral understanding is being explored experimentally by Plantinga's team. Some other questions worth pursuing include: Does the difference between emotions with and without clearly associated actions map onto the difference between real-life structures and fictional characters as objects of emotions proposed in Chapter Six? How variable is the intensity of emotional involvement with fiction film and what parameters explain this variability? What is the relative intensity of involvement with fictional and nonfictional works?

Turning to the question of imaginative resistance I already proposed some future directions for research in Chapter Four. How richly do audiences imagine when engaging fiction films? Do they imagine in non-propositional domains? Is it possible to simultaneously perceive and imagine perceptually? In how much detail do audiences flesh out propositional imaginings? Is imaginative resistance a function of richness of imagining? What are the engagement strategies in dealing with clashing mandated imaginings? Is imaginative engagement with clashing mandated imaginings spontaneous or willed? How much cognitive resources does rich imagining exhaust when compared to minimal imagining?

All these questions require us to collaborate across disciplines. And this entails not only cooperation between film scholars and philosophers of fiction, but psychologists as well. Recently, philosophers of fiction have been more open to participating in the design and interpretation of experimental studies as evinced by Stacie Friend and Gregory Currie who have partnered with a psychologist to work on the Leverhulme Grant Project 'Learning from Fiction: A Philosophical and Psychological Study' (2018–22). But given both philosophers' and psychologists' traditional interest in literature, it is no wonder the study was devoted exclusively to literary fiction. Regardless, film scholars would profit to follow their lead and develop their collaborative projects focusing on film.

Elsewhere, I have argued that while some film scholars inspired by both continental and analytical schools of thought have drawn on empirical studies in their work, even here with very few exceptions the studies themselves have been designed and run by psychologists interested in film (Slugan, 2020). Since then, Carl Plantinga's and Murray Smith's current (2022–5) cooperation with communication scholars and psychologists on character engagement and moral understanding has broken the mould and hopefully this type of interdisciplinary work will set a model for film scholars to emulate. At the very least, the findings of such studies and experiments should become basic information for film scholars working on the subject.

In other words, film scholars stand to gain much by moving away from the discipline's traditional lack of interest in the experimental method and its results. And, as I have argued in the book, anybody who ignores the existing empirical findings does so at their own peril especially when it comes to the key disciplinary assumption that fiction film changes beliefs about the non-aesthetic world. This is not to say that film scholars should become psychologists any more than psychologists should become film scholars. I am not urging film scholars to execute experimental studies or become expert statisticians nor am I asking psychologists to become fluent in the theory of film since Hugo Munsterberg. But a genuine interdisciplinary work would involve more than helping the psychologists with identifying potential films test subject are to watch. It would involve study co-design as well as joint interpretation of the results.

Among the four main groups of questions that I pursued in the monograph – disciplinary, ontological, historical, and phenomenological – the collaborative experimental method is clearly best suited for the last one. We should by no means be prohibited to discuss speculatively the actual audience engagement and effects but at its core these are empirical phenomena and any theories or assumptions about them need to be tested empirically and, if possible, experimentally. In fact, experimental method is well suited for some ontological questions as well, especially those about the nature and taxonomy of imagination and its relationship to other mental phenomena. The method may help with articulating the nature of objectual imagining and necessary entailment in imagining. And we may arrive at a firmer grasp of the role of imagination in mental states like memory and transportation.

The method might even shed some light on more social phenomena including the process of indexing and reasons behind the fictional puzzle discussed in Chapters Three and Five, respectively. Concerning the latter, experiments can reveal how varied the examples when the mandate's authority breaks down are and how much variability there is among individuals in perceiving this failure. Audience members can be asked about their own accounts of the reasons behind the breakdown and their responses can be related to other constructs like ease of imagining, confidence in author, or even political orientation.

While historical analysis of reception reveals how (re)indexing occurred on specific case studies, social psychology may tell us how audiences respond to categorization proposed by producers, distributors, and exhibitors. A study could label one and the same film 'fiction' and 'nonfiction' and ask of participants whether they agree with the categorization. Depending on the films used, a function of resistance to categorization could be plotted in relation to specific standard and contra-standard features. Non-experimental surveys and questionnaires may also reveal the level of coincidence (or divergence) of public categorization established through promotion and databases with personal categorization by audience members. All this can help us identify films likely to undergo re-indexing and the reasons behind it.

Of course, the experimental method can only go so far. It cannot tell us how historical audiences responded to indexing proposals nor can it reveal how audiences imaginatively engaged with mandates. It cannot reveal how films were categorized at the time of their premiere nor which films crossed the fiction/nonfiction threshold over time. And it cannot articulate the reasons behind the dissipation of the mandates to imagine nor those for establishments of authorization to make-believe either. For historical questions the best guide will clearly be historical analysis.

There is little sense of applying experimentation to disciplinary questions of film studies and philosophy of fiction either. Their assumptions, interests, blind spots, etc., will be best revealed by an extensive literature review of the respective fields. Of course, disciplinary membership will make identification and critical outlook on blind spots of one's discipline more difficult. But the silver lining is that a potential collaborator from another partner discipline may help in identifying and overcoming our weaknesses and that we may do the same for them. As I have argued elsewhere (Slugan, 2019a), while film studies stand to gain from a robust theory of fiction as mandated imagining developed by philosophers, philosophy of fiction can only profit from tools necessary to historicizing those mandates.

Furthermore, because fiction is a normative category – one is primarily *supposed to* imagine a fictional work's content – the ontology of fiction cannot be explained through the experimental method either. The same holds for nonfictional works for they are defined by the absence of such a demand. The results of surveys of aggregated audience members' categorizations cannot change a work's fictional status – they are only a measure of (dis)agreement with official categorization. At most, they point to a tension and the possibility that a work may change its status in the future. The same holds for empirical findings on whether audiences actually imagine anything and if they do how richly. In fact, such outcomes are not even informative about the potential for re-indexing but merely describe preferred imaginative engagement strategies with fiction film.

But none of this means that either film studies or philosophy of fiction is sufficiently equipped to pursue the study of film fiction alone. The two ideally need to collaborate and at the very least converse more extensively. And when they tackle actual audience engagement and effects, they should at the very least familiarize themselves with empirical research on the matter.

Finally, if the goal is to provide a more general account of fictional works regardless of the medium, literary studies, linguistics, art history, performance studies, game studies, studies of comics, musicology, etc., must all have their say in the conversation. One of the key questions in such a general account is presumably whether fictional works are necessarily figurative. For instance, while non-figurative experimental films are currently indexed as nonfictional there is no principled reason why there could not be a mandate to imagine the abstract content of a film like *Symphonie Diagonale* (Viking Eggeling, 1924).

A related, and, arguably, more important concern is what the importance of fiction as a category is for a given artform and its discipline. In film studies, I have argued, fiction/nonfiction distinction has organized both films and much of disciplinary work. In literary studies, the distinction appears to be more important for categorization of literary forms than the organization of the discipline. Furthermore, although the distinction can clearly be applied to experimental film with most of such works relegated to nonfiction simply because whatever is not indexed as fiction is relegated to nonfiction, the question is how useful such a categorization is. The same question is even more poignant in music. Similarly, we can ask whether a stand-up (special on Netflix) is nonfiction or fiction because unlike with experimental film and music it is less clear, but will that question help us better understand what stand-up and these specials are? In other words, we should be careful that our conceptualization of fiction and nonfiction does not displace other potentially more informative taxonomies of the artform.

Whatever the answers to these and above questions might be, this monograph will have hopefully shown that they are worth pursuing and that the more disciplinary voices join in the more effective their pursuit will be.

NOTES

Chapter 1

1 A notable exception is Christian Metz (1982) whose proposal I discuss below.

2 The entry for 'fiction film' in Kuhn and Westwell (2020) only points to related terms: 'See diegesis; feature film; narrative/narration; storytelling terminology'.

3 Earlier versions like Currie's (1999) account of documentary as trace excludes animated documentaries.

4 If contact is removed as one of the criteria of indexicality and we insist only on the object's automatic trace, then the photograph is also an index of whatever preceded that object in an automatic casual manner. Say we photograph remains of a forest fire caused by lighting. We would then be forced to say that this is a documentary photograph of not only the charred remains but also of the lighting though the lighting was never in front of the camera.

5 For an account of Italian and Spanish scholarship, I am indebted to Enrico Terrone. Takaheshi Kohei has provided information about scholarship in Japan in his 'Seminar of Japanese Literature and Fictionality' presentation at the 2019 International Society for Fiction and Fictionality Studies inaugural conference. For works in Russian and German, see Bareis and Slugan (2019) and Slugan (2019b).

6 I discuss Matravers' (2014) more nuanced version of this view in Chapter Two.

7 In a further clarification of the definition of documentary Nichols (2017) explains that the understanding of documentary also changes over time through the influence of institutions, filmmakers, films, and audiences. Nichols' approach remains textualist, however, because what matters most is the relationship of these four agents to changing textual conventions. Producers and distributors influence how the film is going to look like usually by exercising pressure to use existing conventions. These may be subverted by filmmakers. Films which are initially outliers may come to popularize new conventions. Audiences, finally, have expectations in line with conventions. In extratextualist approaches, the focus is elsewhere. For Wilson (2011), textual conventions are irrelevant, and the only thing that matters for determining fictionality is the author's intention. For Slugan (2019a), similarly, it is not the change in textual conventions that is crucial but negotiating whether the film should be engaged primarily as a veridical representation or as a prop in a game of make-believe.

8 In personal communication, Carroll clarifies that his indexing 'answers the epistemological question of how audiences determine which films are documentaries

and the Gricean account answers the ontological question of what makes something a fiction or a nonfiction film.' In Chapter Two, we will see there is a difference between determining the fictionality of an utterance as opposed to the fictionality of the whole work. Given that the key authors engaged here talk about works – Carroll, Odin, and Wilson – we can neglect the difference in this chapter.

9 For an example of a feedback loop between audience reception and promotional strategies on the example of phantom rides, see Slugan (2019a: 75–6). For Carroll's response to simultaneous mandates for imaginings and beliefs see Carroll (2016a)

10 For an overview of Odin's semio-pragmatics in English, see Buckland (2000). For another French-language monograph on fiction in film, see Siety (2009).

11 But, see Chapter Three for an exception and the relative stability of promotion in the case of *The Blair Witch Project*.

12 I return to this point in the next section.

13 For how my institutional theory deals with instructional or didactic films, see Chapter Three.

14 https://www.youtube.com/watch?v=C5yhxqkJiAQ.

15 Stars, undeniably, demand special consideration but even when enamoured with Bogart we are also very much interested in Rick.

16 For the reception of Hale's Tours outside of Europe and North America, see Slugan, Hanifee, and Zeng (2025, 2026).

17 Angwar's re-enactment could have even been performed by a star actor, but this would not necessarily make the re-enactment fictional either (albeit the film would lose much of its power which rests on the actual perpetrators performing the re-enactments).

18 I have already pointed out that fiction films may depict things which are true. There is organized crime in the United States and some Italian Americans are a part of it. But, although some or even all aspects of the fictional content may be true, the point of fiction is not to primarily assert what is represented but to primarily imagine it. And I have also admitted that some fictions make nonfictional assertions which invite beliefs through their fictional content – historical dramas or the instructional mode in Odin's account to be found in anti-war films. But here we are not concerned with historical facts or how film's message may generate beliefs but with how explicit fictional representations – stereotypes – may instil beliefs. Although *The Godfather* stereotypes Italian Americans as criminals, neither its historical truths nor its message is, arguably, that all Italian Americans are criminals. For more about the relationship of fictional works to belief, see Chapter Two and Chapter Seven.

19 A related problem known as the paradox of fiction concerns explaining how we engage fictions emotionally if we do not believe that the fictional entities and characters depicted exist. The solutions offered, importantly, circumvent beliefs by emphasizing that emotions might stem from imaginings (Carroll, 1990b and Smith,

1995) or various forms of embodiment understood phenomenologically (Williams, 1991; Marks, 2000; Sobchack, 2004) or in terms of mirror neurons (Smith, 2017). As such they do not provide guidance here. For more, see Chapter Six.

20 An earlier famous account hinges on the analogy of the dream-like state and viewing in the cinema (Jean-Louis Baudry, 1986). The problems with the analogy have been discussed at length (Carroll, 1988a). Moreover, Baudry's account, unlike Metz's, is not applicable to conditions of spectatorship outside of cinema.

21 A version of this view can be found in Carroll (1990a).

22 One of the few film scholars who has picked up on this argument is Torben Grodal who argues that 'even as we watch fictional films it remains true seeing is believing, because to believe incoming information is, as previously mentioned, the default mode and to disbelieve demands a special effort' (2009: 154). But even Grodal adds that whereas cognitive bottom-up processes secure this default belief, top-down processes introduce disbelief, i.e. evaluate the reality status of sensory input.

Chapter 2

1 Most claim that their account of fiction should apply to all media (Davies 2015 and Stock 2017), but only rarely do they spell out how this should work (cf. Currie, 1990: 92–9). When Currie does so and commits to the idea that in visual and literary media 'we make believe that a story is being told as a known fact' (Currie, 1990: 98), he is forced to introduce fictional narrators in film as those responsible for conveying these 'facts'. The idea of the fictional film narrator, however, is controversial to say the least (cf. Curran, 2019 and Slugan, 2015, 2017a, 2019b).

2 A further benefit from moving away from language to games of make-believe is that they are more in line with how fiction developed both phylogenetically and ontogenetically. It is likely that human ability to generate fiction derives from pretence play found in other animals rather than from language use. Children also engage in pretend play before they learn how to speak.

3 In speaking of fictional content as opposed to fictional propositions, Catharine Abell (2020) offers an effective way of not conflating the two. Much like Abell, however, I am forced to speak of propositions because the discussion is usually phrased in those terms.

4 Given that García-Carpintero (2013) treats myths as nonfiction – which, as I explain in Chapter One, would under the model I propose be fictions – he might stick to his guns and insist that early train films are fiction and trick films nonfiction and that they are currently miscategorized. I can only respond that my account better captures how these categories have been and are indexed.

5 Currie might deny that the alleged intention to see Méliès' film as a recording is identifiable in the film as a text (second part of Gricean model) and, therefore, intentions are not secured. I agree that they are not visible for present-day audiences, but they would have been identifiable to the turn-of-the-nineteenth-century ones because of the novelty of the medium. In other words, some contextual knowledge will always be relevant for understanding texts, i.e. drawing inferences about intentions from them.

6 Walton recognizes this difference by calling prop-oriented make-believe as one required for comprehension and content-oriented make-believe as one relevant for a fictional world (Walton, 2015b). But even then, he treats pictures as falling under the latter.

7 Elsewhere, Walton (2015b) claims linguistic metaphors (e.g. 'life is hell') are also games of make-believe because they necessarily prescribe imagining by virtue of having to understand one linguistic structure (life) as another (hell). My point remains the same: even if it turned out that metaphors necessarily involve imagination for comprehension which would, because most of the language is based on metaphors (cf. Lakoff and Johnson, 1980), make most if not all linguistic texts incomprehensible without the faculty of imagination, that would not make all these texts fictions. Mandate is not about whether imagination is needed for comprehension but what attitude to take towards the work once it is understood.

8 We will see in the discussion of imaginative resistance in Chapter Five, however, that what or, better, how richly is spontaneously imagined varies considerably from person to person.

9 Walton provides a few more examples with pictures but again they are only an issue if we accept his theory of depiction.

10 Currie (1995: 150) argues that we regularly end up imagining the former but what we do is distinct from what we are supposed to do.

11 While I am not denying that many such works mandate beliefs, beyond some otherwise widely known facts it is not quite clear what precisely they mandate believing. I develop this point further below and in Chapter Seven.

12 After all, even the category of moving images includes films like *Poetic Justice* (Frampton, 1972) in which there are no images that move (cf. Carroll, 2008).

13 For an overview of what are essentially standard features of documentary at different times, see Winston (2013).

14 For Gibson (2007) the problem with completeness or, as he calls it, comprehensiveness, is a person cannot simultaneously believe and imagine the same thing. To this I ask you to think of a belief you hold such as that the sun will rise tomorrow. Now imagine it. I believe that this solves the matter (and can imagine the same).

15 While Schama's history is nonfiction, no such 'act of narration' envelope exists in it because the act of narration is not a part of content of the work. In *Walking with*

Dinosaurs, because there is an audio and image track, Branagh's voice-over narration is one part of what is represented in the show.

16 The crack is not only in how to accommodate different nondiegetic elements; there is also the question of what to do with what David Bordwell (1991) calls the work's implicit meaning or simply the message. *Don't Look Up* (McKay, 2021) is implicitly about collective denialism of climate change though explicitly it is about the denialism of an incoming meteor. In such cases, we are certainly supposed to believe the message but are we also mandated to imagine it? Is such implicit meaning the relevant content? Perhaps we can say that much like form is different from the content so is the message. For the importance of the explicit message for the film's content and ultimately its status already noted by Davies in his engagement with parables, see discussion of *Neighbours* (McLaren, 1952) in Chapter Three.

17 For Terrone (2020a) this amounts to nonfiction because he does not take into consideration the power of indexing.

18 The two mandates in trick and magic film films that I discuss elsewhere (Slugan 2019a) are not simultaneous. Moreover, the application of the mandate changes the relevant content as I discuss below.

19 Davies' (2015: 50–4) discussion of what counts as an overall organizational principle – respect of fidelity constraint or something else – is similar to the question of primacy. I take didactic fiction example from him.

20 Walton classifies Berkeley's philosophical treaties *Dialogues between Hylas and Philonous* as fiction because, while the main goal is to present Berkley's views of nature and arguments in favour of believing in them, the dialogue is between characters we are supposed to imagine. From my perspective this is nonfiction because, as Walton himself admits, not much would be lost if we did not imagine the titular characters in conversation and, more importantly, because it is indexed under philosophical works. The upshot is that the classification follows the existing categorization.

21 Perhaps Terrone would challenge these moving images as artworks, but by the same token we should also disqualify TV documentaries of the History Channel type then.

22 The same does not hold for the categories of fictional and nonfictional *works*. For instance, musical works in general do not appear to be appropriately described as either fiction or nonfiction. While program music like *The Four Seasons* (Vivaldi, 1723) and *Flight of the Bumblebee* (Rimsky-Korsakov, 1899–1900) exists and while the works mandate imaginings about the eponymous subjects, respectively, most musical works do not represent anything so do not have a relevant content to imagine.

23 I no longer hold the view espoused in Slugan (2021b) that evocative documentaries are hybrids.

24 https://www.youtube.com/watch?v=pIJMwlT7hmQ.

25 Notice that the same does not hold for equivalent phrases in prescribing beliefs. While *Fargo* (Coen, 1996) opens with 'This is a true story' it does not determine which part of the story is to be believed nor does it even necessarily prescribe that any part of the film should be prescribed.

26 In fact, the author's original intention was to publish it as fiction. Only after numerous publishers passed on the book it was pitched as a memoir.

27 Friend appears to accept this only for *A Million Little Pieces*.

28 This is distinct from the claim that this makes both works nonfiction as argued by Koch (2009) and addressed in Chapter One.

29 I discuss photographic verisimilitude in more detail in Chapter Five.

30 Matravers might respond that this type of non-propositional engagement is covered by transportation. For how transportation differs from imagination, see Chapter Four.

31 Admittedly, my partial agreement with Matravers that there is no difference in processing many fictional and nonfictional narratives implies that there need not be any fiction institution-specific content-determining rules involved. Even if I am wrong here this does not bear on my criticism of Matravers (in fact, it strengthens it). Furthermore, the more important difference with Abell concerns her other criterion.

Chapter 3

1 https://www.boxofficemojo.com/release/rl2269611521/; https://web.archive.org/web/20090823002301/http://popwatch.ew.com/2009/07/09/blair-witch/.

2 https://www.grainypictures.com/blairwitch/index.html; https://www.grainypictures.com/splitscreen/epten.html.

3 https://www.indiewire.com/news/general-news/split-screens-first-season-ends-with-a-cliffhanger-83475/.

4 https://www.grainypictures.com/blairwitch/index.html; https://www.grainypictures.com/splitscreen2/ss11.html.

5 https://www.grainypictures.com/blairwitch/index.html.

6 Pierson (7 May 1998) followed up on the debate, clarifying that the trailer content was invented: https://www.grainypictures.com/answers/may7.html.

7 Given that multiple visits by the same person count as different visits, this means there are even less unique visitors let alone fans who visit regularly.

8 In fact, two fans who developed one of the most popular fan websites – Abigail Marceluk and Eric Ivins (http://tbwp.freeservers.com) – were given the role of anthropologists who found the missing students' footage in the mockumentary *Curse* *of the Blair Witch* (Myrick and Sánchez, 1999). Premiering on Sci-Fi Channel on 11 July 1999, the film was a promotional prelude to the theatrical release the next day and used much of the footage that did not end up in *The Blair Witch Project*.

9 Johnsen is also credited with starting the film's first fan website live even before the Sundance premiere. Cf. https://web.archive.org/web/20010124093000/http://www0.delphi.com/blairwitch/.

10 https://web.archive.org/web/20010124093000/http://www0.delphi.com/blairwitch/.

11 The film type information does appear on the Sundance Film Festival website: https://history.sundance.org/films/2082/the_blair_witch_project. But the website itself is from present-day rather than from the time closer to the premiere, unlike, Johnsen's website. Moreover, there is no reason for Johnsen to omit the information on his website (unlike in his call) because, as a die-hard fan, on the same pages he is clear that the film content is invented.

12 In the first paragraph, there is a mandate to imagine oneself being in the woods, but this is distinct from imagining the content of the film.

13 https://web.archive.org/web/20170110015305/http://www.mtv.com/news/2816554/best-movie-publicity-stunts/.

14 https://filmmakermagazine.com/archives/issues/winter1999/into_the_woods.php.

15 https://www.imdb.com/title/tt0185937/reviews?sort=submissionDate&dir=asc&ratingFilter=0.

16 For how the website looked at the time see, http://www.haxan.com/blairwitch/.

17 https://www.imdb.com/title/tt0185937/trivia/.

18 https://www.rogerebert.com/festivals/buzz-on-witch-sweeps-cannes.

19 Among the IMDb user reviews above, one reviewer (Stoney-17) reports that at the time of watching (before 27 May) they believed the film was real but by the time of writing the review found out it was fiction.

20 This is much like Davies' (2015) view of parable mentioned in Chapter Two with the exception that he does not allow for the focus to shift with time.

21 https://blog.nfb.ca/blog/2011/02/27/neighbours-the-nfbs-second-oscar-winner/. This should not come as a surprise as we are talking about a short experimental film.

22 McLaren was first and foremost known to the wider audiences as an experimental filmmaker (cf. Thompson, 1952).

23 My translation.

24 *Los Angeles Times* (20 March 1953: 7); *The Journal* (20 March 1953); *Motion Picture Daily* (20 March 1953: 1); *Variety* (25 March 1953: 4); *Motion Picture Herald* (28 March 1953: 17); *The Exhibitor* (1 April 1953: 24).

25 https://en.wikipedia.org/wiki/Animated_documentary.

26 https://web.archive.org/web/20070809224238/http://www.oscars.org/press/pressreleases/2005/05.10.31.html.

27 At least 100 of these must be mine: https://www.youtube.com/watch?v=pIJMwlT7hmQ.

28 https://www.bfi.org.uk/sight-and-sound/best-video-essays-2020.

29 I suspect that most visual essay scholars would disagree and claim that even these films are hybrid. Their dissent, however, rests on defining fiction and nonfiction based on textual features. More importantly, they have not swayed public indexing.

30 https://www2.bfi.org.uk/sight-sound-magazine/greatest-docs.

Chapter 4

1 For a long history of discussing imagination and its varied functions in philosophy running to at least Aristotle, see Amy Kind (2016).

2 For a discussion on whether supposition and imagining are distinct, see Tamar Szabó Gendler and Shen-yi Liao (2019). For a view that entertaining is distinct from imagining, see Kendall Walton (1990: 19–21).

3 For various typologies, see Lagland-Hassan (2020: 1–3).

4 An important caveat is the condition known as aphantasia or the inability to create mental imagery.

5 But, see Kind (2001) for a dissenting view and Gregory (2016) for the overview of the debate.

6 While speaking of perception as a potential input for simulation Currie does not explicitly address offline perceptions, but these are likely to be understood as perceptual imaginings.

7 In other words, imagining linguistically is distinct from imagining perceptually because imagining even such linguistic objects as words and sentences does not necessarily entail imagining their auditory aspects (e.g. phonetics, prosody, etc.). Only when noticeable stylistic markers such as orthography are deployed are auditory aspects to be imagined.

8 On a less charitable reading, this appears to be the view espoused by Carroll (2008: 112–13, 2009: 199, 2016b: 126). This is certainly how Wilson (2011: 75) understands Carroll.

9 While it is debatable whether *Poetic Justice* (Frampton, 1972) mandates perceptual imaginings, it is possible to think of a film consisting of images of pages telling a fictional story which does not refer to the pages and which would as such involve only propositional imaginings.

10 In the next chapter we will see that some objectual imaginings may involve experiential imagining. But in general, imagining objects perceptually does not involve imagining them experientially.

11 For a less charitable reading of this view construed as 'the illusion thesis', see Carroll (2009: 81–93).

12 Another question of this sort which has generated a lot of debate is whether we are mandated to imagine narrators in fiction films (cf. Curran, 2019 and Slugan, 2019c).

13 For more on imagining contradictions, see Chapter Five.

14 According to some of André Bazin's writings (2004) which were later developed as the transparency thesis (Walton, 1984) we literally see objects and people in photographs much like we see them in mirrors or with binoculars. Whether in the case of photographs this is true or whether we see a representation of objects and people instead is irrelevant for my argument because even in the case of representations they remain representations from a vantage point which is distinct from the position occupied.

15 In fact, I have argued above that a core version of imagining seeing may be indistinguishable from imagining visually in the sense that there may be imagining seeing without a visual field (they still differ in terms of imagining from within and from without). Because visual field is what also defines a vantage point, I suggest that imagining seeing does not necessarily entail imagining seeing from a vantage point.

16 For a plane example, see https://www.youtube.com/playlist?list=PL0zVsgbYOuE9RUXS5RDuo3Y-Hrx3a_N41.

17 Cf. https://birdlyvr.com/.

18 Cf. https://www.youtube.com/watch?v=ztVV54sPOns.

19 The coincidence is, of course, not complete because there are paratexts in the actual film texts like credits.

20 Interestingly, Wilson (2011: 102) does not think that every novel is mediated in the sense that its text coincides with the words produced in a written form in some undetermined fashion. He accepts that in this regard non-epistolary novels differ from epistolary ones. But he does think all fictional radio dramas mandate imagining oneself hearing some type of indeterminately produced audio recordings from within a fictional world (2011: 101). One would think that imagined mediation would apply consistently to all media.

21 In practice, I assume we could not do this simultaneously because it is cognitively taxing, but this is a different type of problem that I address in the next chapter.

22 While the dominant view is that they are ubiquitous, see Slugan (2015) for an alternative.

23 Imagining from within is not contrary to imagining from without but rather its contradictory. In other words, imagining from without does not mean active imagining that oneself is *not* experiencing something, but simply means no cognitive resources are expended to imagine anything about oneself experiencing. That is why imagining from within is only an *addition* to imagining from without rather than deletion and replacement of something in that imagining. This is also why determinate imagining such as inclusion of disembodied presence at vantage point in face-to-face imagined seeing is an *addition* to the indeterminacy about any type of presence at a vantage point in modest imagined seeing. Put differently, imagining from without is simply indeterminately imagining when it comes to imagining oneself experiencing.

24 Video games would deserve far more attention than given here. While many genres such as point-and-click adventure games, arcades, sports games, etc., clearly do not mandate imagining any access, I am less certain about real-time strategy games established by *Dune II* (1992) which might be described in terms of mediated imagined seeing.

25 Some epistolary novels do seem to establish the mandate that we are reading the fictional texts, but they do so explicitly as for instance Choderlos de Laclos' *Dangerous Liaisons* (1782) which opens both with a publisher's and editor's notes to establish the reader as an imaginary reader as well. Admittedly, the same can be said of non-epistolary novels which use phrases such as 'Dear reader'.

26 *Cloverfield* could be an exception given that it opens with a test screen overlaid with textual information about where in the fictional world the footage derives from. This arguably works similarly to publisher's and editor's notes in *Dangerous Liaisons* in the sense that it implies imaginary *viewing* of the fictional footage. While in *The Blair Witch Project* there is also a text explaining what we are to see this does not seem to be the part of the film derived from the fictional world in the way publisher's and editor's notes and the opening test screen are parts of the fictional texts.

Chapter 5

1 See Flory (2013) for an exception.

2 Notice that unintentional errors like noticeable cameramen in *Gladiator* (Ridley Scott, 2000) or coffee cup in *Game of Thrones* (HBO, 2011–2019) are not puzzles, because there is no mandate to imagine these things in the first place. In other words, there is neither a failure to prescribe the presence of that entity in the fictional world nor a refusal to accept it as prescribed.

3 https://www.youtube.com/watch?v=_lK4cX5xGiQ.

4 The results of their latest study (Barnes and Black, 2023: 202–3) are approximately the same with conceptual contradiction being the most difficult to imagine at 36 and fantastical scenarios being the easiest to imagine at 71.8. There is a slight variation in morally deviant examples which now score a bit below 50 at 45.6. This would make them cases of imaginative resistance proper under the 50-cutoff interpretation. Even so, they remain less problematic than conceptual contradictions. Moreover, it must be kept in mind here that this is an aggregate of morally deviant examples with most of them hovering around 50 and only one scoring considerably lower at 36.

5 There are examples where attractive actors undergo a considerable physical transformation and genuinely lose or, at least, considerably diminish their shine such as Charlize Theron in *Monster* (Jenkins, 2003) or Christian Bale in *The Machinist* (Anderson, 2004). These I do not class as evoking imaginative resistance.

6 https://www.rottentomatoes.com/m/plan-9-from-outer-space.

7 Cf. https://quora.com/Are-actors-and-actresses-aged-23-to-26-too-old-to-play-high-school-students-in-movies; https://www.quora.com/What-older-actress-actor-was-the-most-egregious-portrayal-of-a-middle-high-schooler-1.

8 https://www.quora.com/What-are-some-good-examples-of-actresses-who-play-ugly-roles-on-screen.

9 https://www.quora.com/Who-are-some-actors-who-were-either-too-pretty-or-too-ugly-for-the-roles-they-played-in-movies-or-TV-shows.

10 I thank the anonymous reviewer for raising this objection.

11 Notice that this differs from Derek Matravers's point discussed in Chapter Two that there is no need for imagination in fiction (film) at all. The objection here is that there is just no need for perceptual imagination.

12 It might be argued that there is also a discrepancy with the effect in the examples of moral deviations. There, a typical reaction to female infanticide is one of disgust yet the mandate is to imagine that this is morally right. The difference is that while laughing or not determines whether a joke is funny or not, and being frightened or not ascertains if something is scary or not, feeling disgust or not does not quite map onto moral right or wrong.

13 Moreover, unlike the *Trainspotting* example from Chapter Three, there is no stylistic strategy here which would mandate perceptual and experiential mandating.

14 If imagining logical contradictions were impossible due to some constraints in cognitive architecture, there would not be so much variation in individual responses in Barnes and Black's experiment.

15 Although it could be possible that part of the reason why people report that they cannot or are even unwilling to imagine is because the richer imagining is the more cognitively taxing it is.

16 More mandated imaginings can also work in the opposite way and disarm the need to think about this in more detail as is, arguably, the case of the longer version of 5 plus 7 is and is not 12 stories which causes less imaginative resistance than its shorter counterpart (cf. Barnes and Black, 2023).

17 Cf. https://www.quora.com/What-are-some-of-the-flaws-scientific-errors-and-plot-holes-scientific-or-otherwise-in-the-Interstellar-movie.

18 https://www.quora.com/What-are-some-of-the-technical-or-scientific-errors-in-the-movie-Gravity.

19 It is likely that in this case the knowledge of real-life physics paired with the tacit assumption that low-level facts in SF should be realistic impels the viewer to richer and therefore more problematic imagining. In fact, the commentator, Saul Hoffman, describes himself as 'Former Electronics Tech'. I, for instance, do not experience this difficulty because I do not assume low-level realism and because I know less about real-life physics than Saul.

Chapter 6

1 For a more detailed overview going beyond the tripartite taxonomy of which the premise is denied, see Jerrol Levinson (1997).

2 https://www.quora.com/Why-do-I-have-no-empathy-for-real-people-only-fictional-characters; https://www.quora.com/Why-do-I-prefer-fictional-characters-over-real-people; https://wrongplanet.net/forums/viewtopic.php?t=166190; https://www.reddit.com/r/sociopath/comments/6pawq0/does_anyone_else_feel_empathy_for_fictional/.

3 The point is to illustrate the problem with one (personal) example and then draw attention to the fact that this experience is quite common. After all, the discussion of the paradox of fiction in terms of its three premises also starts from what we *personally* experience as intuitively correct. The personal example could have easily been transformed into a third-person account such as Walton's 'Charles', but this merely clothes what are regular arguments starting from personal intuitions into academically more acceptable frames.

4 It is undeniable that the presentation of these entities is crucial for actual effects on media consumers as opposed to what they ought to be. But this does not disarm the underlying *moral* demand: irrespective of how somebody's suffering is presented, the *fact* of somebody's suffering *should* suffice for strong emotional involvement. To focus briefly on two nonfictional representations, whether we are watching a ninety-minute documentary focusing on a single person or a five-second report citing death statistics, both presentations give sufficient information about suffering which *should*

bring about the same level of emotional involvement. The *moral* paradox is that they do not appear to do so. To get to the moral paradox of fiction, we simply need to replace a documentary with a fiction film in this example.

5 The other obvious example is the pity for Anna Karenina which I discuss in the following section.

6 The other important fear in horror films is fear *for* the protagonist. I have already discussed how fear for fictional characters can be articulated when discussing the example of Tyrion so will not address it further.

7 The reason is that whereas his interest is primarily in the plot structure, mine is in the relation of the plot and the fear-inducing strategies.

8 To discuss suspense as one way of inducing fear and horror is coherent with Carroll's view (1990b) that suspense on its own is a different emotion than horror.

9 https://www.youtube.com/watch?v=-fDzdDfviLI.

10 I believe this also explains why the horror genre is among the most challenging to execute successfully. So much of its effect rests on the revelation of the monster but once it is revealed, it is difficult to keep the audience afraid.

11 Yanal denies the same solution can apply to Anna and Edward because for him no real-life person could be a vampire. Under my irrational hypotheticals framework, this is not necessarily excluded.

12 I would like to thank Anna Abraham for drawing my attention to this.

13 That there is a clear associated action does not mean that the action has to be executed, just that there is a potential for one. Under this framework, frequenting instead of running away from horror films is no more mysterious than riding roller coasters instead of avoiding them – they both present fear-inducing real-life structures.

Chapter 7

1 For the project website, see https://aetna.uniri.hr/.

2 Thomson-Jones (2005) is an exception, but her real focus is the second claim about the aesthetic value and how it relates to the broader version of epistemic part of aesthetic cognitivism. Christensen, Cardillo and Chatterjee (2025) are similarly interested in this broader version of the epistemic value of aesthetic cognitivism.

3 I assume an ecumenic position where a fictional work qualifies as a fictional work of art.

4 Makers of fictional works arguably also become better at making that art through continuing practice.

5 For one notable exception discussing narratological knowledge, see Carroll (2013).

6 It is no surprise that the taxonomy is reminiscent of the taxonomy of imagining discussed in Chapter Four given that imagination and belief do not differ in content but in the attitude taken towards the content.

7 I am deliberately not including the discussion of how objects sound because these regularly come from pre-recorded studio sound libraries which were often made with very different objects. For voice, see the next footnote.

8 The reason I hesitate is that in radio drama actors often deliberately try not to sound like they usually do. The same often holds for fiction film where actors regularly sport accents different from their own. Certainly, even then fiction films and radio dramas confer perceptual knowledge about how the actors sounded at the time of the performance, but that type of knowledge seems to be less relevant because it is not really knowledge about how the actor sounds in general.

9 There seems to be an equivalent to medium-based perceptual knowledge in the propositional domain. In literary fiction, it is hard to deny that the texts *qua* texts impart a range of non-aesthetic information about syntax and semantics. Ernest Hemingway's fictional works, for instance, teach us a lot about how a grammatical sentence in American English of the first half of the twentieth century looks. The main difference is that this type of knowledge is not as easily extractable for the audiences as perceptual knowledge in film fiction is but would rather need more expert engagement by linguists or students thereof. (In another version of this, foreign language speakers can acquire knowledge about a language through reading or watching films in that language but again the learning is due to texts *qua* texts).

10 While imagining perceptually does not necessarily entail imagining experientially, perceiving does necessarily entail experiencing.

11 McGregor also discusses moral knowledge in part under counterfactual knowledge or knowledge of how things should be.

12 For a more detailed debate, see Slugan (2021a) and McGregor (2021b).

13 Unlike for beliefs, they determine that attitudes, desires, and behaviours are influenced by fiction suggesting that broad aesthetic cognitivism and in particular aesthetic cognitivism focusing on morality stands on a firmer ground. That fictions change behaviours may on first inspection contradict my claim in the previous chapter's conclusion that fictional entities do not change them. But this is not the case because fictional works are distinct from fictional entities – in the previous chapter's parlance fictional works clearly include or invoke real-life structures and as such may change behaviours.

14 Interestingly, they do not mention Braddock and Dillard (2016) but provide proposals for why studies which report effects should instead be construed as showing something else.

15 It might be objected that I am taking narrow aesthetic cognitivists to a different standard than the one I have provided in this chapter. I have referred to no empirical

studies when claiming standard knowledge acquisition among art fiction makers and aesthetic knowledge acquisition among audiences. That is true, but in these cases the situation is different in the sense that empirical proof is already embedded in standard fiction making and consumption practices. Concerning audiences, it is uncontroversial that at least a significant subset understands the stories they are consuming. If our everyday conversations with fellow moviegoers, TV show watchers, or novels readers are not proof enough, then psychological literature I have already cited should be for it already assumes this basic comprehension in its questionnaires. Turning to fiction makers, it is unclear how, unless using something like ChatGPT or having a ghost writer, a writer of historical fiction like Mantel could produce her work without extensive historical research. And if that is not sufficient, I can point to the words of Mantel herself who admits that it took her five years to research the book (Alter, 2009). Similar observation can be made for filmmakers like Nolan and actresses like Streep and their subjects (Ebiri, 2023, NPR staff, 2011).

16 I would like to thank the anonymous reviewer for these comments.

17 A somewhat different meta-analysis which looks at the difference in long-term persuasion effects (attitudes, intentions, and beliefs) between narratives and non-narratives reveals that nonfictional narratives are more persuasive than (nonfictional) non-narratives, but that fictional narratives are only as persuasive as (nonfictional) non-narratives (Oschatz and Marker, 2020). When it comes to beliefs as opposed to intentions and desires, narratives are no more persuasive than non-narratives regardless of whether narratives are fictional or not.

18 In 2011, the Chinese government notably banned films and TV shows involving time travel plots: https://www.hollywoodreporter.com/news/general-news/china-bans-time-travel-films-177801/.

19 Cf. Enrico Terrone's 2022 ERC Project 'The Philosophy of Experiential Artefacts': https://pea.unige.it/node/2. Moreover, as Terrone himself points out, his view of artworks as artefacts for generating experiences is not incompatible with the institutional theory presented here: if artworks are artefacts and if their non/fictional status also boils down to one of the ways in which they are used, there is nothing strange with artefact's use changing over time.

Conclusion

1 I thank the anonymous reviewer for drawing my attention to the connection.

2 https://templetonreligiontrust.org/explore/developing-moral-understanding-at-the-movies/.

BIBLIOGRAPHY

Abell, C. (2020), *Fiction: A Philosophical Analysis*, Oxford: Oxford University Press.

Allen, R. (1997), *Projecting Illusion: Film Spectatorship and the Impression of Reality*, Cambridge: Cambridge University Press.

Alter, A. (2009), 'How to Write a Great Novel', *The Wall Street Journal*, 13 November. Available online: https://www.wsj.com/articles/SB10001424052748703740004574513463106012106?mod=WSJ_hpp_sections_lifestyle.

Alter, N. M. and T. Corrigan, eds. (2017), *Essays on the Essay film*, New York: Columbia University Press.

Althusser, L. (2001), 'Ideology and Ideological State Apparatuses', in *Lenin and Philosophy and Other Essays*, 85–126, trans. Ben Brewster, New York: Monthly Review Press.

Altman, R. (1999), *Film/Genre*, London: British Film Institute.

Aristotle (1987), *Poetics*, trans. R. Janko, Indianapolis: Hackett.

Bareis, J. A. and M. Slugan (2019), 'Introducing Fiction in Central and Eastern European Film Theory and Practice', *Apparatus* 8. http://dx.doi.org/10.17892/app.2019.0008.169.

Barnes, J. and J. E. Black (2016), 'Impossible or Improbable: The Difficulty of Imagining Morally Deviant Worlds', *Imagination, Cognition and Personality* 36 (1): 27–40.

Barnes, J. and J. E. Black (2023), 'Can You or Will You Imagine? Ability and Willingness to Imagine Fictional Scenarios Depend on the Type of Imaginary World', in H. Kapoor and J. C. Kauman, eds., *Creativity and Morality*, 201–20, London: Academic Press.

Bathbun, J. R. (1913), 'Motion Picture Making and Exhibition', *Motography* 9 (13): 471.

Baudrillard, J. (1994), *Simulacra and Simulation*, trans. S. F. Glaser, Ann Arbor: University of Michigan Press.

Baudry, J.-L. (1986), 'The Apparatus: Metapsychological Approaches to the Impression of Reality in Cinema', in P. Rosen, ed., *Narrative, Apparatus, Ideology: A Film Theory Reader*, 299–318, New York: Columbia University Press.

Bazin, A. (2004), *What Is Cinema?* Vol. 1. ed. and trans. H. Gray, Berkeley: University of California Press.

Bell, N. (2020), *How to Write a Horror Movie*, New York: Routledge.

Benshoff, H. M. and S. Griffin (2011), *America on Film: Representing Race, Class, Gender, and Sexuality at the Movies*, Malden: John Wiley & Sons.

Black, J. E. and J. Barnes (2017), 'Measuring the Unimaginable: Imaginative Resistance to Fiction and Related Constructs', *Personality and Individual Differences* 111: 71–9.

Blake, M. and S. Bailey (2013), *Writing the Horror Movie*, London: Bloomsbury.

Bogdanovich, P. (1963), *The Cinema of Alfred Hitchcock*, New York: Museum of Modern Art.

Boileau-Despréaux, N. (1674), *L'Art poetique*, Paris: Denys Thierry.

Bordwell, D. (1985), *Narration in the Fiction Film*, Madison: University of Wisconsin Press.

Bordwell, D. (1991), *Making Meaning: Inference and Rhetoric in the Interpretation of Cinema*, Cambridge: Harvard University Press.

Bordwell, D., J. Staiger and K. Thompson (1985), *The Classical Hollywood Cinema: Film Style & Mode of Production to 1960*, New York: Columbia University Press.

Borenstein, M., L. V. Hedges, J. P. T. Higgins and H. R. Rothstein (2009), *Introduction to Meta-Analysis*, Malden: John Wiley & Sons.

Bottomore, S. (1999), 'The Panicking Audience?: Early Cinema and the "Train Effect"', *Historical Journal of Film, Radio and Television* 19 (2): 177–216.

Boyd, B. (2018), 'The Evolution of Stories: From Mimesis to Language, from Fact to Fiction', *Wiley Interdisciplinary Reviews: Cognitive Science* 9 (1): e1444. https://doi.org/10.1002/wcs.1444.

Braddock, K. and J. P. Dillard (2016), 'Meta-analytic Evidence for the Persuasive Effect of Narratives on Beliefs, Attitudes, Intentions, and Behaviors', *Communication Monographs* 83 (4): 446–7.

Branigan, E. and W. Buckland, eds. (2014), *The Routledge Encyclopaedia of Film Theory*, New York: Routledge.

Brodie, M., U. Foehr, V. Rideout, N. Baer, C. Miller, R. Flournoy and D. Altman (2001), 'Communicating Health Information through the Entertainment Media', *Health Affairs* 20 (1): 192–9.

Buckland, W. (2000), *The Cognitive Semiotics of Film*, Cambridge: Cambridge University Press.

Campbell, R. (2019), 'Moral Epistemology', in E. N. Zalta, ed., *The Stanford Encyclopedia of Philosophy*. https://plato.stanford.edu/archives/win2019/entries/moral-epistemology.

Carroll, N. (1983), 'From Real to Reel: Entangled in Nonfiction Film', *Philosophic Exchange* 14 (1): 5–45.

Carroll, N. (1988a), *Mystifying Movies: Fads and Fallacies in Contemporary Film Criticism*, New York: Columbia University Press.

Carroll, N. (1988b), *Philosophical Problems of Classical Film Theory*, Princeton: Princeton University Press.

Carroll, N. (1990a), 'The Image of Women in Film', *The Journal of Aesthetics and Art Criticism* 48 (4): 349–60.

Carroll, N. (1990b), *The Philosophy of Horror: Or, Paradoxes of the Heart*, New York: Routledge.

Carroll, N. (1995), 'Review: Mimesis as Make-Believe', *The Philosophical Quarterly* 45 (178): 93–9.

Carroll, N. (2003), 'Fiction, Non-fiction, and the Film of Presumptive Assertion: A Conceptual Analysis', in *Engaging the Moving Image*, 193–224, New Haven: Yale University Press.

Carroll, N. (2004), 'Sympathy for the Devil', in R. Greene and P. Vernezze. eds., *The Sopranos and Philosophy*, 121–136, Chicago: Open Court.

Carroll, N. (2008), *The Philosophy of Motion Pictures*, Madison: University of Wisconsin Press.

Carroll, N. (2009), 'Narration', in P. Livingston and C. Plantinga. eds., *The Routledge Companion to Philosophy and Film*, 196–206, New York: Routledge.

Carroll, N. (2013), '*Memento* and the Phenomenology of Comprehending Motion Picture Narration', in *Minerva's Night Out: Philosophy, Pop Culture, and Moving Images*, 203–20, Chichester: Blackwell.

Carroll, N. (2016a), 'Fiction', in N. Carroll and J. Gibson, eds., *The Routledge Companion to the Philosophy of Literature*, 359–71. New York: Routledge.

Carroll, N. (2016b), 'Motion Picture Narration', in K. Thomson-Jones, ed., *Current Controversies in Philosophy of Film*, 115–27, New York: Routledge.

Cavell, S. (1979), *The World Viewed: Reflections on the Ontology of Film*, Cambridge: Harvard University Press.

Charlton, W. (1984), 'Feeling for the Fictitious', *The British Journal of Aesthetics* 24 (3): 206–16.

Charlton, W. (1986), 'Radford and Allen on Being Moved by Fiction: A Rejoinder', *The British Journal of Aesthetics* 26 (4): 39–394.

Christensen, A. P., E. R. Cardillo and A. Chatterjee (2025), 'Can Art Promote Understanding? A Review of the Psychology and Neuroscience of Aesthetic Cognitivism', *Psychology of Aesthetics, Creativity, and the Arts* 19 (1): 1–13. https://doi.org/10.1037/aca0000541.

Coëgnarts, M. (2019), *Film as Embodied Art: Bodily Meaning in the Cinema of Stanley Kubrick*, Boston: Academic Studies Press.

Coleridge, S. T. (1817), *Biographiae Litteraria; Or Biographical Sketches of My Literary Life and Opinions*, London: S. Curtis.

Curran, A. (2016), 'Fictional Indeterminacy, Imagined Seeing, and Cinematic Narration', in K. Thomson-Jones, ed., *Current Controversies in Philosophy of Film*, 99–114, New York: Routledge.

Curran, A. (2019), 'Silly Questions and Arguments for the Implicit, Cinematic Narrator', in N. Carroll, L. T. Di Summa and S. Loht, eds., *The Palgrave Handbook of the Philosophy of Film and Motion Pictures*, 97–117, Cham: Palgrave MacMillan.

Currie, G. (1990), *The Nature of Fiction*, Cambridge: Cambridge University Press.

Currie, G. (1995), *Image and Mind: Film, Philosophy and Cognitive Science*, Cambridge: Cambridge University Press.

Currie, G. (1999), 'Visible Traces: Documentary and the Contents of Photographs', *The Journal of Aesthetics and Art Criticism* 57 (3): 285–97.

Currie, G. (2020), *Imagining and Knowing: The Shape of Fiction*, New York: Oxford University Press.

Davies, D. (2015), 'Fictive Utterance and the Fictionality of Narratives and Works', *British Journal of Aesthetics* 55 (1): 39–55.

Davies, D. (2022), 'Definition of Fiction: State of the Art', *British Journal of Aesthetics* 62 (2): 241–55.

Deleuze, G. (1983), *Cinema I: The Movement-Image*, Minneapolis: University of Minnesota Press.

Deleuze, G. (1986), *Cinema II: The Time-Image*, Minneapolis: University of Minnesota Press.

Derrida, J. (1976), *Of Grammatology*, Baltimore: Johns Hopkins.

De Sousa, R. (2010), 'The Mind's Bermuda Triangle: Philosophy of Emotions and Empirical Science', in P. Goldie, ed., *The Oxford Handbook of Philosophy of Emotion*, 95–117, New York: Oxford University Press.

Dobson, N. (2017), *Norman McLaren: Between the Frames*, London: Bloomsbury.

Dobson, T. (1994), *The Film Work of Norman McLaren*, PhD dissertation, University of Canterbury.

Dubourg, E. and N. Baumard (2023), 'Do Fictions Impact People's Beliefs? A Critical View', in A. James, A. Kubo and F. Lavocat, eds., *The Routledge Handbook of Fiction and Belief*, 141–58, London: Routledge.

Dyer, R. (2013), *The Matter of Images: Essays on Representations*, 2nd edn, Hoboken: Taylor and Francis.

Eaton, A. W. (2015), 'Literature and Morality', in N. Carroll and J. Gibson, eds., *The Routledge Companion to Philosophy of Literature*, 433–50, New York: Routledge.

Ebiri, B. (2023), 'An Action Movie about Scientists Talking', *Vulture*, 17 July. Available online: https://www.vulture.com/article/oppenheimer-christopher-nolan-cillian-murphy-behind-the-scenes.html.

Eitzen, D. (1995), 'When Is a Documentary?: Documentary as a Mode of Reception', *Cinema Journal* 35 (1): 81–102.

Flory, D. (2013), 'Race and Imaginative Resistance in James Cameron's Avatar', *Projections* 7 (2): 41–63.

Friend, S. (2012), 'VIII–Fiction as a Genre', *Proceedings of the Aristotelian Society* 112 (2): 179–209.

Friend, S. (2014), 'Believing in Stories', in G. Currie, M. Kieran, A. Meskin and J. Robson, eds., *Aesthetics and the Sciences of Mind*, 227–48, New York: Oxford University Press.

Friend, S. (2017), 'Fiction and Emotion', in A. Kind, ed., *The Routledge Handbook of Philosophy of Imagination*, 217–29, New York: Routledge.

Gallese, V. and M. Guerra (2019), *The empathic screen: Cinema and neuroscience*. Oxford: Oxford University Press.

García-Carpintero, M. (2013), 'Norms of Fiction-Making', *British Journal of Aesthetics* 53 (3): 339–57.

García-Carpintero, M. (2021), 'Documentaries and the Fiction/Nonfiction Divide', *Studies in Documentary Film* 15 (2): 163–74.

Gasser, L., Y. Dammert and P. K. Murphy (2022), 'How Do Children Socially Learn from Narrative Fiction: Getting the Lesson, Simulating Social Worlds, or Dialogic Inquiry?' *Educational Psychology Review* 34 (3): 1445–75.

Gaut, B. (2005), 'Art and Knowledge', in J. Levinson, ed., *The Oxford Handbook of Aesthetics*, 436–50, New York: Oxford University Press.

Gaut, B. (2010), *A Philosophy of Cinematic Art*, Cambridge: Cambridge University Press.

Gendler, T. S. (2000), 'The Puzzle of Imaginative Resistance', *The Journal of Philosophy* 97 (2): 55–81.

Gendler, T. S. (2006), 'Imaginative Resistance Revisited', in S. Nichols, ed., *The Architecture of the Imagination: New Essays on Pretense, Possibility, and Fiction*, 149–73, New York: Oxford University Press.

Gendler, T. S. (2008), 'Alief in Action (and Reaction)', *Mind and Language* 23 (5): 552–85.

Gendler, T. S. and S. Liao (2016), 'The Problem of Imaginative Resistance', in N. Carroll and J. Gibson, eds., *The Routledge Companion to Philosophy of Literature*, 405–18, New York: Routledge.

Gerrig, R. J. and D. A. Prentice (1991), 'The Representation of Fictional Information', *Psychological Science* 2 (5): 336–40.

Gerrig, R. J. and D. N. Rapp (2004), 'Psychological Processes Underlying Literary Impact', *Poetics Today* 25 (2): 265–81.

Gibson, J. (2007), *Fiction and the Weave of Life*, Oxford: Oxford University Press.

Gibson, J., W. Huemer and L. Pocci, eds. (2012), *A Sense of the World: Essays on Fiction, Narrative, and Knowledge*, London: Routledge.

Gilbert, D. T. (1991), 'How Mental Systems Believe', *American Psychologist* 46 (2): 107–19.

Gottschall, J. (2008), *Literature, Science, and a New Humanities*, New York: Palgrave MacMillan.

Graham, G. (1996), 'Aesthetic Cognitivism and the Literary Arts', *Journal of Aesthetic Education* 30 (1): 1–17.

Green, M. C. and T. C. Brock (2000), 'The Role of Transportation in the Persuasiveness of Public Narratives', *Journal of Personality and Social Psychology* 79 (5): 701–21.

Gregory, D. (2016), 'Imagination and Mental Imagery', in A. Kind, ed., *The Routledge Handbook of Philosophy of Imagination*, 97–110, New York: Routledge.

Grodal, T. (2009), *Embodied Visions: Evolution, Emotion, Culture, and Film*, Oxford: Oxford University Press.

Hakemulder, J., M. M. Kuijpers and E. S. Tan, eds. (2017), *Narrative Absorption*, Amsterdam: John Benjamins Publishing Company.

Hall, S. (1973), 'Encoding and Decoding in the Television Discourse', in *Colloquy on Training in the Critical Reading of Televisual Language*, 1–20, Birmingham: University of Birmingham.

Hayward, S. (2017), *Cinema Studies: The Key Concepts*, 5th edn, London: Routledge.

Hediger, V. (2009), 'Von Überhandnehmen der Fiktion', in G. Koch and C. Voss, eds., '*Es ist, als ob*': *Fiktionalität in Philosophie, Film- und Medienwissenschaft*, 163–84, Paderborn: Wilhelm Fink.

Herbert, F. (1966/2005), *Dune*, London: Hodder & Stoughton.

Hjort, M. (2011), *Lone Scherfig's Italian for Beginners*, Seattle: University of Washington Press.

Hjort, M. (2019), 'The Public Value of Film: Moving Images, Health and Well-Being', *Journal of Scandinavian Cinema* 9 (1): 7–23.

Hjort, M. (2022), 'The Benefits of Genre: Feel-Good Films as a Path to Health and Well-Being', in M. Hjort and T. Nannicelli, eds., *A Companion to Motion Pictures and Public Value*, 558–75, Chichester: John Wiley & Sons.

Hoare, F. A. (1953), 'Production Techniques in the Making of Educational Films', *British Kinematography* 22 (6): 176–81.

Hopkins, R. (2008), 'What Do We See in Film?', *The Journal of Aesthetics and Art Criticism* 66 (2): 149–59.

Horace (1990), *Epistles Book II and Ars Poetica*, trans. N. Rudd, Cambridge: Cambridge University Press.

Howell, R. A. (2011), 'Lights, Camera … Action? Altered Attitudes and Behaviour in Response to the Climate Change Film the Age of Stupid', *Global Environmental Change* 21 (1): 177–87.

Hume, D. (1757/1875), 'Of the Standard of Taste', in *Essays: Moral and Political and Literary*, 245–55, London: Longmans, Green, and Co.

Hutto, D. D. (2012), *Folk Psychological Narratives: The Sociocultural Basis of Understanding Reasons*. Cambridge: MIT Press.

Johnson, M. P. A. (2001), *Online, Onscreen: Motion Picture Promotion via the Internet*, MA thesis, Carleton University.

Kahneman, D. and A. Tversky (1973), 'On the Psychology of Prediction', *Psychological Review* 80 (4): 237–52.

Kim, H., M. Kneer and M. T. Stuart (2019), 'The Content-Dependence of Imaginative Resistance', in F. Cova and S. Réhault, eds., *Advances in Experimental Philosophy of Aesthetics*, 143–65, New York: Bloomsbury.

Kind, A. (2001) 'Putting the Image Back in Imagination', *Philosophy and Phenomenological Research* 62 (1): 85–109.

Kind, A., ed. (2016), *The Routledge Handbook of Philosophy of Imagination*, New York: Routledge.

Koch, G. (2009), 'Tun oder so tun als ob?' in G. Koch and C. Voss, eds., *'Es ist, als ob': Fiktionalität in Philosophie, Film- und Medienwissenschaft*, 139–50, Paderborn: Wilhelm Fink.

Koch, G. and C. Voss, eds. (2009), *'Es ist, als ob': Fiktionalität in Philosophie, Film- und Medienwissenschaft*, Paderborn: Wilhelm Fink.

Konrad, E. (2016), 'Panfiktionalismus', in T. Klauk and T. Köppe, eds., *Fiktionalität: ein interdisziplinäres Handbuch*, 235–54, Berlin: Gruyter.

Konrad, E., T. Petraschka and C. Werner (2018), 'The Paradox of Fiction – A Brief Introduction into Recent Developments, Open Questions, and Current Areas of Research, including a Comprehensive Bibliography from 1975 to 2018', *Journal of Literary Theory* 12 (2): 193–203.

Kracauer, S. (1960), *Theory of Film: The Redemption of Physical Reality*, New York: Oxford University Press.

Kroon, F. and A. Voltolini (2019), 'Fiction', in E. N. Zalta ed., *The Stanford Encyclopedia of Philosophy*. https://plato.stanford.edu/archives/win2019/entries/fiction.

Kuhn, A. and G. Westwell (2020), *A Dictionary of Film Studies*, 2nd edn, Oxford: Oxford University Press.

Lagland-Hassan, P. (2020), *Explaining Imagination*, Oxford: Oxford University Press.

Lakoff, J. and M. Johnson (1980), *Metaphors We Live By*, Chicago: University of Chicago Press.

Lamarque, P. and S. H. Olsen (1994), *Truth, Fiction, and Literature: A Philosophical Perspective*, Oxford: Clarendon Press.

Levinson, J. (1997), 'Emotion in Response to Art: A Survey of the Terrain', in M. Hjort and S. Laver, eds., *Emotion and the Arts*, 20–34, Oxford: Oxford University Press.

Levinson, J., ed. (1998), *Aesthetics and Ethics*, Cambridge: Cambridge University Press.

Liao, S. and T. Gendler (2019), 'Imagination', in E. N. Zalta, ed., *The Stanford Encyclopedia of Philosophy*. https://plato.stanford.edu/archives/win2019/entries/imagination/.

Liao, S., N. Strohminger and C. S. Sripada (2014), 'Empirically Investigating Imaginative Resistance', *British Journal of Aesthetics* 54 (3): 339–55.

London, I. (2024), *Hollywood Online: Internet Movie Marketing before and after the Blair Witch Project*, London: Bloomsbury.

Marks, L. U. (2000), *The Skin of the Film: Intercultural Cinema, Embodiment, and the Senses*, Durham: Duke University Press.

Marsh, E. and L. Fazio (2006), 'Learning Errors from Fiction: Difficulties in Reducing Reliance on Fictional Stories', *Memory & Cognition* 34 (5): 1140–49.

Marsh, E. J., M. L. Meade and H. L. Roediger III (2003), 'Learning Facts from Fiction', *Journal of Memory and Language* 49: 519–36.

Matravers, D. (2014), *Fiction and Narrative*, Oxford: Oxford University Press.

McCormick, P. J. (1988), *Fictions, Philosophies, and the Problems of Poetics*, Ithaca: Cornell University Press.

McGinn, C. (2005), *The Power of Movies: How Screen and Mind Interact*, New York: Pantheon.

McGregor, R. (2021a), *A Criminology of Narrative Fiction*, Bristol: Bristol University Press.

McGregor, R. (2021b), 'Response to Frauley, Simecek, Slugan, and Whitecross', *Journal of Theoretical & Philosophical Criminology* 13: 148–57.

Metz, C. (1982), *The Imaginary Signifier: Psychoanalysis and the Cinema*, London: MacMillan Press.

Moran, R. (1994), 'The Expression of Feeling in Imagination', *The Philosophical Review* 103 (1): 75–106.

Morgan, D. and J. Schonig (2023), 'Introduction: Camera Movement and the Necessity of Criticism', *Film Criticism* 47 (1). https://doi.org/10.3998/fc.4730.

Nichols, B. (2013), 'Irony, Cruelty, Evil (and a Wink) in the Act of Killing', *Film Quarterly* 67 (2): 25–9.

Nichols, B. (2017), *Introduction to Documentary*, 3rd edn, Bloomington: Indiana University Press.

Nichols, S., ed. (2006), *The Architecture of the Imagination: New Essays on Pretense, Possibility, and Fiction*, New York: Oxford University Press.

Niver, K. R. (1971), *Biograph Bulletins, 1896–1908*, Los Angeles: Locare Research Group.

NPR staff (2011), 'From Meryl to Margaret: Becoming the Iron Lady', *NPR*, 19 December. https://www.npr.org/2011/12/19/143962896/from-meryl-to-margaret-becoming-the-iron-lady.

Nussbaum, M. C. (1990), *Love's Knowledge: Essays on Philosophy and Literature*, New York: Oxford University Press.

Odin, R. (1988), 'Du spectateur fictionnalisant au nouveau spectateur', *Iris* 8: 121–40.

Odin, R. (1995), 'For a Semio-Pragmatics of Film', in W. Buckland, ed., *The Film Spectator*, 213–26, Amsterdam: Amsterdam University Press.

Odin, R. (2000), *De la fiction*, Brussels: De Boeck Université.

Ohayon, A. (2011), 'Neighbours: The NFB's Second Oscar Winner'. https://blog.nfb.ca/blog/2011/02/27/neighbours-the-nfbs-second-oscar-winner/.

Oschatz, C. and C. Marker (2020), 'Long-term Persuasive Effects in Narrative Communication Research: A Meta-analysis', *Journal of Communication* 70 (4): 473–96.

Paskins, B. (1977), 'On Being Moved by Anna Karenina and *Anna Karenina*', *Philosophy* 52 (201): 344–7.

Pierson, J. (1999), 'John Responds (Blair Witch and Haxan Films)', 7 May. https://www.grainypictures.com/answers/may7.html.

Plantinga, C. (2005), 'What a Documentary Is, after All', *The Journal of Aesthetics and Art Criticism* 63 (2): 105–17.

Plantinga, C. (2018), *Screen Stories: Emotion and the Ethics of Engagement*, New York: Oxford University Press.

Plantinga, C., ed. (2023), *Screen Stories and Moral Understanding: Interdisciplinary Perspectives*, Oxford: Oxford University Press.

Plato (1997), '*The Republic*', in J. M. Cooper, ed., *Complete Works*, 971–1223, Indianapolis: Hackett.

Prentice, D. A. and R. J. Gerrig (1999), 'Exploring the Boundary between Fiction and Reality', in S. Chaiken and Y. Trope, eds., *Dual-Process Theories in Social Psychology*, 529–46, New York: Guilford Press.

Prentice, D., R. Gerrig and D. Bailis (1997), 'What Readers Bring to the Processing of Fictional Texts', *Psychonomic Bulletin & Review* 4: 416–20.

Proctor, W. (2018). '"I've Seen a Lot of Talk about the #blackstormtrooper outrage, but Not a Single Example of Anyone Complaining": The Force Awakens, Canonical Fidelity and Non-toxic Fan Practices', *Participations: International Journal of Audience and Reception Studies* 15 (1): 160–79.

Pudovkin, V. (1958), *Film Technique and Film Acting*, trans. and ed. I. Montagu, New York: Grove Press.

Putnam, H. (1978), *Meaning and the Moral Sciences*, London: Routledge & Kegan Paul.

Rabinovitz, L. (2012), *Electric Dreamland: Amusement Parks, Movies, and American Modernity*, New York: Columbia University Press.

Radford, C. (1975), 'How Can We Be Moved by the Fate of Anna Karenina?', *Proceedings of the Aristotelian Society, Supplementary Volumes* 49: 81–93.

Rascaroli, L. (2009), 'The Essay Film: Problems, Definitions, Textual Commitments', *Framework* 49 (2): 24–47.

Renov, M. (1993), 'Introduction', in M. Renov, ed., *Theorizing Documentary*, 1–11, New York: Routledge.

Roe, A. H. (2013), *Animated Documentary*, Basingstoke: Palgrave MacMillan.

Rubeša, D. (1999), 'Post festum 52. Cannesa', *Hrvatski filmski ljetopis* 5 (18): 133–7.

Schama, S. (2003), *A History of Britain III: The Fate of Empire, 1776–2000*, London: Random House.

Schiller, F. (1794). *Über die ästhetische Erziehung des Menschen*, Stuttgart: Cotta.

Schneider-Mayerson, M., A. Gustafson, A. Leiserowitz, M. H. Goldberg, S. A. Rosenthal and M. Ballew (2020), 'Environmental Literature as Persuasion: An Experimental Test of the Effects of Reading Climate Fiction', *Environmental Communication* 14 (1): 1–16.

Schreier, M. (2004), '"Please Help Me; All I Want to Know Is: Is It Real or Not?": How Recipients View the Reality Status of the Blair Witch Project', *Poetics Today* 25 (2): 305–34.

Searle, J. (1975), 'The Logical Status of Fictional Discourse', *New Literary History* 6 (2): 319–32.

Sharpe, D. and S. Poets (2020), 'Meta-analysis as a Response to the Replication Crisis', *Canadian Psychology/Psychologie Canadienne* 61 (4): 377.

Shelley, P. B. (1891), *A Defense of Poetry*, Boston: Ginn.

Sidney, P. (1974), *The Defense of Poesie*, Oxford: Oxford University Press.

Siety, E. (2009), *Fictions d'images: Essai sur l'attribution de propriétés fictives aux images de films*, Rennes: Presses universitaires de Rennes.

Sinnerbrink, R. (2016), *Cinematic Ethics: Exploring Ethical Experience through Film*, Oxon: Routledge.

Sitney, P. A. (1978), *The Avant-garde Film: A Reader of Theory and Criticism*, New York: New York University Press.

Slugan, M. (2015), 'Deixis in Literary and Film Fiction: Intra-Ontological Reference and the Case of the Controlling Fictional Narrator', in J. A. Bareis and L. Nordrum, eds., *How to Make Believe: The Fictional Truths of Representational Arts*, 185–202, Berlin: De Gruyter.

Slugan. M. (2017a), *Montage as Perceptual Experience: Berlin Alexanderplatz from Döblin to Fassbinder*, Melton: Boydell and Brewer.

Slugan, M. (2017b), 'Taking Bazin Literally', *Projections* 11 (1): 63–82.

Slugan, M. (2019a), *Fiction and Imagination in Early Cinema: A Philosophical Approach to Film History*, London: Bloomsbury.

Slugan, M. (2019b), 'The Film Narrator and the Early American Screenwriting Manuals', *Early Popular Visual Culture* 17 (2): 192–206.

Slugan, M. (2019c), *Noël Carroll and Film: A Philosophy of Art and Popular Culture*, London: Bloomsbury.

Slugan, M. (2019d), 'Theorizing Fiction in Film Non/Fiction: Some Thoughts on Recent German Film Theory', *Apparatus* 8. http://dx.doi.org/10.17892/app.2019.0008.161.

Slugan, M. (2020), 'Film Studies and the Experimental Method', *NECSUS* 9 (2): 203–24. https://necsus-ejms.org/film-studies-and-the-experimental-method/.

Slugan, M. (2021a), 'Fiction, Knowledge and Cinematic Realism', *Journal of Theoretical & Philosophical Criminology* 13: 99–110. http://www.jtpcrim.org/OCT2021/Mario.pdf.

Slugan, M. (2021b), 'Textualism, Extratextualism, and the Fiction/Nonfiction Distinction in Documentary Studies', *Studies in Documentary Film* 15 (2): 114–26.

Slugan, M. (2022a), 'Early Cinema and the Philosophy of Imagination', in M. Slugan and D. Biltereyst, eds., *New Perspectives on Early Cinema History: Concepts, Approaches, Audiences*, 103–30, London: Bloomsbury.

Slugan, M. (2022b), 'Pandemic (Movies): A Pragmatic Analysis of a Nascent Genre', *Quarterly Review of Film and Video* 39 (4): 890–918.

Slugan, M. (2023), 'Fiction as Challenge for Text-Oriented Film Studies', *New Review of Film and Television* 21 (3): 427–50.

Slugan, M. and E. Terrone (2021), 'The Fiction/Nonfiction Distinction: Documentary Studies and Analytic Aesthetics in Conversation', *Studies in Documentary Film* 15 (2): 107–13.

Slugan, M., A. Hanifee and W. Zeng (2025), 'Hale's Tours in Singapore and Hong Kong', *Early Popular Visual Culture* 23 (1–2) [forthcoming].

Slugan, M., A. Hanifee and W. Zeng (2026), 'Chinese-, Malay-, and English-Language Reception of Early Cinema in Malaya', in D. Roig Sanz, S. Van de Peer and A. C. Rodagut, eds., *Global and Feminist Perspectives on Cinema Histories: Reframing Cinema Through a Decentered Lens*, Amsterdam: Amsterdam University Press [forthcoming].

Smith, M. (1995), *Engaging Characters: Fiction, Emotion, and the Cinema*, Oxford: Clarendon Press.

Smith, M. (2011), 'Just What Is It That Makes Tony Soprano Such an Appealing, Attractive Murderer?', in W. Jones and S. Vice, eds., *Ethics at the Cinema*, 66–90, Oxford: Oxford University Press.

Smith, M. (2017), *Film, Art, and the Third Culture: A Naturalized Aesthetics of Film*, Oxford: Oxford University Press.

Sobchack, V. (1999), 'Toward a Phenomenology of Nonfictional Film Experience', in J. Gaines and M. Renov, eds., *Collecting Visible Evidence*, 241–54, Minneapolis: University of Minnesota Press.

Sobchack, V. (2004), *Carnal Thoughts: Embodiment and Moving Image Culture*, Berkeley: University of California Press.

Sperber, D., F. Clément, C. Heintz, O. Mascaro, H. Mercier, G. Origgi, G. and D. Wilson (2010), 'Epistemic Vigilance', *Mind & Language* 25 (4): 359–93.

Spivak, G. C. (2012), *An Aesthetic Education in the Era of Globalization*, Cambridge: Harvard University Press.

Springer, J. P. and G. D. Rhodes (2005), 'Introduction', in G. D. Rhodes and J. P. Springer, eds., *Docufictions: Essays on the Intersection of Documentary and Fictional Filmmaking*, 1–9, Jefferson: McFarland.

Stam, R. and T. Miller (2000), *Film and Theory: An Anthology*, Malden: Blackwell.

Stecker, R. (2011), 'Should We Still Care about the Paradox of Fiction?', *The British Journal of Aesthetics* 51 (3): 295–308.

Stock, K. (2011), 'I–Kathleen Stock: Fictive Utterance and Imagining', *Aristotelian Society Supplementary Volume* 85 (1): 145–61.

Stock, K. (2016), 'Imagination and Fiction', in A. Kind, ed., *The Routledge Handbook of Philosophy of Imagination*, 204–16, London: Routledge.

Stock, K. (2017), *Only Imagine: Fiction, Interpretation, and Imagination*, New York: Oxford University Press.

Stolnitz, J. (1992), 'On the Cognitive Triviality of Art', *The British Journal of Aesthetics* 32 (3): 191–200.

Strange, J. J. and C. C. Leung (1999), 'How Anecdotal Accounts in News and in Fiction Can Influence Judgments of a Social Problem's Urgency, Causes, and Cures', *Personality and Social Psychology Bulletin* 25 (4): 436–49.

Suits, D. B. (2006), 'Really Believing in Fiction', *Pacific Philosophical Quarterly* 87 (3): 369–86.

Sullivan-Bissett, E., H. Bradley and P. Noordhof, eds. (2017), *Art and Belief*, Oxford: Oxford University Press.

Terrone, E. (2020a), 'Documentaries, Docudramas, and Perceptual Beliefs', *The Journal of Aesthetics and Art Criticism* 78 (1): 43–56.

Terrone, E. (2020b), 'Imagination and Perception in Film Experience' *Ergo: An Open Access Journal of Philosophy* 7. https://philarchive.org/archive/TERIAP.

Thomson, H. (1952), 'Norman McLaren: Expert on the Unorthodox', *New York Times*, 27 June: X5.

Thomson-Jones, K. (2005), 'Inseparable Insight: Reconciling Cognitivism and Formalism in Aesthetics', *The Journal of Aesthetics and Art Criticism* 63 (4): 375–84.

Tuna, E. H. (2020), 'Imaginative Resistance', in E. N. Zalta, ed., *The Stanford Encyclopedia of Philosophy*. https://plato.stanford.edu/archives/sum2020/entries/imaginative-resistance.

Turvey, M. (2020), 'Mirror Neurons and Film Studies: A Cautionary Tale from a Serious Pessimist', *Projections* 14 (3): 21–46.

Tversky, A. and D. Kahneman (1973), 'Availability: A Heuristic for Judging Frequency and Probability', *Cognitive Psychology* 5 (2): 207–32.

Van Laer, T., K. De Ruyter, L. M. Visconti and M. Wetzels (2014), 'The Extended Transportation-Imagery Model: A Meta-Analysis of the Antecedents and

Consequences of Consumers' Narrative Transportation', *Journal of Consumer Research* 40 (5): 797–817.

Vidmar Jovanović, I. (2019a), 'Cognitive and Ethical Values and Dimensions of Narrative Art', in I. Vidmar Jovanović, ed., *Narrative Art, Knowledge and Ethics*, 17–85, Rijeka: Filozofski fakultet Sveučilišta u Rijeci.

Vidmar Jovanović, I. (2019b). 'Literature and Truth: Revisiting Stolnitz's Anti-Cognitivism', *Croatian Journal of Philosophy* 19 (56): 351–70.

Walsh, D. (1969), *Literature and Knowledge*, Middletown: Wesleyan University Press.

Walton, K. L. (1978), 'Fearing Fictions', *The Journal of Philosophy* 75 (1): 5–27.

Walton, K. L. (1984), 'Transparent Pictures: On the Nature of Photographic Realism', *Critical Inquiry* 11 (2): 246–77.

Walton, K. L. (1990), *Mimesis as Make-Believe: On the Foundations of the Representational Arts*, Cambridge: Harvard University Press.

Walton, K. L. (1994), 'Morals in Fiction and Fictional Morality', *Proceedings of the Aristotelian Society, Supplementary Volumes* 68: 27–50.

Walton, K. L. (1997), 'Spelunking, Simulation, and Slime: On Being Moved by Fiction', in M. Hjort and S. Laver, eds., *Emotion and the Arts*, 37–49, Oxford: Oxford University Press.

Walton, K. L. (2006), 'On the (So-called) Puzzle of Imaginative Resistance', in S. Nichols, ed., *The Architecture of the Imagination: New Essays on Pretense, Possibility, and Fiction*, 137–48, New York: Oxford University Press.

Walton, K. L. (2008), 'Seeing-In and Seeing Fictionally', in *Marvelous Images: On Values and the Arts*, 133–42, Oxford: Oxford University Press.

Walton, K. L. (2015a), 'Fiction and Imagination – Mind the Gap', in *In Other Shoes: Music, Metaphor, Empathy, Existence*, 17–35, Oxford: Oxford University Press.

Walton, K. L. (2015b), 'Metaphor and Prop Oriented Make-Believe', in *In Other Shoes: Music, Metaphor, Empathy, Existence*, 175–95, Oxford: Oxford University Press.

Weatherson, B. (2004), 'Morality, Fiction, and Possibility', *Philosophers' Imprint* 4 (3): 1–27.

Welsh, I. (1993/2013), *Trainspotting*, Croydon: Vintage.

Weston, M. (1975), 'How Can We Be Moved by the Fate of Anna Karenina?', *Proceedings of the Aristotelian Society, Supplementary Volumes* 49: 81–93.

Williams, L. (1991), 'Film Bodies: Gender, Genre, and Excess', *Film Quarterly* 44 (4): 2–13.

Wilson, G. M. (1997), '*Le Grand Imagier* Steps Out: The Primitive Basis of Film Narration', *Philosophical Topics* 25 (1): 295–318.

Wilson, G. M. (2011), *Seeing Fictions in Film: The Epistemology of Movies*, New York: Oxford University Press.

Winston, B. (2013), 'Introduction: The Documentary Film', in B. Winston, ed., *The Documentary Film Book*, 1–32, London: British Film Institute.

Wollen, P. (1969), *Signs and Meaning in the Cinema*, Bloomington: Indiana University Press.

Wollheim, R. (1980), *Art and Its Objects*, Cambridge: Cambridge University Press.

Yabblo, S. (2008), 'Coulda, Woulda, Shoulda', in *Thoughts: Papers on Mind, Meaning and Modality*, 103–50, Oxford: Oxford University Press.

Yanal, R. J. (1999), *Paradoxes of Emotion and Fiction*, University Park: Penn State Press.

Žižek, S. (1992), *Enjoy Your Symptom! Jacques Lacan in Hollywood and Out*, New York: Routledge.

INDEX